To Pamela [illegible] —
who calls San Pedro [illegible]
and whose ancestors were
Shipbuilders and Sea-Faring
Men at Searsport -

Oliver Vickery

HARBOR HERITAGE

Tales of the Harbor Area of Los Angeles, California

by Oliver Vickery

ISBN 0-89430-036-9

Library of Congress Catalog Number: 79-89082

An Authors Book Company Publication

Manufactured in the United States of America

THIS BOOK IS DEDICATED TO GRACE

– MY WIFE, MY HELPMATE, AND MY INSPIRATION

Introduction and Acknowledgments

The source material for this book was gleaned over a period of almost fifteen years of research of unpublished manuscripts, old letters, and other family records found in private homes, some of them left by early pioneers who settled in the Los Angeles harbor area. Among them were the heirs of Phineas Banning, father of the harbor, the Sepulveda Clan, Pio and Andreas Pico, the Dominguez family, and others.

Much valuable knowledge was derived from files of old newspapers, the agendas and reports of chambers of commerce and the city libraries of San Pedro, Palos Verdes, Wilmington, Los Angeles, Avalon, Santa Barbara, Sacramento, and San Diego, plus the files of the Los Angeles Harbor Department.

In 1965 the author visited the National Archives in Mexico City to search files for early deeds of California land grants. This search was repeated in 1969 under the guidance of Dr. Antonio Sanchez of the University of Mexico.

The urge to tell, to write history, is as old as the first hunt. Cave paintings thousands of years old, as precious as they are as early art, are among man's earliest attempts to chronicle his times. However, modern history scholars often overlook significant items that lie outside the usual centers of historical research, such as dates and messages on tombstones in local cemeteries, portfolios in old attics, and messages written in family Bibles. Our landmark buildings, handicrafts, art, and folksongs often tell the life and the spirit of the pioneer, too often neglected in history books.

A community that neglects to know its own history is limited to the short present of the present generation. We cannot mature without an intelligent awareness of our past, and reading about it in the present takes on a deeper meaning in the context of time. No two history writers are alike; that is why two manifestly conscientious historians may give different versions of the same period.

For instance, Macaulay's History of England is a literary masterpiece, but Macaulay said quite frankly that he would sacrifice a minor fact for the sake of a balanced sentence. Nevertheless, if you read Macaulay's history you will be well informed on the history of England. There are bound to be statements in *Harbor Heritage* that some historians may not accept, but which the author himself has reasons to believe are true.

In the present moment the past is all we know. In telling the story of what our forefathers did should inspire us in two directions: to respect their achievements, great in their day, and to strive to equal their resourcefulness and courage in our day.

If you find much folly in this book, you will, I'm sure, find much of interest. If there are mistakes revealed, you will find, hopefully, many moments of good reading pleasure. The author has tried to draw word pictures in the text, and to write them clearly, alertly, compactly and factually.

Acknowledgments

The author is deeply indebted to George Hugh Banning, grandson of Phineas Banning, who has supplied him with much unpublished memorabilia and helpful information, without which this book could not have been written. He is most grateful, too, to Dr. and Mrs. John D. Kegler, for their inspiring leadership, showing the way to dig deep for historical facts, and to Ann Rumery, Librarian of the San Pedro library, and to former Librarian Margretta Marshall of the Wilmington library, for their loyalty and dedication in locating rare books of reference.

Orchids to Louis Sepulveda and to Margerie Sepulveda Bellew, for their help in researching the roots of the Sepulveda and the other leading harbor families; to Mrs. Fred Lorenzen, President of the Society for the Preservation of the Civil War Drum Barracks, and to her board of directors including Walter Holstein, Wilmington educator, all of whom have helped and encouraged the author to write this book.

Also grateful thanks and votes to Hon. Glenn Anderson, and to Hon. John S. Gibson, Jr., for their combined counsel and close friendship in matters of harbor interest, and to Hon. Vincent Thomas, himself a history buff, who wrote the foreword to *Harbor Heritage.* The author thanks especially Jim Groth, managing editor of the San Pedro *News-Pilot,* for his patient and careful editing and arrangement of the author's history columns which have appeared weekly in the *News-Pilot* for years.

A special accolade is affectionately reserved for the untiring efforts of Peter Mandia, harbor official, for his critical analysis and helpfulness in the preparation of the manuscript of *Harbor Heritage,* and to my old 1921 Stanford roommate, Ralph S. Scott, now of Florida, who has been generous in helping the author achieve the goal of his years: the completion of the manuscript of *Harbor Heritage.*

During the 14 years of research in the harbor alone, there are many others whom the author wishes to thank for their interest and encouragement, many of whom invited me to visit their homes, examine their Bibles and records, and to review significant historical items. The partial list concludes these remarks.

O.V.

Akerson, Bess
Anaker, Edward
Andreassen, Capt., H.J.
Ash, George
Askew, Harold L.

Barich, Frank, Jr.
Bennett, Paul
Bershad, Bob
Binns, Judge Walter
Bird, Wilmot
Bolstad, Sam
Brower, Ernest
Bush, Steve
Bustamonte, Eva

Cleveland, Herbert H.
Coats, Roy
Coghlan, Frank
Comparsi, Dominick
Cross, Vern
Coulter, Tom

Denni, Joe
Dills, Hon. Ralph G.
DeWitt, Dr. Ward

Ehrke, Ernie

Fahy, Leslie and Margaret
Ferkich, Roy
Foster, Mike
France, Dewey
Frlekin, Slavko

Grinnell, Marian
Goerlitz, John, Jr.
Goode, Dr. John R.

Hadsell, Geraldine B.
Hauck, Ed
Heim, Fredrick
Higbee, Adm. Frank D. (USCG-Ret)
Holland, John
Houston, John
Hughes, Glenn

Jorovick, Joe

Kemmerer, Walter
King, Percy
Kittell, Wade

Levitt, Mike
Lippman, B.B.
Loy, Leonard
Lucas, Marga Jean

McClintock, John
McNerney, Bob
McNett, Renee
McPolin, Father Patrick J.
Martin, Mel
Medak, Marty

Olds, Bud
Olesen, Bill
Oliver, Dwight
Olguin, Capt. John
Ostoich, Clara

Papadakis, Angie
Papadakis, Katie
Pauluzzi, Gerardo
Pennington, Dr. Howard
Podesta, Steve

Regan, Joseph E.
Reilly, George R. Hon.
Robings, Edward W.
Rowan, Dr. Melvin L.
Russell, William D.

Schwartz, Maurice
Scott, Msgr. George
Shonafelt, Paul
Schenz, Robert F. Ph.D.

Trani, Frank
Trani, Nick S.
Thomas, Bruce
Thomas, Eddie
Trudnich, Vince

Van Camp, Gilbert, Sr.

Vanderlip, Elin

Warren, Kenneth

Zabica, Vince
Zitco, Lee

PHOTOGRAPH CREDITS

Photographs, courtesy of Gus Ley, Security Pacific National Bank; Southwest Instrument Co.; George Hugh Banning; Title Insurance and Trust Co.; California Historical Society; Ernie Ehrke; Security First National Bank, and Port of Los Angeles Public Relations Department.

Foreword
By Vincent Thomas

In the year 66 B.C. Cicero wrote: "Not to know what happened before one was born is to remain a child."

To know what happened, how it happened, and to whom it happened belongs in the category of historical researchers and investigators.

Because I was reared in San Pedro and initiated at an early age to the colorful docks and streets of the entire harbor district, the heritage of the Los Angeles Harbor has always been an absorbing and fascinating subject to me.

For a number of years, Oliver's popular weekly columns entitled, "Harbor Heritage," have appeared on the editorial page of the daily News-Pilot. His manuscripts for this book are the compilation of the best of those articles and graphically reveal the happenings in the Los Angeles Harbor District before one was born.

Much of the early history of the area has been lost, either by fire, accident, or by negligence and indifference. It would be almost impossible to record every interesting event that has played a part in the development of the community, but Vickery has uncovered most of the significant and important events and placed them in their proper historical perspective, even if some of the text is in capsule form.

His thorough research into local history has greatly intrigued me because some of the events of which he writes I vividly recall, while others were related to me when I was a child.

Vickery's narrative revives the drama and romance of the Los Angeles Harbor Area. Since each of his columns is a complete story in itself, it makes for easy reading and should have wide appeal to our modern and busy readers.

At a luncheon aboard the SS Princess Louise, on January 15, 1975, the Los Angeles Board of Harbor Commissioners presented Vickery with a certificate making him an Honorary Commodore for his outstanding contributions as a writer and for his historical research.

For over 10 years, he has been a designated lecturer in history for the Los Angeles Unified School System. A quote from its printed brochure which is distributed to over 600 schools states: "Oliver Vickery presents a romantic history of Phineas Banning, father of the harbor, San Pedro, Wilmington, Palos Verdes, and the people who have made the Los Angeles harbor area an outstanding district. It is a timely subject with facts never before revealed to the public."

George Hugh Banning, grandson of the late Phineas Banning, the man who founded Wilmington and the first man to start in 1851 the physical development of the Los Angeles Harbor, a water complex which has won world-wide renown as a maritime miracle, conferred a great honor upon Vickery, when he selected him as one of the few people to be given access to several historical memorabilia in his possession.

Vickery is Curator Emeritus of the 113-year-old Phineas Banning Mansion and Museum, and presently, is Acting Commandant of the 115-year-old Civil War Drum Barracks in Wilmington. In 1967 the Society For the Preservation of Drum Barracks, upon motion by its president, Mrs. Fred (Joan) Lorenzen, sent Vickery to Sacramento to seek a legislative appropriation for the reconditioning of the barracks premises. Vickery came directly to my office, and I arranged for him to speak before the Finance Committee. Because I fully endorsed the concept of his presentation, I took a special interest in the project and urged the committee to appropriate $125,000, which they did. After the bill was approved by the Legislature, I personally took it to Governor Ronald Reagan, who signed it into law.

Vickery's roots are very deep in our community. Some of you may not know that Vickery's name made world-wide headlines on April 17, 1952, when he left San Pedro to make a free enterprise speech before the International Economic Conference in Moscow advocating the American approach to economic justice. A report of this unprecedented speech was carried over the radio by Drew Pearson, and later in a national radio interview with Fulton Lewis, Jr., which attracted nation-wide attention.

Life Magazine, with a world-wide circulation of some 20 million monthly copies, in its June 2, 1952 issue, featured an 11-page article by Vickery which described a 6,000-mile trip he made into the interior of Russia and from which he successfully brought out uncensored 1,500 feet of 16mm motion pictures. This was during the period when China and Russia were on good terms. Vickery's film shows a large group of Chinese, some of whom are now the new leaders of China. On Thursday, September 4, 1952, Eleanor Roosevelt highly complimented Vickery in one of her nationwide articles released by the United Features Syndicate.

While on a lecture tour showing his pictures of the USSR, the editor of the *Oak Ridger* in Oak Ridge, Tennessee, called U.S. Senator John Sherman Cooper, former Ambassador of the United Nations, inquiring about Vickery's reputation and credentials.

Cooper's reply, published on the first page of the *Oak Ridger* of their December 7, 1954 issue, was one of the greatest compliments Vickery has ever received:

"I've known Oliver Vickery for 30 years. He originally came from Kentucky. At the time he was considering making a trip to Russia in 1952 for an international economic conference, he came to Washington and talked to me about it. I told him of the dangers he was running. I counseled him as to the type of speech he expected to make and helped him edit parts of it. He was certainly courageous in making a speech for free enterprise in view of the Russian attitude toward strangers at the time."

"I told Vickery before he went that I was worried about two things: First, that he might not get back; and second, that the circumstances of the conference and his trip might not be understood. But before he left, he got clearance from both the State Department and the F.B.I.

"Vickery is an adventurer," Senator Cooper said, "and by that, I mean he likes to take chances like this. But I would vouch for him 120 percent. He is not only highly regarded by me but by a large number of others I know who have worked with him in his business."

As Assemblyman of the 52nd Assembly district, and one who has dedicated over one-half of his lifetime representing the interests of the Los Angeles Harbor District in Sacramento, I am very happy to recommend this book by Oliver Vickery. If you enjoy an adventure into the heritage, the romance and the history of our beloved Los Angeles Harbor Community, you will find it fascinating reading.

Vincent Thomas

September 20, 1978

Table of Contents

1
SEBASTIAN VIZCAINO

Vizcaino was the most prolific name-giver of coastal places. He named all the offshore islands, honoring saints, including the towns of San Diego, San Pedro and Santa Barbara.

MOST EVERYONE HAS heard of Juan Rodriquez Cabrillo, who discovered California and the San Pedro Bay in 1542 for the King of Spain. But few people have ever heard of Sebastian Vizcaino, who has had more influence on California and the Pacific Coast than possibly any other man.

The Spanish Viceroy, Zuniga Y. Acaveda, Conde de Monterrey, outfitted Vizcaino with three ships to explore and chart the entire California coast.

The voyage started from Acapulco May 6, 1602. On November 10th, Vizcaino noted a large bay, which he named San Diego. He left there on November 19th, with his ships—San Diego, Santo Tomas and Tres Reyes—sailing northward to reconnoiter and take soundings.

On November 21st, he passed the first of the offshore islands, which he named San Clemente. On November 24th, 1602, Vizcaino found another but larger island, which he named Santa Catalina.

The Indians welcomed Vizcaino and his crew, generously supplying his ships with fresh fish, abalone, wild cabbage, and sweet potatoes.

On November 28th, Vizcaino observed a lunar eclipse, calculated to be a good omen. The next day, he pulled anchor and sailed to the mainland to a place noted on his ship log as Bahia de Fumos, a name given by Cabrillo in October, 1542.

Vizcaino anchored his ships approximately off where Fort MacArthur now stands. He went ashore and placed a cross on an Indian idol. The Indians ran away. Returning to his command ship, San Diego, he named the Indian community in honor of St. Peter (some historians say it was in honor of St. Peter of Alexandria).

Thus, on November 29, 1602, San Pedro was born, making it the second oldest named community in California—just 10 days after San Diego was named. Most historians concede that San Diego is California's oldest community, but few people realize that San Pedro is the second oldest named town in California.

After leaving San Pedro Bay on December 1, 1602, Vizcaino sailed to the other offshore islands, naming each one for a saint, including San Miguel, Santa Barbara, Santa Cruz, Santa Rosa, and Saint Nicholas—all of them except Anacapa, a mile-long rocky reef unworthy of a saint. By that time, perhaps Vizcaino had run out of saints!

After sailing from San Pedro, Vizcaino discovered an inlet which he named Hueneme. Then sailing northward, he discovered a large Indian village, which he named Santa Barbara.

He remained there only two days. Then, sailing up the coast, he noted a protruding land mass and named it Point Concepcion.

Hugging the coast at a safe distance, Vizcaino discovered and fell in love with a bay he named Monterey, in honor of the Viceroy Conde de Monterrey, who had sent him on this voyage.

Sailing all the way to Cape Mendecino, Vizcaino gave place names that to this day are still recorded on graphs, maps, and globes.

I like to refer to Sebastian Vizcaino as the Marco Polo of the sea, and I remember vividly writing a paper with this title in a college history class more than 50 years ago, and getting an "A" grade from my professor and mentor, Dr. Herbert Bolton, University of California at Berkeley.

Like Marco Polo of ancient Cathay, Vizcaino left a record of his adventure into unknown realms. He was the first to map the California coast, first to discover and make note of dangerous reefs and inlets and, like Marco Polo, first to leave records of the fauna and flora observed in his travels.

Monuments and parks have been named for Cabrillo, but few, if any, have been named for Vizcaino. The fact that most of the major place names along the California coast were given by him is often not remembered, or not known.

2

John Charles Fremont: Heroic Pathfinder

No man ever lived who has done more good for California, faced so many critics, and had such a lovely and loyal wife—An unsung hero.

POSSIBLY NO MAN IN California was more controversial, provocative, significant, or illuminating than John Charles Fremont (1813-1900). His devotees claim he did more for the conquest of the West and for California than any other man. His detractors say he became prominent only because he married the daughter of a famous U.S. Senator.

Some historians think Fremont tried to shine in too many fields by undertaking tasks for which he was ill equipped, and courted the charge of false pretensions. But both sides styled Fremont the Pathfinder. He was essentially a geographer, a mathematician, a surveyor and an explorer, and research shows he excelled in all four categories.

Fremont was the first to scientifically explore and survey the West, and to report his voluminous data of California, the topography, climate, soils, vegetation, the Indians, and wild animals, and a wealth of other sought-after general information about California, which our president and the congress were eager to get. Fremont's fate carried him through the uncharted frontiers of the West from 1841 to 1850, and into the clash of national politics, through the thick of the Civil War, gold mining, and finance. He rose from poverty to millions and died penniless in 1900.

Fremont's four pioneering journeys into California stirred much comment and apprehension. He endeared himself to the Californios, most of whom owned large ranchos. They told Fremont that they heard rumors that Mexico, fearing defeat if war should come, offered to sell California to England, France, and even to Russia. To them this would be unbearable, although being Mexicans they were in sympathy with Fremont and the United States if war started.

Shortly after the Mexican-American War was declared on July 7, 1846, Fremont established a headquarters in San Pedro. When Gen. Stephen W. Kearny lost the Battle of San Pasqual and the Battle of Dominguez Rancho in December 1846, Fremont came to Kearny's rescue, gathered the dead and buried them at Dead Man's Island in San Pedro Bay. Kearny retired to San Diego waiting for reinforcements. From San Pedro Fremont used a surprise tactic capturing the Presidio at San Francisco. While there he gave the name of Golden Gate to the entrance of San Francisco Bay, and also named California the Golden State.

Fremont's detractors are loud in blaming him for flying the Bear Flag at Sonoma and proclaiming the "California Republic" on June 14, 1846. But the United States was already at War with Mexico over Texas. Apparently Fremont knew this and was bidding for time.

From Captain John Sutter's Fort at Sacramento Fremont received large amounts of blankets, tents, guns, ammunition, horses, grain, food, and tools. Mexican General Mariano Vallejo became a staunch friend of Fremont's plan for the conquest of California, was put in charge of ordnance, and visited San Pedro and other sections on inspection trips.

When Fremont brought large reinforcements to the San Fernando Valley for a showdown battle, General Andreas Pico, in charge of the Mexican troops, and brother of Governor Pio Pico, offered to negotiate for a surrender. The war in California was thus officially ended by the Capitulation of Cahuenga, signed on January 13, 1847. Three days later, when General Kearny approached Los Angeles with his reinforcements, Fremont met him and exclaimed, "General, the war is over, here is the signed surrender." Kearny was raving mad and retorted, "Lieut-Colonel Fremont, I'm a general! you should have waited for me! I'll have you courtmartialed for insubordination!"

Fremont faced a heated trial before officer graduates from West Point. The trial lasted for weeks in Washington, D.C. The newspapers were filled with the charges and counter-charges as the trial proceeded. Public sympathy was on Fremont's side, but Fremont was found guilty. His father-in-law, Senator Thomas Hart Benton, swore revenge. President James K. Polk cancelled the punishment. "Lieut-Colonel Fremont," he ordered, "will be released from custody, will resume his sword, and report for duty." But Fremont resigned and returned to California. When California became a state in 1850, Fremont was appointed the first U.S. Senator from California. He was military governor in 1847.

The picturesqueness of Fremont's life reflects many difficulties, but he lived an active and meaningful life throughout his 87 years. He was swindled out of his vast Mariposa Estate and gold ventures in the 1850s. Fremont was the first candidate for president under the new Republican Party, but Buchanan beat him at the polls. Fremont became a major general in the Civil War. The Republican Party nominated him to run again in 1864, but he withdrew in favor of Lincoln. Fremont was governor of the Arizona Territory in 1878, and helped Phineas Banning get the right-of-way for the Southern Pacific Railroad for the track system to New Orleans.

Research shows that Fremont surveyed a road for the government in 1836 which was used for the forced march of the Cherokee Indians to Oklahoma, which Fremont chronicled in his Memoirs as the cruelest act in our national history. During Fremont's Third California expedition in 1945, he hired Edward Kern as a topographer while surveying parts of the San Joaquin Valley and named a river for Kern, from which a county was later named Kern. Fremont was also the first to draw plans for the Colorado River to irrigate the Salton Sink area. Many cities, streets, schools, and hotels are named for him, and he gave the name to the poinsettia flower.

In Charleston, S.C., where Fremont lived with his mother as a youngster, he met Joel Robert Poinsett, when he returned as the first American Minister to Mexico. He gave the youth some flower seeds to plant. When they bloomed, he yelled to his mother, "Look, mom, at these pretty flowers! Let's name them for Poinsett." Thus the new flower became known as poinsettias. Poinsett became Secretary of War under President Van Buren, and in 1838 commissioned Fremont a second lieutant in the Topographical Corps.

Fremont's marriage to Jesse Benton was a runaway affair. Her father, Senator Thomas Hart Benton, of "I'm from Missouri, you've got to show me" fame, was wrathfully opposed to the match. They had a hard time finding a minister who would marry them. Jesse was 17. She appealed to her good friend, Mrs. J.J. Crittenden, wife of the Senator from Kentucky, who had watched the romance in Washington with warm interest, and fully approved of the match. She found a minister who would perform the ceremony, regardless of Senator Benton's wrath.

A few days after their marriage on October 19, 1841, Jessie urged Fremont that they should face her father together. When they told the senator about the secret marriage, Benton blazed with anger, and gave a sharp command, "Get out of my house and never cross my door way again! Jessie shall stay here!" Jessie held Fremont's arm tighter and silenced her father by the words of Ruth: "Whither thou goest, I shall go, and where thou lodgest, I will lodge; thy people shall be my people, and thy God, my God." Her father softened and invited Fremont to live in the house with Jessie.

Kit Carson's tribute to Fremont, written in 1856 was most complimentary, as well as revealing: "I was with Fremont from 1842 to 1847. The hardships through which we passed I find impossible to describe, and the credit which he deserves I am incapable to do him justice in writing. . . . I have heard that he is rich. I wish to God that he may be worth ten times as much more—all that he has or may ever receive he deserves. I can never forget his treatment of me while in his employ, and how cheerfully he suffered with his men when undergoing the severest of hardships!"

His widow, Jesse, wrote in her memoirs: "To the end my husband retained his ardent enthusiasm for wild nature. He would not let his children cut down a healthy tree, he never hunted or fished, and he taught his children not to kill animals except under necessity. He is gone now but I am happy in his memory. He always retired early that he may be outdoors with the dawn."

3
Thomas Hart Benton Duels with Andrew Jackson

Benton helped California in many ways in getting statehood status and in becoming a great state of the Union.

SOMETIMES HISTORY proves stranger than fiction. A case in point is the early life story of Thomas Hart Benton, father-in-law of John Charles Fremont, California's famous pathfinder.

Benton, among other things, fought a duel with Andrew Jackson, who became the seventh president of the United States.

Benton was born March 14, 1782, at Hillsboro, N.C., and was raised by his widowed mother on a farm near the Tennessee frontier. He wanted to be a lawyer. In those days, as there were no law schools as we know them, all he had to do was to be apprenticed to a practicing lawyer and read law books. In colonial times the basis of legal education was centered in Blackstone's Commentaries, and young Benton learned them well.

He was a big man and physically hardened. It is said that he was rough and tough, with a bobcat aggressiveness mixed with a keen sense of subtle humor.

He started his law practice in Nashville, Tennessee where he met another Carolinian lawyer—Andrew Jackson.

Benton had a brother, Jesse, after whom he named the daughter who married Fremont. According to the St. Louis *Globe Democrat,* June 19, 1976, brother Jesse also was an aggressive character, and fought a duel in 1813 with Jackson's close friend, Maj. William Carroll. Both men were wounded, but Jesse more seriously and shamelessly. He got it in the seat of his pants, and couldn't sit down like other respectable people.

Brother Thomas felt compelled to defend his family's honor and forced a quarrel with Jackson. The *Globe Democrat* commented, "There were angry letters between Jackson and Benton, and on September 4, 1813, the Benton brothers got embroiled in a tavern with Jackson and his guest, Col. John Coffee. During the scuffling, stabbing, clubbing and gunfire, Jackson was shot in the arm, Jesse was stabbed, and Thomas was wounded, and fell down a flight of stairs."

When it was over Thomas Benton figured there was no future in Tennessee for a man who brawled with Andy Jackson, and wrote a letter stating, "I am literally in hell here, the meanest wretches under heaven to contend with, liars, false affidavit makers, and shameless puppies. The scalping knife of Tecumseh is mercy compared to these villains."

In September, 1815, Benton moved his law practice to St. Louis. Two years later Benton received a challenge to a duel by Charles Lucas, another Missouri lawyer. "I understand you applied to me the epithet of 'puppy', Lucas said. "If so, I shall expect that satisfaction which is due one gentleman to another for such an indignity." Benton accepted the challenge.

On August 12, 1817, they fought at 10 paces. Both Benton and Lucas were wounded. Six weeks later, after they had recovered, Lucas challenged Benton again. This time they faced each other at 10 feet. Lucas was mortally wounded. Benton would never again offer or accept a duel challenge.

When Missouri became a state of the Union in 1821, Benton was the leading lawyer in the state and was appointed U.S. senator. He served in Washington for 30 years, where he matched his legislative skill in debates with Daniel Webster, Henry Clay, and John C. Calhoun. In 1823, Tennessee sent Jackson to the U.S. Senate, where he and Benton patched up their old quarrels and became good friends.

Benton used to twist the tail of the British Lion over the Oregon boundary line, and coined the phrase, "Fifty-Four Forty or Fight." He was one of the deciding factors in making California a state of the Union in 1850. Three days before Benton's death on April 10, 1858, he called President James Buchanan to his bedside and delivered a plea to preserve the Union and avoid a civil war.

Fremont died in 1900. His widow, Jesse, lived for several years after his death in a modest house in Los Angeles, where she wrote her memoirs.

(The Eschscholtzia Chapter in Los Angeles of the Daughters of the American Revolution gave the author a pamphlet recently which shows that Jesse Benton Fremont was the founder of the chapter in 1894, and was its first regent.

4

Phineas Banning Transformed the Mud Flats

The Early History of Wilmington and San Pedro.

THE HISTORY OF San Pedro and Wilmington, California, is the history of Phineas Banning. When Banning arrived on the scene in 1851, the state was just one year old, and California needed creative imagination, guidance, and leadership. Almost everyone who came to California during the mining boom caught "gold fever," but Phineas Banning did not. He was tempted many times, even urged by passengers on the ship that brought him to California, but he resisted to the very end and was happy that he did.

Banning's immunity to gold fever was simple. He had visions of greater things, and before he died, by an untimely accident (he fell off a cable car in San Francisco in 1885), he had built an economic empire from the wharves and the stables of the harbor and touched greatness in founding Wilmington.

In 1858 Banning forsook San Pedro and dug his way five miles up the channel. With the aid of mud scows and hand pumps, he siphoned water from 2400 acres of tule waste, bought from the Dominguez estate for $1.10 an acre. It was situated in a hunter's paradise, called "Goose Town." People stood in awe of Banning's handiwork, and he named the settlement Wilmington in honor of his home town in Delaware.

Banning was wise to choose this site, because Rattlesnake Island, now Terminal Island, afforded protection for his lighters and shallow draft ships anchored in the open harbor at San Pedro against the miserable Santana winds that blew intolerable waves.

Phineas Banning was the first to draw blueprints for a breakwater, and first to submit them with characteristic resolve to an understanding, if reluctant, congress.

Banning left many landmark firsts in the harbor community. One of the most historic occurred on July 4, 1858, when he landed in Wilmington onto his newly created wharf with the first merchandise cargo. He invited one hundred guests from far and near to meet him in San Pedro, to share in this memorable trip up the estuary, and to enjoy the new sights as the first bale of cargo was unloaded on the docks of the new Wilmington port, five miles from San Pedro. Had a picture been taken of this historic event, we would venture that a thousand ships that now ply the seas bringing cargo to Wilmington, California, would proudly display it in their bridge quarters as a maritime miracle.

When this first ship landed with its precious cargo, another 100 men lined the well-decorated area at the foot of Canal Boulevard, now Avalon Boulevard, and helped pull the hawser line that signalled Wilmington's beginnings as a world-famous port of call. No other port in the world can match its achievements. Thereafter, Phineas Banning surveyed his handiwork, and he was pleased. The new port of Wilmington lifted him to a new socioeconomic level, like a tidal wave bringing blessings of good things yet to come.

Phineas Banning became the transportation king of Southern California. He employed more than 500 people. He maintained a wagon manufacturing company near Fries Avenue, with 1,000 mules and about as many horses; however, his inventory varied according to needs. It is said that one could see miles of Banning's wagon trains stretching through the desert waste all the way to Ft. Yuma and the Pacific Southwest, hauling needed equipment from Wilmington to the United States Army and frontier settlements, including urgent trips to Salt Lake City. Brigham Young was ever grateful.

The town of Banning, California, was named for Phineas, honoring his camping in that area with his caravans on their way to the Colorado River.

Banning built the first railroad in Southern California and owned over half of the stock of the Los Angeles and San Pedro Railroad, which was completed in 1869. It ran from Los Angeles to Wilmington. When Collis P. Huntington of the Southern Pacific Railroad bought it from Banning in 1876, he extended the line to San Pedro in 1881.

During Banning's brilliant lifetime he was an honorary admiral, an active brigadier general, a judge, and a California state senator. No one who has lived in California has achieved a more enviable record. Banning did not seek publicity and refused to have his picture taken for historical books popular in his day.

To his enemies Banning was like the whine of a mosquito, not loud, but too piercing for comfort. In this respect his name was often omitted from lists in history on which it clearly belonged. Banning and Wilmington have been more or less lost in history. This writer has been assigned the task as historian to research Banning and Wilmington and try to put these entities into their rightful, historic perspective.

Banning was never backward in taking a giant step forward. An historic step into the future, he knew, could be most rewarding. Because of the Civil War, Banning hesitated to start the foundation for his new 30-room mansion in Wilmington until he was convinced the designs would meet all structural requirements even through the twentieth century. Nevertheless, Banning used architectural concepts of solid design and workmanship, gracious function, and artistic simplicity. Most of his help was enlisted from shipwrights, carpenters, blacksmiths, and artisans through the courtesy of clipper ship captains whom Banning entertained lavishly while they were in port.

He generously supplied these ships with kegs of high-grade tar for caulking purposes without charge. Of course, Banning got his tar from the Brea Tar Pits, likewise without charge. It was easy to convince the clipper captains who came into port that their ships were leaking and needed weeks of caulking repairs. The mansion was completed in 1864, and it is amazing that the structure has not experienced any physical defects during its first century.

From the vantage point of the cupola atop the mansion, Banning would take his telescope and scan the horizon. The Wilmington harbor was ever in focus, with ships from foreign ports loading and unloading. He could see modern beauty with ancient trappings, rich and exciting. Then, pointing his scope toward the Palos Verdes and the Dominguez expanse, Banning could behold the Spanish panoply—carritas loaded with hides and tallow, pulled by single oxen, dashing Dons on horseback, cattle by the thousands, flocks of sheep, and a burgeoning of adobes and corrals.

With the installation of the Civil War Drum Barracks in 1862 named by Banning in honor of Major Richard Coulter Drum, who was sent by President Abraham Lincoln to confer with Phineas Banning relative to building a barracks, Wilmington had a greater population than Los Angeles from 1862 through 1865. At times over 7,000 troops were camped in Wilmington. Ft. MacArthur in San Pedro was never as large.

In 1864 General Banning personally took A Battery to Catalina Island and subdued some southern pirates who were harassing the ships carrying Comstock silver and gold from San Francisco, gold which was sorely needed by Lincoln's government.

Banning was steadfast with his Breakwater Bill, which over the years took on the aspects of a political football before he won the game. Fourteen years after his death in 1885, work was started in 1899. In 1910 the breakwater was completed. Because of Banning's foresight, Wilmington became a thriving port city and even today more cargo per ton is handled through the Port of Wilmington than through the Port of San Pedro. The citizens of Wilmington should be proud of their romantic heritage, and to be the possessor of both the 117-year-old Drum Barracks and the 115-year-old Banning Residence and Museum.

Many thousands of visitors come yearly to Wilmington to view and glory in its rich history, and to learn for the first time that Wilmington itself is more varied, more strange, and more richly endowed perhaps than any other part of California.

Exxon officials will tell you that they are taking another 75 million barrels of crude oil out of Wilmington through a new pressurization system; calculated at $12 per barrel, it totals almost a billion dollars of new wealth. In 1975 Wilmington had a population of approximately 50,000 people, with 15 schools and six commercial banks. As a corporate entity, Wilmington is 30 years older than the City of Long Beach.

Banning's father was a graduate of Princeton University, and his grandfather, John Banning, was one of the electors for George Washington. Banning's roots are deep in Americana, but in 1642, when Rembrandt was doing his best painting, he portrayed one of Phineas' ancestors, who happened to be the Burgomaster of Amsterdam, in a masterpiece now worth many millions of dollars, known as "The Night Watch."

The Banning Mansion and Museum was opened to the public in 1937, and is now managed by Beverly Bubar for the Los Angeles Department of Recreation and Parks, at 401 East "M" Street in Wilmington. When Banning lived there his yard and garden embraced 50 acres. He had almost every variety of fruit and flowering tree imaginable. It was carriage trade living at its best. But, alas, only a few trees are left, and the size of the yard has been cut to 20 acres. However, the oldest California eucalyptus tree is still standing in leafy majesty just off the front porch.

The 25th Annual Wisteria Festival was held on April 2nd, 1978, in honor of a 90-year-old vine thought to have been brought from China by Charlie Lim Yong, Banning's major-domo. About 4,000 visitors attend each year to celebrate the memory of a romantic, long-gone era, amid music, song, and beauty competition.

One hundred years have wrought a profound change in human perspective and moral values, but still found here at the Banning Residence is a vivid representation of the gracious living of the horse-and-carriage era. One can easily imagine the festivities that took place in this mansion where Phineas Banning lavishly entertained the elite of the social, economic, and political world of his time.

5
'Till Death Do Us Part'

This story should convince the non-believer that true love can exist between husband and wife.

IT IS NO EASY task to describe in a few lines the beautiful courtship and marriage of Phineas Banning and Rebecca Sanford. Rebecca was the only sister of William Sanford, owner of a rancho near the La Brea Tar Pits. It was

Banning's courtly philosophy to praise without hyprocrisy, rebuke without malice, rejoice without envy, and assist without ostentation. He was brilliant in conversation, knightly in manners, eloquent in oration, and independent and fearless in spirit.

Rebecca was impressed with his transcendent wit and with his dialectical acumen; he stood apart from all other men whom she had met. Phineas had aristocratic manners, by turns affable and haughty, but this stamped him as an extraordinary man, which he was.

Rebecca was the personification of sympathy, human in her impulses and divine in grace. She was bright, amiable and affectionate, and exuded feminine charm, pride and dignity.

Though blushing with modesty, she overcame her shyness and accepted his bid. Phineas and Rebecca were married, November 16, 1854, in San Pedro. She was 17, he was 24. Her caresses had spiritual fervor, her thoughts and words rich with meaning. During her 15 years of married life, her soul was kindled by lofty sentiments and divine vigor.

They moved into their new 30-room mansion in Wilmington in 1864. Phineas gave her security, and her home inspired poetry. Their relationship was based on a devoted love as helpmates and companions, tied together in connubial bonds with a common purpose in philanthropy, art, and in caring for children. They had a boundless veneration one for the other; they knew the glories of self-sacrifice and religious contemplation.

The premature deaths of four of their children caused a sadness that only a divine love could endure. These misfortunes tended to bind them closer than ever before, with a new force of love that enabled them to seek the solution to life's mysteries; consoled by prayerful benedictions wrapped in songs of thankfulness and adoration of their three living sons, William, Joseph, and Hancock, they enriched the lives of their family and of all who knew them.

Phineas was a gracious host. His larder was kept filled for courtly entertaining, his friendship was sought far and wide by the leading political and business leaders of his day, and the great and near-great knocked at his door seeking his advice and his courtesies.

During this time Rebecca reigned supreme as hostess in their famous mansion, and Phineas was proud.

But the time came, as it always must, for the severing of all earthly ties. Rebecca died in Phineas' arms January 7, 1868. At 31, she was in her prime. Throughout her life Rebecca radiated a spiritual character without contradiction that commanded the deepest respect and the most profound admiration.

We venture to say that whatever heights to which woman may rise and however exalted the spheres she may fill, as wife, teacher, author, actress, singer, painter, poet, artist, or queen of society, no woman can hope to excel in purity, in peerless charm or noble courage, or to live the sanctity of womanhood more wonderfully and with more love than Rebecca Sanford Banning. She and Phineas lived in mutual love, admiration, and respect. Her home life was one of serene tranquillity. If any woman may stand as a model of a wife and mother in all her glory, it is Rebecca.

6

ANNE SMITH BANNING AND THE ASSISTANCE LEAGUE

Anne Banning was a great lady who lived in the elegant horse-and-buggy days, and who left a rich legacy of service through her founding of the Assistance League of California.

PHINEAS BANNING had three sons, William, Joseph, and Hancock. William, the eldest, never married. Hancock married Anne Smith, a blushing 18, in 1889. Her father was Colonel George Hugh Smith, a commander of a Virginia regiment in the Civil War, who moved to Los Angeles to practice law, eventually to become Justice of the California Supreme Court.

Anne's mother, born Susan Glassell, came to Los Angeles a war widow. She was first married to Colonel George S. Patton, grandfather of General George Smith Patton, World War II hero. The romance of Susan Patton began when Colonel Smith joined Susan's brother, Andrew Glassell, in a law partnership. This marriage united her illustrious Patton background with the prominent and affluent Banning family.

Among the clients of this law firm were Benjamin Davis Wilson, who married Ramona Yorba, daughter of Don Bernardo Yorba, owner of the Rancho Santa Ana, a great portion of which today is Orange County. When Ramona died, Wilson married Margaret Hereford. Two daughters were born of this union, Annie and Ruth. George Patton, son of Susan Glassell Patton, married Ruth Wilson. By this time, B.D. Wilson, Ruth's father, owned most of the land on which the cities of Pasadena and San Gabriel are situated today.

Their son, George S. Patton III, was born on November 11, 1885, on the 1,800 acre Wilson-Patton ranch in San Marino. The event was recorded in his mother's Bible, and in the books of the Church of Our Saviour, the oldest Episcopal Church in Southern California, built by his grandfather, B.D. Wilson, mayor of Los Angeles in 1851. Wilson helped Phineas Banning in the hauling business between San Pedro and Los Angeles.

George S. Patton III married Beatrice Ayer on May 26, 1910, at Salem, Massachusetts. Her mother was married to her first cousin, Joseph Banning, son of Phineas Banning.

The *Los Angeles Examiner* on December 20, 1951, stated, "The Hancock Banning home at 240 West Adams Street became a Southern California show-place. Almost every distinguished person visiting Los Angeles in three decades was its guest. So completely did the personality and charm of Mrs. Banning dominate society that none could be said to be socially known who had not figured on her guest list."

Possibly her influence could be compared with that of Mrs. John Jacob Astor's leadership in the Society of The Four Hundred in New York City, then at its zenith. There was a significant difference, however. Mrs. Banning did not relish being head of a society clique and brushed aside any idea that she was a social leader.

The fact is that Anne Banning was never ostentatious and looked upon society, in its true sense, as an organization of persons, each one to be treated with the dignity and respect due a human being, no matter what color, creed, or economic status. It is said that her social philosophy was as sound as it was simple. She believed that the workings of social welfare should be local, voluntary, intimately personal, and autonomous. Life for Anne Banning was not of material splendor. She devoted most of her life helping others through the Assistance League of Southern California, which she founded in 1919.

When the San Francisco earthquake and fire came in 1906, Mrs. Banning organized a relief unit. They collected supplies of food and clothing. The group, headed by Mrs. Banning, went to San Francisco, where they personally worked on the relief distribution. They were known as the Good Samaritans. This was the first time that these women had worked as a unit for relief of suffering people, although most of them had been charitable to local individuals and families, as was the custom of their time and social level.

During World War I, these same ladies were the nucleus of Los Angeles' Red Cross unit, which Mrs. Banning organized, and which she served as director. Their best fund raising activity was the Red Cross Shop. Donations sold in the shop included clothes, furs, lace, tapestries, toys, jewelry, books, pictures, art, needlework, vegetables, jams and jellies—and quite often treasured heirlooms. The Shop was staffed six days a week by volunteers.

Among the early interests of the League, which are still reflected in its community services, are family and individual counseling on pressing problems, day care of the young, and in-depth study of the elderly and their needs. Operation School Bell, founded in 1966, provides clothing for needy school children.

Center of activities for Assistance League of Southern California is Anne Banning Community House, opened in 1964 as a new building especially planned to concentrate League administrative offices, meeting rooms and record storage at 1370 North Saint Andrews Place, Los Angeles 90028. Expansion of services and readjustment of present programs are continuously studied by volunteers and professional staff in order to meet changing needs of those seeking aid. A growing population of elder citizens, more sophistication in boys and girls, and a larger transient society challenges the League to ever greater efforts.

Mrs. Banning originated the League's motto, "All for Service and Service For All."

"On these principles Mrs. Banning founded the Assistance League. Also on these principles she conducted her own private charities. Among them was the first restoration and donation of period furniture, buggies, and artifacts to the Banning Museum in Wilmington in 1937. Anne was the impersonation of sympathy, human in her impulses and divine in her graces. She wanted Los Angeles and the harbor area to become a city of culture, of literature and art, schools and libraries and museums where scholars and others could congregate and discuss their opinions and philosophy. It was these principles, not social leadership, that attracted people to her home," according to Fanchon Eggenberger, Director of Public Relations, of the Assistance League of Southern California.

On the occasion of Mrs. Banning's birthday, February 25, 1952, the Assistance League unveiled a large portrait of her in the League Club Room. It was followed by an impressive eulogy by Dr. Rufus von KleinSmid, chancellor of the University of Southern California, who said, "Although cloaked with prestige by others, Mrs. Hancock Banning herself was without pretension, and her own interest was in her family and her charities, always active through the years on behalf of the Community Chest, Children's Hospital, museums, and other worthy causes."

Mrs. Banning also was an effective member of the Daughters of the Confederacy and the Colonial Dames. Throughout the portrait unveiling exercises stood her favorite and proud and beautiful grandchild, Marianne Banning, daughter of George Hugh Banning.

Mrs. Hancock Banning, 80, died on December 19, 1951, and was buried at the Inglewood Park Cemetery. She left two sons, Hancock Banning, Jr., of San Marino, and George Hugh Banning, of La Jolla. Both sons are living and in fairly good health. Robert Banning, son of Hancock, Jr., was president in 1977 of the California Historical Society; another son, William Hancock Banning III, of Newport Beach, is the fiscal agent of the Banning business and industrial holdings.

Anne Smith Banning lived through some of the adobe days of Los Angeles, and the horse-and-buggy era of graceful living in the harbor area. Her spirit still lives at the 115-year-old Banning Residence and Museum in Wilmington.

Anne Banning was indeed a great lady who lived in an era which will long be remembered in our harbor heritage.

7

Lucy Banning—A Girl Who Had Everything but Love

A story of one of the most unhappy experiences of a beautiful girl of society seeking love and not promises.

LUCY BANNING was a blue-blood, to the manner born into a family of culture and wealth. She won honors for being the prettiest girl in all of California. She was one of the first Rose Bowl Princesses, even before the stadium was built.

As noted in the family Bible, she was born Feb. 11, 1876, at 9:30 p.m. Lucy was nine years old when her famous father, Gen. Phineas Banning died, March 8, 1885, leaving her a fortune.

Lucy was a normal, play-loving girl. She had a tousled head of wavy blond hair and loved to sit perched on the yard fence and wave at visitors. She blew soap bubbles and rolled hoops across the wide green lawn of the 50-acre Banning manor. She especially loved her older half-brother, William, and blew kisses as he sat high in his coach of four bumping along the lane leading into the archway of her home. Lucy often stood beside Charley Lim Yong, the family major-domo, while he turned a roast on a long spit over an open fire. She was ever fascinated by the large buttermaking churn.

When she went to town she pressed her cute little nose against show windows of the candy merchants. Also, like most nineteenth century girls, she learned to sew and do needlework. At Christmas holidays she sang carols with her friends in candle-lit houses.

On Sunday she accompanied her parents to St. John's Episcopal Church of Wilmington, a religious facility which her father donated to the community in 1881, and, with her parents, prayed. At home they would read from the big family Bible kept on a table in the parlor. The Bible is still there. Certain pages are given to vital statistics of the Banning family.

At an early age Lucy learned to ride and had a pony of her own. She observed visiting ladies of fashion step out of hansom carriages, protecting their wide sweeping skirts from the mud and dust.

In the evening, soon after supper, Lucy went upstairs to her bedroom. Her doting mother went along with a candle to light the way. After kneeling for prayers, she was tucked lovingly into her deep featherbed.

When 13 years old, Lucy was sent to the Field Seminary in Oakland, where she studied the social graces, French, and other subjects. She was skilled in music and dancing and conversant in history. She was hospitable, fine looking, and cultivated. Lucy received good grades—she was on her way.

But Lo! At 17, John Bradbury, meeting Lucy at a formal dance, swept her off her pretty little toes while she was still a student at the seminary. They were married Dec. 4, 1893. This was her first marriage. Three more were to follow.

For their honeymoon, they first went to the Chicago's World's Fair, then to Paris to visit U.S. Consul General and Mrs. Adam E. King, old friends of Lucy's parents. After nine years, their passionate love turned into passionate frustration and turmoil. Lucy divorced Bradbury Nov. 17, 1902.

Surely she could do better.

On Sept. 20, 1906, Lucy married Mace Eustace Greenleaf at Santa Ana. His family were orange growers. Mace was a sport and loved horse racing. He loved other things too, some of them not in keeping with his marriage vows. Their marriage went sour long before he died in Philadelphia, March 23, 1912.

During this marriage Lucy built a fine Spanish-type home with thick walls, reinforced timbers, and a patio. This home is presently occupied and in excellent condition at 1110 W. Anaheim St., Wilmington. Nine days after Greenleaf died, Lucy married Robert E. Ross at Riverside. She divorced Ross for infidelity.

Lucy was now frightfully frustrated, lonely and depressed. Life for her seemed empty and lacking in direction. She wanted to meet a man who would love her for herself and not for her money.

In 1919 Lucy was one of five heirs, along with her half-brothers, William, Joe and Hancock, and her sister Mary, who sold Catalina Island to William Wrigley for three million dollars. Lucy's mother died about this time, Aug. 22, 1919, leaving her another fortune. Lucy went into retirement.

When she emerged again, she was still a gorgeous creature. Her figure was flexible and elegant, her head well poised showing a rosy mouth, red cheeks, pearly teeth, blond curly hair, and soft, expressive eyes.

At elite social parties she carried herself in a manner indicative of culture and pride and with a face warm with good-nature and sympathy. So remarkable was her beauty that murmurs of admiration permeated the salon. Lucy had many suitors. They promised incense and myrrh; she wanted love, love for herself and not for her material possessions. She was still infinitely more stimulating and exciting than the whiff of any attar.

Lucy's next marriage was tragic. In her desperation she married an Oriental, Setsuza Ota, June 5, 1926. He was a graduate of the Imperial University of Tokyo, but the best he could do was wrestle for a living and make love to other women. We quote from the *Los Angeles Examiner,* Feb. 11, 1942: "Ota, now 43 and an enemy alien Japanese, was the fourth and last husband of the late Lucy, daughter of Gen. Phineas Banning, and considered in her day the most beautiful girl in all California. A speckled existence in more recent years found Ota being named defendant in a breach of promise suit in 1939, another 'East-West' tangle, and convicted in 1940 for kidnapping . . . Sentenced to five years in federal prison, Ota appealed and is in jail here."

The article mentions Lucy's estate, valued in excess of $350,000. Also mentioned is the Los Angeles home of the Bannings at 514 N. Broadway just purchased for the new County Courts Building." The $45,000 paid for the property was credited to the estate of the late Lucy Banning Bradbury Greenleaf Ross Ota. The executor of the Will is Attorney Ware Chapman." Such is the unhappy story of Lucy Banning's four marriages.

In 1929 Lucy was determined to "find" herself and return to the moral code of her childhood. She needed a change, maybe an extended trip to Italy. The center of the cultural arts would provide the right environment. In such a place, perhaps some of the freshness of her childhood at the old Banning manor in Wilmington would return, with a feeling of filial love, relaxation and restoration of the joy of living. It was worth a try.

In Tuscany and the Appennines of Lombardy, she fancied the earth would look good, smell good, taste good, and in all its texture of bark and blossom, leaf and blade, would have an invigorating effect. Perhaps she would meet a real man there.

In Florence she would try to make the most of her unhappy life. She would taper off and slow down. Her solitude and loneliness was painful, but her vivacity and good spirits never deserted her. She would glide in the Arno and bathe in the Po.

She would visit the famous art galleries and museums, journey to the La Scala Opera in Milan, relax in the music of Puccini, Rossini, and Verdi. She would go to Rome and feast her eyes on the paintings and sculptures of Michelangelo, Leonardi Di Vinci, and glory in the Sistine Chapel of St. Peters.

Before leaving Florence, she was invited to a royal party. This was fatal—the beginning of the end. At the reception she met a royal dandy, a tall, handsome man beautifully groomed and cultured. He was greatly impressed by this languorous beauty. Lucy was mesmerized by the first touch. Since there was no time like the present, he lost no time taking her to the Uffizi Palace to prove his title of Count.

Lucy accepted his bid to go with him to Venice, to the Dolomites, and to the Brenner Pass in Austria. But alas! When they returned to Florence, Lucy learned the Count was married and she was confronted with his lorgnette Countess.

Lucy settled out of court.

It was another snare and a delusion. She knew this kind of affair, based on lust rather than on love, could not endure. Lucy bore the reverses of her affairs and marriages with an equanimity peculiar to the Banning clan—a blood heritage that went back even to the Renaissance, when Rembrandt painted one of her ancestors in his famous "Night Watch."

Lucy was a lovely person. She may have coquetted more than would be decorous in a lady of fashion and culture, but if so, it was due to vanity and hunger for admiration. An appetite that grew as her hunger for true love went unsatisfied.

To the end she was devoid of anger and hostility. Her life came to an abrupt end. Lucy died mysteriously—some say it was a natural death—in Florence, Italy, Feb. 20, 1929, at the age of 53, still a ravishing beauty, unheralded, unsung, and unloved.

She is buried in the Banning plot, Rosedale Cemetery in Los Angeles, close to her father, her mother, and her sister, Mary.

8

The Early Sepulveda Clan

A brief history of the celebrated Sepulveda family from 1804 to Louis Sepulveda in 1979. They are a highly respected landmark family whose achievements are indelibily imprinted on local history.

THE QUESTION OF whether the adobe hide-house located at the Middle Reservation of Fort MacArthur was the first structure and business in San Pedro will soon be decided by the State of California Historic Resource Board.

The site of the old hide-house, recently found by Flora Baker and a committee of the San Pedro Bay Historical Society, may not have been the first commercial enterprise in San Pedro because historical research indicates that Delores Sepulveda, the first of the large and prominent Sepulveda family of the Palos Verdes, had an active and sometimes booming commercial business in San Pedro possibily 20 years before the hide-house, built in 1823, and made famous by Richard Henry Dana.

Delores built a depot warehouse in San Pedro to store sea otter and cattle hides, where early traders came in sailing ships to barter their wares, and load their ships with hides and tallow. He also maintained a ship chandlery business supplying ships with galley stores of grain, meats, wood, and water. Moreover, the San Gabriel Mission had a vested interest with Dolores in these commercial enterprises.

The old hide-house was constructed by ship agents, McCulloch and Hartnell, a company formed to facilitate and centralize trading with ships. They established other depots along the coast, including Santa Barbara, Monterey, and San Diego. Before this they dealt directly with the Sepulveda and the Dominguez families.

History reveals that trade restrictions were relaxed under the Mexican regime after 1822, but before then, Spanish officials permitted ships to enter the San

Pedro harbor for needed supplies, long before 1822. This was the business of ship chandlery, which also maintained lighters and rowboats to meet the ships anchored in the harbor. The old hide-house, no doubt, was the first large commercial enterprise in the harbor, but certainly it was not the beginning of San Pedro business.

The historic facts are that Dolores Sepulveda settled here in 1804 in the Rancho San Pedro land grant, first issued to Juan Dominguez in 1784, which embraced all of what is now the City of San Pedro. Before leaving Spain, Dolores married Maria Ygnacia Avila, both families representing pure Castilian blood and both families having long been identified with court life with king and royalty.

On the old Sepulveda Rancho Dolores and Maria gave birth to five children who lived, Jose Loreto, Jose Diego, Teresa, Juan and Ygnacio. During their married life, they had twelve children, only the five surviving.

Dolores, the father, was killed by Indians near San Luis Obispo, while returning from a trip to Monterey to see the governor about his land grants. Jose Diego Sepulveda, born in 1813, succeeded his father and became best known of the Sepulveda clan. His holdings were considerable, and in 1842 he added the Rancho San Bernardino and Yucaipa Valley. During the Mexican War, Jose Diego remained loyal to the United States and rendered aid to John C. Fremont's battalion, and to other troops that came West.

In the 1830s, Jose Diego Sepulveda married Maria Francesco Elisalde, daughter of the overseer of the San Diego Mission. He built a large home where Channel Street is now located in San Pedro, added large corrals and adobe houses for his caballeros and retainers, and directed the management of his vast estate from San Pedro. Don Jose Diego also died by an accident in 1872 by falling off a ladder. When his widow died a few years later she left three children, Aurelio W., Ramon D., and Rudecinda Florencia.

"In the 1870s my grandfather Don Jose Sepulveda sold the townsite in Yucaipe Valley at such a low price," said Louis Sepulveda, "that it was practically a gift." Ella Ludwig, in her book *Harbor District,* wrote that Mormons from San Bernardino used to come to the Sepulveda rancho bringing buffalo and deer skins to trade for ponies. Ludwig also records that Jose Diego gave three acres of land to the government for the Point Fermin Lighthouse in 1874. The government sent a check for $35, but Sepulveda sent it back uncashed. "The check is on display in archives at Washington, D.C.," according to Ludwig.

Ramon D. Sepulveda was born in San Pedro, August 9, 1854. After his schooling at St. Vincent's College in Los Angeles, he returned to San Pedro and dealt in real estate and contracting. He established the San Pedro Water Works, pumping water into reservoirs and tanks from his water lots, located back from about 1400 North Gaffey Street. He was one of the organizers of the First

National Bank of San Pedro, and a long-time member of the San Pedro City Council. Ramon also developed the warm sulphur springs at the White Point hotel and resort, and leased the facilities to responsible Japanese leaders. He also owned the land in the 1920s which was leased to the San Pedro Golf Club situated in the South Shores district. Ramon improved the facilities at Royal Palms, built a wharf for fishing, and helped beautify the shoreline all the way to Redondo.

Records show Ramon hauled the brick and lumber used in building the Point Fermin lighthouse from Crawfish Landing at Timms Point in 1874. At age 14 he also worked for Phineas Banning in Wilmington keeping time for workers on the San Pedro and Los Angeles Railroad.

The story is told that during Holy Week in Los Angeles, Jose Diego would command his son, Ramon, to hitch ox teams to carts and carrates for the long 10-mile a day trip to the fiesta with the family. Rawhide was stretched in lattice work across the interior of the carts to serve as a bed at night. The old wooden axles required constant greasing.

On one occasion, the report shows, Ramon neglected to grease in time, had to stop and hunt for a certain cactus, used after being ground to keep the axle and wheel from catching fire from friction. "These wagon wheels," he wrote, "could be heard for miles and was a signal to the church to toll the bells and celebrate, for the Sepulveda family was coming!"

Ramon married Caroline Oden in 1878. They had eight children, Albert G., William F., Caroline, Phillip R., Benjamin P., Elenita, Modesta, and Louis M. Only Louis M. and Modesta survive. They are the last of the direct Sepulveda clan from Dolores who came to San Pedro in 1804. Louis M. maintains offices in San Pedro and is the fiscal agent in charge of the Sepulveda interests.

9

Rudecinda Florencia de Sepulveda Dodson

Rudecinda contributed greatly to the welfare of San Pedro and to the Harbor Area. She was one of the most celebrated of the Sepulveda clan.

RUDECINDA FLORENCIA Sepulveda was a Castilian blueblood, to the manner born, and protected throughout her Christian life by proud parents and a coterie of devoted servants. She had 35,000 acres in which to romp, ride, and play. The Palos Verdes was her sunrise and her sunset.

Both her father and mother, the Jose Diego Sepulvedas, were religious and studious, read good books, and practiced the virtues which their religion ever enjoined—almsgiving to the poor, kindness to the sick and infirm, truthful, chaste, temperate and God-fearing.

Rudecinda was one of several children. She was a pretty baby with warm sparkling eyes, rosy cheeks, and dark wavy hair. Her birth on October 27, 1857, signalled the preparation of a long drive by oxcart and mule caravan of relatives from San Bernardino, Newport, Los Angeles, and Santa Barbara, to come see the newborn baby of Jose Diego Sepulveda, head of their clan. They would cross miles of plains, of mountains and sand, averaging about 15 miles a day for the trek to the distant Palos Verdes. They brought many gifts in grateful appreciation—not incense and myrrh, but a new pledge of love and loyalty to the growing importance of the Sepulveda families. Rudecinda became their favorite child, and she lived to make them proud.

Although Rudecinda was not sullied by moral sins as a teen-age girl, she was like most other girls, fond of fine dresses and perfumes, lace and ornaments, and elaborate hair-dressing. Her companions were likewise alert young ladies of rank, as fond of living as she was, and whose morals were equally above reproach.

The history of the Sepulvedas is a history of the San Pedro district, for it was here, on the Palos Verdes land grant, that the progenitor of the family on this continent, Dolores Sepulveda, settled in 1804 and brought to California some of the romantic splendor and customs of Castilian Spain. According to Ella Ludwig, in her history *Harbor District,* "Back in the seventeenth and eighteenth centuries, the Sepulvedas and their Avila kin were a part of the aristocracy and court life of old Castile. Provinces were named for both families and they had great influence with king and court."

In early life, Rudecinda was inclined to be overly strict to the ritualism of her church, but as she grew up she became moderate in reforms and spurned any suggestion toward religious bigotry. She was never parsimonious in helping worthy causes and aiding the poor.

She literally cut her teeth on righteousness, good manners and hospitality. Her father, Jose Diego, once owned Yucaipa Rancho, also La Mesa Rancho, where Newport now is, San Bernardino Rancho, and San Joaquin Rancho, embracing miles and miles of land near San Juan Capistrano. Phineas Banning had contracts to haul goods and passengers to most of these outlying districts. Banning was foremost in transportation from 1851 to 1885. He was contemporaneous and a good friend to most all the dashing Dons during this period. Rudecinda and her family were guests at the 30-room Banning Mansion in Wilmington on many occasions.

Rudecinda often wore a mantilla and heavy veils, both to protect her complexion and to fend the glances of strangers. And at large family fiestas she was wont to dance a mean fandango with her castanets in rhythmic accompaniment to song and dance.

In 1905 she donated land also for the building of the first San Pedro Women's Club, 11th and Gaffey Streets, of which her dutiful daughter, Florence Schoneman, was an active member up to her death in 1969. Rudecinda had three children who lived to maturity—Carlos, Florence, and James H. All of them, including her husband, lie buried under the careful supervision of the Los Angeles Department of Recreation and Parks in the Rudecinda Chapel at Harbor View Memorial Park, end of Grand Avenue South, San Pedro.

Rudecinda was a feminine first in many undertakings in San Pedro: first in the suffragist movement, first in driving an automobile, first in having a bank account in her own name, first in keeping her own books, and first in supervising the moral code of her vast establishment. She donated the crypt and the Rudecinda Chapel. Rudecinda died September 11, 1929, and is buried there with her family. She was indeed a great lady, and her spirit, thanks to the students and faculty of Dodson Junior High School, who have done much to memorialize her, should live on forever.

In 1881 Rudecinda married James H. Dodson, Sr., who was a Junior partner in the firm of Vickery and Hinds, wholesale butchers with offices in San Pedro and Wilmington. This writer claims kin to the Vickery part of this firm. Dodson was born in Palos Verdes, February 26, 1861, and was himself from a long line of prominent pioneer stock, including the eminent Dominguez family.

Dodson lived to contribute greatly to the advancement and progress of the San Pedro-Wilmington complex. He served five years as postmaster of San Pedro. He was a trustee of the local school board, marshal and license collector and a former president of the San Pedro Chamber of Commerce. His home was moved from Beacon and 7th Street to where the present San Pedro High School is now located.

The residence was later moved to its present location at 13th and Parker Streets in San Pedro. Dodson was one of the few who attended Wilson College, possibly the oldest college in California, established in 1874 from the buildings of the abandoned Civil War Drum Barracks. After two years, the school burned down. The college was named for Don Benito Wilson, who aided Phineas Banning in donating 60 acres of prime land in Wilmington for the establishment of Drum Barracks, named in honor of Richard Coulter Drum, who became a brigadier.

The facility was completed in 1862. Due to the Civil War, conditions in the harbor and Los Angeles were tense, exciting, and explosive. The records show two Sepulvedas enlisted. In front of the Officers' Quarters, 1053 Clay Street, is indelibly imprinted in cement the fact that these barracks saved California and the Pacific Southwest for the Union cause. Abraham Lincoln was grateful.

The Native Daughters of the Golden West have named two parlors in the names of the Dodson and Sepulveda families, Rudecinda Parlor No. 230, and

Sepulveda Parlor No. 236. Both organizations have been generous in contributing historic items to the Banning Museum, including several horse-drawn vehicles, which may be seen in the carriage house at the mansion.

For the past 14 years, this writer has researched old manuscripts, newspaper files, and family records. He has made two trips to the National Archives in Mexico City, in search of lost history of our harbor pioneers to put them into proper historic perspective.

We believe the Los Angeles Harbor district is one of the most unique districts in California, and the whole Pacific Coast. The students of Dodson Junior High School can be proud of their heritage and glory in the privilege of attending a school bearing the names of Dodson and Sepulveda. Both lived a life that was like a blessing to the poor and a benediction to the affluent.

10

The Amazing Pio Pico

His brother, Gen. Andreas Pico, ended the Mexican-American War by surrendering his troops to Lt. Col. Fremont at Cahuenga Pass in 1847. Gen. Stephen W. Kearny had Fremont court martialed for this act.

OF ALL THE Mexican governors who served in California from the time Mexico took over the territory from Spain in 1822, Pio Pico, the last governor, conformed less to the tyrannical rules from Mexico than any of his predecessors.

Pico exercised absolute power, but not in a harsh, cruel, or oppressive manner. He was, in general, a generous but maverick governor. His life was divided into two parts, the Mexican and the American. Pico became an important figure in California's transition from Mexican to American rule, and he became a leader in the cultural and economic development of American California.

Pico was born on May 5, 1801, the second son of ten children, while his soldier father was stationed at the San Gabriel Mission. Pio states in his memoirs, "I was born in a brush shelter, not even a house. When I was 18 years of age my father died, and I had to support the large family."

In his early manhood Pio was first and foremost a revolutionist. It seemed the revolution and counter-revolution in the Mexican period were the accepted manner for political advancement. During most of his revolutionary exploits Pico used the port of San Pedro as ordnance and supply headquarters.

Pico's political life began in 1826 with his appointment to the advisory committee to the governor at Monterey. In 1834 he married Governor Juan

Alvarado's niece, Maria Ignacia Alverado. They had no children, and when she died in 1860 he did not remarry. Pio received a land grant from Governor Alverado of some 10,000 acres, known as Rancho Jamul. This parcel of land was the beginning of Pico's vast empire.

Pico's first revolution was against Governor Manuel Victoria in 1831. Victoria led an army from Monterey to crush the rebel Pico at Los Angeles. Victoria lost, and Pio Pico became governor, but because of a counter-revolution Pico served only a few months, and was forced to resign on February 16, 1832.

In 1838 the ambitious Pico led an unsuccessful revolt against his old friend, Governor Alvarado. Pico was defeated, captured, taken prisoner and chained to his prison cell at the Santa Barbara barracks. Alvarado's niece and wife of Pio, Maria Ignacia Alvarado, pleaded to her uncle for Pio's life and safety. After a few weeks Pico was released, but the revolutionary spirit was still in his blood. In 1845 he led an army of rebels against Governor Manuel Micheltorena, and won it at the Battle of Cahuenga Pass.

This victory established Pio Pico as governor of California for a second time. This event ended the internal strife for leadership in California. The American troops had arrived and were waiting on the horizon.

Pico, unable to fight the war against the United States without adequate finances and supplies, escaped to Mexico in 1846 to seek aid. Mexico's failure to give aid eased the way for Gen. Stephen W. Kearny, Commodore Robert R. Stockton, and Col. John C. Fremont to win the Mexican War quickly. When General-In-Charge Jose Castro fled to Mexico, Gov. Pio Pico put his brother, Gen. Andreas Pico, in charge of the Mexican troops.

General Andreas likewise was ready to give up, but first he would sign an official treaty with Fremont at Cahuenga Pass, surrender all Mexican troops and cannon, and put an end to the Mexican-American war.

This act should have put a feather in the cap of Fremont. On the contrary it caused Fremont to be court-martialed. When Fremont met Gen. Kearny two days later near the outskirts of Los Angeles, upon Kearny's march with reinforced troops from San Diego, Kearny was furious about the surrender without a fight, stating that only generals win wars. He ordered Fremont arrested for insubordination.

Fremont went before a courts marshal in Washington, D.C. Commodore Stockton testified on behalf of Fremont, but Fremont was summarily reprimanded for accepting the treaty of surrender—a treaty that ended the war with Mexico without further bloodshed. Kearny's action established a legal precedent, which has become one of the most controversial cases in courts-martial history.

There is a Pio Pico State Historical Park in Whittier with Pico's 13-room mansion open to the public. Pico died in 1894 almost penniless, but he lived a vigorous 93 years, linking an exciting period in California history between two cultures that merged to make California a great state.

11
More About Pio Pico

The intrigues of Pio Pico were many and varied. The port of San Pedro played an important role in his life.

THE AREA THAT NOW comprises the highly developed complex of the Los Angeles harbor was originally an open roadstead in San Pedro Bay, subject, before the completion of the breakwater in 1910, to the ebb and flow of treacherous tides and winds that swept everything not securely fastened into the ocean's undertow.

During the years from 1822 to 1847, when Mexico controlled California, the San Pedro Bay was its busiest port. Monterey Bay was close second. San Diego Bay was a safer anchorage because of inland protection, but commerce there during the Mexican period was negligible. San Francisco Bay, with its scant population, did not become an important port until after the discovery of gold in 1849. Santa Barbara enjoyed some shipping, and Long Beach did not come into existence until 1888.

San Francisco's rise to popularity as a seaport began after the Treaty of Guadalupe Hidalgo was signed on Feb. 2, 1848, ending the Mexican War, and when California became a state on Sept. 9, 1850.

Before that time San Pedro Bay was the busiest port in California; more ships anchored and traded, or anchored to take on supplies than any other port in California. During this period none of the California ports had landing berths or docks; all of them had to anchor in their respective bays and were served, as in San Pedro Bay, by lighters to take people and goods ashore.

The San Pedro Bay is rich in historical folklore and anecdotes. It is recorded that one of the most important military events at San Pedro occurred during the waning days of Mexican domination with the deportation of Governor Michael Micheltorena and his rugged undisciplined army after Pio Pico defeated him at the Battle of Cahuenga. On Feb. 23, 1845, Pico allowed Micheltorena to depart with his ragged army with military honors, drums beating and flags flying, from Los Angeles to San Pedro for deportation to Mexico.

But the soldiers were not allowed to march through the streets of downtown San Pedro. It is said the citizens had a vivid recollection of the many raids on their orchards, barns, and chicken coops, by Micheltorena guerrillas over a long period of time.

The soldiers had to encamp three weeks on the plain where the lower reservation of Ft. MacArthur is now located, just below the old enlarged hide house. The hide-house was quadrangular in form with transverse wings, made famous by Richard Henry Dana. Even during this encampment night raids were made in San Pedro for more chickens and eggs. The raids practically cleaned out the harbor area; irate citizens demanded that Pico hurry up and find a ship that would take this undesirable group back to Mexico.

Pico and his friends, Jose Figueroa, Antonio Maria Lugo, and Jose Antonio Carillo, grandfather of the late Leo Carillo, pledged financial help. They found a suitable sailing vessel, the Don Quixote, in the harbor; her master, Capt. John Paty, agreed to take Micheltorena and his soldiers to the port of San Blas for $11,000. The agreement called for payment of $1,000 when the ship left San Pedro, March 12, 1845, and another $1,000 when the ship arrived at Monterey, where Pico would go to become the governor to succeed Micheltorena and issue a permit for the trip to San Blas. The remainder of the payment was to be taken from customs receipts.

In 1832 the people of Los Angeles and San Pedro had to put up money to deport another Mexican governor, Manuel Victoria, who lost to Pico in the deciding battle fought also in the Cahuenga Pass. Two of Victoria's personal staff lost their lives, many were wounded, and Victoria himself was badly disabled. After the battle Pico allowed Victoria to be sent to San Gabriel Mission for care and convalescence.

Fortunately for Victoria, Pico arranged to have the surgeon of the brigantine Ayacucho anchored in San Pedro to go to San Gabriel and treat him. The surgeon pronounced the wound dangerous, but not fatal. When he was able to travel, he was escorted with a courteous bodyguard and taken to San Pedro for deportation to Mexico. During this interval Pico was already sworn in as governor at Monterey.

But when Pico became governor again after the defeat of Micheltorena in 1845, Pico moved the Mexican Capitol from Monterey to Los Angeles because he wanted to be near the Port of Los Angeles, just in case. . . .

12

The Original Palos Verdes Land Grant

How the Sepulvedas obtained the Palos Verdes land grant from Pio Pico, the last Mexican Governor in 1846.

ONE OF THE rarest items in California history is an original land deed or grant dating from the Spanish or Mexican period. The originals of such instruments usually were kept by the grantees, but few have survived due to being misplaced, or by fire, or by neglect and indifference. Even a trip to the National Archives in Mexico City will reveal a scant few.

For almost 15 years the author has diligently searched archives and old family records of pioneers, determined to find a copy of the significant land deed issued by Mexican governor Pio Pico in 1846, when he deeded the important Palos Verdes property, including San Pedro, to the Sepulveda family. Recently, Marjorie Sepulveda Bellew, daughter of the late Albert G. Sepulveda, grandson of Jose Diego Sepulveda, provided the author with a copy of the Palos Verdes deed.

The deed is from an original land grant issued to Don Juan Dominguez by Spain in 1784, embracing some 75,000 acres and known as the San Pedro Rancho, from which many communities have been formed, including Redondo Beach, Torrance, Gardena, Compton, San Pedro, Wilmington, Lomita, Harbor City, Carson, and Dominguez.

Albert Sepulveda was a son of the late Ramon Sepulveda and a brother of San Pedran Louis Sepulveda, fiscal agent of the Sepulveda estate, who seldom misses a day at his Pacific Avenue office. The deed reads as follows:

> *Pio Pico, Constitutional Governor of the Department of California*
>
> Whereas, the citizens Jose Lareto and Juan Sepulveda, brothers have claimed for their personal benefit and that of their families, the tract known by the name of Palos Verdes which they have possessed provisionally under grant made by the government of this country 19 years ago, the investigations in that behalf having been taken. In the exercise of the powers wherewith I am invested, in the name of the Mexican Nation, I do now by decree of this day grant unto them the aforesaid tract, declaring unto them the ownership thereof by the present letters in conformity with the law of August, 1824, under reservation of the approval of the Departmental Assembly and under the following conditions: They may enclose it without prejudicing the crossroads, highways and rights of way; they shall enjoy it freely and

exclusively, devoting it to the use and improvement which it may behoove them.

They shall request the competent magistrate to give them juridical possession by virtue of this patent, which magistrate shall assign the proper landmarks.

The tract hereby granted is that known by the plan filed with the minutes of proceedings. The judge who gives the possession will cause it to be measured conformably to ordinance and shall report to the Government the number of ranges (sitios) for meat cattle which it contains.

They shall leave on the beach of San Pedro five hundred varas (unit of linear measure, varying from 32 to 43 inches) in each direction of the four cardinal points. Neither shall they have power to prevent the persons who traffic at the port of San Pedro from using water and pasturage.

In consequence, I order that the present title, being held as firm and valid, be entered of record in the appropriate book and delivered to the parties in interest for their protection and future ends.

Given on common paper, there being none stamped, on the third day of the month of June, One Thousand Eight Hundred and Forty-Six.

Pio Pico (Signature)
Jose Matias Moreno, Secty. ad interim (Witness).

This deed caused considerable controversy and legal complications between the Dominguez Estate and the Sepulveda family. After California was annexed to the United States in 1850, federal land commissioners sustained the Pio Pico grant on behalf of the Sepulvedas, but the resulting appeals and court litigation froze the deed in escrow up to the late 1870s.

The drought of 1863-65 destroyed most of the Sepulveda cattle, and legal fees and high interest rates during this period caused great hardship on the Sepulveda family. They eventually won clear title, but the damage was done.

Even the 16,000-acre plot which Frank Vanderlip bought from Jotham Bixby in 1913-1915 was a foreclosure by the Bixby against this Sepulveda property. The Sepulveda clan, however, had other property which they proudly retained intact. One of the largest and best-known boulevards in Los Angeles is named in honor of the Sepulvedas.

13

Brief History of Early San Pedro

Intriguing history from Cabrillo in 1542 to Vizcaino in 1602, to Portola and Serra in 1769, to Phineas Banning in 1851.

WHEN JUAN RODRIGUEZ CABRILLO came ashore in San Pedro on October 8, 1542, and named the area "Bahia Los Fumos," it became the most notable historic event that ever happened to our community. However, during the years since that significant epic, 437 years ago, San Pedro has matured.

Looking down the corridors of history, it is plain to see that San Pedro would inevitably become the main gateway port of Southern California: There was no other natural harbor between San Diego and San Francisco.

Most maritime navigators and engineers consider Long Beach as a part of the San Pedro bay, because their port was made possible by the breakwater program started in San Pedro in 1899, and it was only natural that Long Beach would hitch-on and take advantage of this jackpot landfall. But geography has been even more kind to San Pedro in its location.

San Pedro is 21 miles south of Los Angeles, which itself is the center of and adjacent to an enormous agricultural, educational and financial complex with its leadership in aircraft manufacturing, automobile assembly plants, rubber and tire factories, furniture manufacturing, men's and women's cloth spinning centers, and fruit and vegetable processing plants. And San Pedro itself is the home of the largest and most successful tuna and fish canneries in the nation, two large shipbuilding yards, and miles of cargo space, piers, docks, berths, slips and warehouses, besides 20,000 acres of ocean water providing safe anchorage for ships from storm, fire, and quake. Also, San Pedro has close proximity to modern refineries and prolific gas- and oil-producing fields.

All United States shipping companies have offices or representatives in the San Pedro area, and most all the world-wide trading firms have close connections with the port. Several cargo and passenger vessels enter the Los Angeles Port every day of the year, and the in-and-out passenger and freight cargo is steadily increasing, according to harbor department records.

It is no accident that San Pedro is the center of all this activity. It did not just happen. San Pedro was founded and nurtured by human dreams, human toil, and human initiative with vision to see, faith to believe, and courage to do. These has been the guidelines and the blueprint ever since Cabrillo in 1542 was welcomed to these shores by the friendly Chumash Indians who provided him with generous provisions.

Sebastian Vizcaino was likewise welcomed by the Indians when he came in 1602 and changed the name of the area to San Pedro. Over the ensuing years other pioneers came to the San Pedro Harbor and contributed their bit, Juan Dominguez in 1784, Dolores Sepulveda in 1804, John Charles Fremont in 1846, and Phineas Banning in 1851. But Phineas Banning gets the honor of being the Father of the Port.

And let us not forget the exploits of Gaspar Portola and Fr. Junipero Serra, who came to San Pedro in 1774 to convert the Indians and plant the seeds of culture and progress, and George Vancouver, British explorer, who sailed into the harbor in his ship Discovery on November 6, 1794, and met Fr. Fermin Francisco Lasuen, who camped here planning to build a mission. The mission was later built in San Fernando. Vancouver named Point Fermin in honor of Lasuen's sojourn in San Pedro.

The modern Los Angeles Harbor, created by Phineas Banning out of an expansive mud-flat is today the greatest man-made port in the world. It is known throughout all the shipping ports as a maritime miracle. San Pedro is heading toward a new profitable trade era because of the port's modern technology.

To a careful observer it appears San Pedro has contributed greatly in the making of history, based on the fact that the port is envied, respected, and copied by other nations; also that our local citizens and businessmen have had a strong sophisticated grassroots foundation in their thinking, acting, doing and understanding of where the community has been and where it is headed.

Obviously, the alert and progressive San Pedro spirit has gone right along over the years with the old motto uppermost, "It is better to light a candle than to curse the darkness."

14

Smugglers Are Smug

Dr. John Kemble, eminent authority, explains the hazards that the sea otter faces in a comeback along the Pacific Coast and how smugglers first popularized its fur.

THE SAN PEDRO BAY Historical Society hit a jackpot of information on smuggling in San Pedro at its Sept. 22, 1976 meeting.

"Smuggling began in California," Professor John Kemble said, "in the late eighteenth century under Spanish rule, during which time Spain did not allow trade with any other country."

"This smuggling lingered on even after the Mexican takeover from Spain in 1822," he said, "and on until the Treaty of Guadalupe Hidalgo was signed on Feb. 2, 1848. The fur of the sea otter started the first smuggling in California, and San Pedro became one of the favorite trading and outfitting centers in the smuggling and contraband enterprise."

Records show that during the Spanish period, from 1769 to 1822, foreign vessels were seldom seen on the California coast. Those that did anchor did so under pretense of needing repairs and urgent supplies.

"And under surveillance," Kemble said, "they succeeded in doing considerable smuggling in sea otter furs by bartering sorely needed items with Mission padres and the rancheros."

The sea otter potential in food and furs was discovered by Denmark's Vitus Bering's 24 shipwrecked castaways in 1741 on the islands off Alaska that are named for him.

These survivors subsisted wholly on sea otter meat and the warmth of the furs from Nov. 6, 1741, to Aug. 17, 1742. Bering's records state that during this time they killed several hundred otters.

The Russians zealously entered into the illicit trade and worked down the coast to Bodega Bay, where they established Fort Ross in 1812.

The news of the vast profits in sea otter trade brought many sailing ships to the coast and was a means of making San Pedro and California well-known to the outside world.

"Furs could be bought from the Indians and others for from $1 to about $5 each," Kemble said, "and in China a good pelt would fetch as much as $500."

Kemble also said that in the Bay of San Pedro and off Dead Man's Island, Santa Catalina, San Clemente, the Channel Islands and in every inlet along the coast where kelp beds were abundant, sea otters multiplied; there were hundreds of thousands of them to about 1870. Then, like the plains buffalo, they almost became extinct by ruthless slaughter.

"The smuggler anchored his ship in some safe shelter on the leeward side of Santa Catalina," Kemble said, "and when the opportune time came and the coast was clear, a quick dash was made for San Pedro. After a rapid exchange of goods for furs, away he sailed. The ship Leila Byrd accomplished this feat several times."

Spain did not charter trading companies as did England, France and Holland, but herself became a monopoly. At first the colonists were forbidden olives, grapes and many other products which the Mission padres urgently needed.

"It was inevitable, therefore," Kemble said, "that a policy of illicit and illegal trade would flourish, and smuggling would become rampant between the stranger and the Spaniards."

The padres were adept at smuggling, always ready to furnish furs and negotiate terms when a ship agent visited them.

Mexican Gov. Arguello, speaking of contraband in 1824, said, "I see not why we should prevent it, since our people are the gainers."

It is said that revenue officials, merchants, traders, the missions and the people all became smugglers by collecting furs, pelts, and whale oil, ready to sell to the first outbound vessel.

Before the arrival of the new England hide droghers, the padres and the people depended upon the coming of Spanish supply ships, which were few and far between. The people demanded foreign products, and the officials were in sympathy with them.

The playful sea otter became the tragedy of the fur world. The sea otter is a child of the ocean. It is born in a sea bed of kelp, rocked in the waves, plays in the sea, submerges for abalone, then comes up to crack them open with a rock on its belly.

Sea otters are protected by law now and are slowly making a comeback. Abalone fishermen, afraid the sea otters are robbing them of their livelihood, are suspects in preventing their propagation.

Dr. Herbert Bolton, this writer's history professor at the University of California, Berkeley, described the beauty of the sea otter fur as of very fine texture, dense, soft and silky, by paraphrasing Sir Isaac Walton's tribute to the strawberry: "God might have made a more beautiful fur, but doubtless he never did."

15
Whaling in San Pedro Bay

Whales were once so plentiful off the California coast and even in San Pedro Harbor "We took little notice of them."

WHALING BECAME an important industry early in San Pedro's history.

Father Crespi, chronicler for Father Junipero Serra and the early missions, left a record saying he saw many whales spouting when he arrived in San Pedro Bay in the spring of 1772.

He wrote that large numbers of whales of different varieties passed south in December, January and February, returing north in March, April, May and June.

Richard Henry Dana also tells of whales in his book, *Two Years Before the Mast,* published in 1845: "This being the spring season, San Pedro, as all other ports upon the coast, are filled with whales that had come to make their annual visit upon the soundings . . . for the first few days that we were here . . . we watched them with great interest, calling out 'thar she blows' every time we saw the spout of one breaking the surface of the water, but they soon became so common that we took little notice of them."

The first whalers were Norwegians, history shows. Pictures carved in rocks thousands of years ago show these men hunting whales from canoes.

American Indians also hunted whales, including the California gray whales that pass between San Pedro and Catalina Island in their annual migrations. The Indians used harpoons with points made of stone, bone, or wood.

About 1815, America began whaling in a big way. In the 1840s there was a record 750 American whaling ships. New Bedford, Mass., was the whaling capital of the world.

Whalers hunted the Arctic toothless baleen whales that provided whalebone for women's corsets, bustles and hoopskirts, buggy whips, umbrella ribs, fishing rods, and other articles that had to be strong, light, and elastic.

The sperm whale, found in all oceans, grows to about 65 feet in length and weighs 60 tons. It is the largest toothed whale with 36 to 56 cone-shaped teeth in the lower jaw. These teeth were made famous by Herman Melville in Moby Dick in 1851. This whale provides materials for certain salves and face creams and substances to lubricate machinery and soften leather; their ambergris is the base for many expensive perfumes.

The oil from the large blue whale, the largest mammal that ever lived—much bigger than pre-history's reptilian dinosaurs—is used chiefly for margarine, glycerine and soap; the meat is used as food in zoos. Some people in Japan and Norway eat whale meat, and many Eskimoes thrive on whale blubber.

San Francisco and San Pedro became Pacific coast centers for outfitting whaling ships. The main rendezvous point, however, during this period was the Sandwich Islands, now known as the Hawaiian Islands.

The *California Chronicle* on May 20, 1856, mentions a whaling station at Portuguese Bend and some whaling activity on Dead Man's Island, as well as shark catching at Santa Catalina Island. Sharks were prized for their liver oil. Shark hunters were also adept at catching the gray whale, which was plentiful then.

The demand for whale oil—used for lamp fuel and wagon axle grease—declined with the growth of the U.S. petroleum industry.

John Olguin, director of the Cabrillo Marine Museum and a local authority on whales, pointed out that the killer whale, found in all oceans, averaging 30 feet in length, weighing 10 tons and having 40 to 48 teeth, is an enemy to California gray whales, as is the sword fish.

Olguin said, "Like other mammals, whales bear their young alive and nurse on their mother's milk for the first year. All whales breathe through lungs, and they must hold their breath when they dive under water. When the whale reaches the surface after a long dive, it blows out its hot breath, (which) when it strikes the colder, outside air . . . condenses, forming a spout of fog.

"Our whalewatch program is geared to observe the migration of the California gray whales," Olguin continued. "These whales were on the verge of extinction by reckless, indiscriminate slaughter a few years ago, but they are now protected by an international treaty signed in 1938. We want to give the few remaining whales their freedom from the harpoon forever."

In 1975, the last of the California whaling vessels, centered at Richmond, was dismantled. There are no more whaling stations or whale oil factories on the California coast, and the protected whales are slowly increasing in numbers for everyone to enjoy as they swim along our coast, grunting grateful grunts, spouting to and from Alaskan Waters.

16
Captain James Cook and His Alaskan Voyage

The early story of how the Russians slaughtered the sea otter along the California coast, and the establishment of Fort Ross in 1812. Also a folklore love story between a Russian count and a beautiful Spanish Senorita.

CAPTAIN JAMES COOK sailed from Plymouth, England, in 1776 to explore the north Pacific Coast of Alaska. Cook sailed around Cape Horn and continued northwest until he reached the Russian settlement around Nootka Sound. While there, he was amazed to discover the extent of the rich Russian sea otter fur trade.

Because of Cook's discovery the Spanish government, fearing the encroachment of Russian ships upon its territory of California, and wishing to avoid the consequences of a fight, ceased to lay claim to any territory along the Pacific Coast above what now is the boundary between California and Oregon. Don Gaspar Portola and Father Junipero Serra were notified to confine their explorations to the 42 degree north latitude. But Spain was still apprehensive and alerted to any Russian movements southward, especially along the California coast.

Disregarding the Spanish warning, the Alaska Russians were urged by Moscow to investigate the Spanish settlements in California and take note of all sea otter fur possibilities.

Russia's first ship, the Juneo, came all the way to San Pedro Bay and slaughtered enough sea otter on Catalina Island to fill the holds of their ship. They processed the skins there, sold some to China, and some to American traders. Thus the first economic venture with California by Russia was solely with the sea otter fur trade. The cattle hide and tallow industry came into being later, then only after the sea otter was almost exterminated.

The Russian profit motive was whetted. They began to kill sea otters right and left, and showed no compassion for the female otters even when giving birth to their young. The Russians clamored for more furs, and established the large settlement which became known as Fort Ross in 1812 and made it their California headquarters.

A crew of 95 Russians and 40 Aleuts came from Alaska and built this stockade fort with heavy redwood timbers. The fort was 30 miles north of Bodega Bay, and 13 miles northwest of a large flowing stream which they named the Russian River. They built a fleet of sailing barks and finally slaughtered almost all the sea otters off our coast and the off-shore islands. It is recorded that one of the Russian ships returned to Sitka with 2,350 sea otter pelts and a greeting that the California coast was clear with an abundance of food resources. There was no danger with a fight with the Spanish.

The Russian czar was delighted, self-assured, and brave. The czar issued a "ukase" closing the Pacific Coast north of San Francisco to all but Russian ships. This order prompted an emergency meeting of President James Monroe's cabinet and their advisers, resulting in the Monroe Doctrine, proclaimed before the United States Congress in 1823, guaranteeing independence of Americans against any European or foreign interference on the North American Continent. This act sealed the fate of Fort Ross.

By the end of 1839, Russian officials ordered their colonists to sell out and return to Alaska. Captain John A. Sutter bought Fort Ross property in 1841. After 1845 the fort area became the center of a large ranch. The fort itself collapsed in the earthquake of 1906. The site was then purchased and rebuilt by the Landmarks Committee of San Francisco and presented to the state of California the same year. It is now a popular all-year tourist attraction.

The first Americans to come into California were fur traders and trappers, blazing the trail overland from the east. In 1826 Jedediah Smith led an expedition from Great Salt Lake and traveled southward toward the Colorado River. They reached the Mojave Desert and traveled along the Mojave River to the San Bernardino Mountains, crossing the Cajon Pass to the San Gabriel Mission.

After several months at the mission as the special guest of Father Jose Sanchez, Smith was ordered out of the state by the Mexican authorities, and returned to Utah. Most of Smith's reports were turned over to the federal government and given to John Charles Fremont and his guide, Kit Carson, and used by them in their later trail blazing into California.

Even while hunting sea otter, the Russians were attracted by the great herds of whales splashing through the water between San Pedro and the Palos Verdes

Peninsula and Catalina Island, often harpooning one or more for food and oil, and carving their bones for utensils.

The author found an old folklore love story at the Bancroft Library at Berkeley. It is connected with the early Russian fur traders. When the Russian bark Juneo sailed into Monterey Bay after leaving San Pedro, it had aboard a Russian count, Nicolai Rezanoff. In the course of negotiations with the Spanish officals he was introduced to the beautiful daughter of Spanish Governor Jose Arguello, Senorita Dona Concepcion. After a brief romance, they became engaged with the blessing of all concerned, and when Rezanoff set sail for Sitka, he promised to return to Monterey to marry her and take her to the family castle in Moscow.

Years went by and Concepcion who, for many months, used to stand on the Monterey cliffs scanning the horizon for her lover, and not hearing from him, became a Catholic nun. She later learned that Rezanoff had died soon after leaving California. It is said the story of this romance was told for many years, through the Spanish and Mexican regimes, and became known as California's most famous love story.

That honor now, however, probably belongs to the Spanish girl, Ramona, and her Indian lover, Allesondro.

17
Richard Henry Dana in San Pedro

There was a flogging in San Pedro Bay. Henry Mellus, who became mayor of Los Angeles in 1860, was a passenger aboard the Pilgrim.

WHEN THE BRIG Pilgrim came to San Pedro in 1835 with Richard Henry Dana, there was another passenger who became prominent in the economic and political life of Los Angeles and the harbor. His name was Henry Mellus.

Mellus paid Capt. Edward H. Faucon a large bribe to leave the Pilgrim in San Pedro. Mellus was a guest of the Sepulveda family until he entered the mercantile business in Los Angeles.

In 1860 he became mayor of Los Angeles, when the City showed a population of 4,339. He invested in real estate and profited greatly.

According to W. W. Robinson, in his book on the pueblo of Los Angeles, Mellus was a cultured romanticist, genial and gracious. His new political office taught him that prosperity did not necessarily create a demand for good government. Mellus found the citizens of Los Angeles much too engrossed in their own private affairs and only occasionally took time to ponder the vicissitudes of city officers. It was difficult for him to appoint responsible committees to carry out civic projects.

Mayor Mellus helped Phineas Banning organize the Southern California chapter of the Sanitary Commission, a forerunner of the American Red Cross. The sick and wounded had multiplied due to the hazards of reckless mining techniques during the gold rush. During Mellus' tenure in office, the Newhall Hills were producing considerable gold and Santa Catalina Island became the center of a mining stampede. Accidents and prolonged droughts caused some untimely deaths. Many were hopelessly crippled for life. There were no hospitals, and certainly no Medicare.

Mellus donated his private library, consisting of a large chestful of books which he brought from the east coast aboard the Pilgrim, to the Los Angeles Public Library. All of Dana's books and most of his manuscripts, which Mellus accumulated later, were part of the donation. Dana's *Two Years Before the Mast,* published in 1840, later became a masterpiece.

Ann Rumery, librarian at the San Pedro Library, is having a search made at the main Los Angeles Library to find some of this Dana memorabilia for the benefit of the San Pedro community.

The Pilgrim sailed up and down the Pacific Coast for two years before its holds were filled with hides and sea otter furs. After arriving in Boston, Dana returned to Harvard Law School and, after graduation, specialized in maritime cases.

While aboard the "Pilgrim" in San Pedro Harbor, Mellus was an eye witness to a flogging. We'll let Dana tell it:

> "Now for you," said the captain, walking up to John, and taking his irons off.
>
> "What do you want to flog me for?" asked John. "Have I ever refused to do my duty, sir?"
>
> "No," said the captain, "it is not that, that I flog you for. I flog you for your interference, for asking questions."
>
> "Can't a man ask a question here without being flogged?" John asked.
>
> "No," shouted the captain, "nobody shall open his mouth aboard this vessel but myself," and began laying blows upon John's back, swinging half around between each blow to give it full effect. As the

captain went on, his passions increased, and he danced about the deck, calling out as he swang the rope; "If you want to know what I flog you for, it's because I like to do it! It suits me! That's what I want to do it for!"

The man writhed in pain until he could endure it no longer, when he called out, with an exclamation more common among the foreigners than with us: "Oh, Jesus Christ! Oh, Jesus!"

"Don't call on Jesus Christ," shouted the Captain. "He can't help you. Jesus Christ can't help you now!"

"At these words, which I shall never forget, my blood ran cold. I could look on no longer. Disgusted, sick, I turned away and leaned over the rail and looked down into the water."

18
SEARSPORT CLIPPERS

Searsport, Maine, built most of the clipper ships that sailed to San Pedro for the rich haul in hides and tallow. One of the ships was named for Phineas Banning.

SAN PEDRO has not been the same since the active maritime days from 1850 to the 1900s, when the port was visited with all kinds of sailing vessels, including windjammers, schooners, barks, brigs, and clippers.

Every local history buff who has pictures of these ships is eager to show them off. Some of the vessels are seen anchored in the bay, but most of them are shown lining the wharves of the expanding port, unloading lumber. The majority of all the sailing ships that came to San Pedro and Wilmington were launched at Searsport, Maine. This is the place where the adjacent forest furnished a fine supply of the best shipbuilding wood, consisting of oak, spruce, maple, and hackmatack.

Clarence M. Bailey, formerly of Searsport, and kin to an old shipping family there, gave the author a rare maritime casebound book with about 300 pictures of the finest looking, proud and well-disciplined former sea captains he has ever seen in a book.

Many of these masters had sailed their ships into the port of San Pedro. The first clipper ship ever built was named Rainbow, launched at Searsport in 1845. It made a trip in 1851 for a cargo of hides picked up in stops at Santa Barbara,

San Pedro, and San Diego. To quote the book, "Searsport furnished more ship masters to the square mile than any others community in the United States."

The book also reveals an interesting episode in the personal history of Phineas Banning. There are 12 Captain Blanchards in the book. One of them, Capt. William H. Blanchard, sailed his bark, Wealthy Pendleton, onto a mud flat near Dead Man's Island, on February 17, 1879. Two days later Phineas Banning's S. S. Crickett pulled the bark off the sand bar while Mrs. Blanchard was giving birth to a healthy son, and she named it Phineas Banning Blanchard.

In 1904 this son, Phineas Banning Blanchard, obtained his shipmaster's papers at Searsport; three months later he sailed the Bark Willard Mudgett for Wilmington, and followed it with several more trips from Boston via Cape Horn. Each time he arrived in Wilmington he met Capt. William Banning, son of the late Phineas Banning, who taught him all he needed to know on how to run a successful stevedoring company, a business Blanchard was eager to learn.

In 1915 Capt. Blanchard retired from the sea and became a partner in the new firm of Turner & Blanchard Stevedores, in Brooklyn, N.Y. The company is still in business.

Captain Blanchard's mother was a daughter of Wealthy Pendelton, a prominent Searsport ship owner. Blanchard's father, Capt. William H. Blanchard, retired in 1904 from his long experience as master of at least 10 sailing vessels, including Ship Alice Buck; Ship Bosphorus, 1863-65, wrecked in Valencia, Spain; Bark Wealthy Pendleton, 1874-83; Ship Phineas Pendleton, burned in Manila Bay, 1885; Ship Governor Robie, 1886-88; Bark Evenell, 1891-95; Bark Henry Buck, 1898; Bark Herbert Black, 1890-91, 1896, 1900-01; Bark Addie Morrell, 1902; Bark Tijuca, 1903; Bark Czarina, 1904.

On September 10, 1904, he sailed from Norfolk, Virginia, for Bangor, Maine, as a passenger on the bark Willard Mudgett, which he owned and which was commanded by his son, Fred Blanchard. After the ship left Norfolk, nothing was heard of the vessel or the crew of 12 sailors. It was presumed that she floundered in a heavy southeast gale which was prevailing along the coast. His widow moved from Searsport in 1915 to be with her son, Phineas Banning Blanchard. She became bookkeeper of his profitable stevedoring business in Brooklyn. She died there in 1931.

The first people to sail the seas may have been the Arabs who traveled across the Indian Ocean in small sailing ships called dhows. About 1500 B.C. Egyptians had a fleet of galleys, propelled mostly by chained slaves with oars, under the stern commands of the bosun's whip. The ship had one sail with 15 men on each side, and two men with oars at the stern for steering.

Phoenician sailors traveled all parts of the Mediterranean Sea, perhaps as far as the British Isles. The Greeks also became expert sailors early in their long history. According to Homer, their oar power slaves carried their ships to the shores of Troy during the Trojan War about 1200 B.C. Their wooden ships were the first to have a curved stern and a tall bow with a handsomely carved figurehead.

Decorative hand-carved maple figureheads were installed on many ships that came to San Pedro Bay, and Clarence Bailey will try to obtain one from the Searsport Marine Museum, for our Los Angeles Maritime History Museum, which hopefully should be ready by the end of 1979.

19
ROMANTIC CLIPPERS

In song and poetry clippers sang their way into the hearts of all historical buffs. Cow hides from our port made Boston a famous city.

NO EPISODE IN California history can surpass in song and poetry or in economic importance the old clipper ships that sailed from Boston and New England to our shores. They brought items to be bartered for hides and tallow.

Each hide was worth $2, and when the clipper was loaded with about 40,000 hides and a few tons of tallow, she would pull anchor and head for Atlantic waters around Cape Horn. One-way clipper ship trips averaged 100 days, about 30 days faster than most other sailing vessels.

Most of the hides were unloaded in Boston. From the hides they made leather, and from the leather they made shoes and luggage. Thus Boston became the shoe center of the United States and other New England towns became world centers for candles and soap made from tallow, thanks to the port of San Pedro.

It can be said that the port of San Pedro was the source from which Boston became a powerful entity in the economic trade lanes of America.

During the busy period of the clippers, Los Angeles county was about twice as large as it is today and most all of it was given to cattle raising from large ranchos and San Pedro was the main hide port in California.

Orange County was sliced from L.A. County in 1889. Later most of Riverside and other adjacent counties took enormous land areas from L.A. County. All of San Bernardino County at one time belonged to Los Angeles County.

There were 159 vessels in the clipper fleet that touched the shores of San Pedro Bay at least once. Some of them unloaded cargo here and headed with hides and tallow for the China tea trade and for the teak-wood and mahogany trade in the Philippines. Some of the clippers went to Australia and on around the world.

The clipper ship was a speed ship. According to old files of the Pacific Marine Review, the clipper embodied two main principles of construction: To cleave the water with least possible resistence and to carry the greatest possible spread of sail. "Her hull was long, slim and concave, and she slipped along with fish-like ease through the waves. And she was beautiful."

Clippers had poetic names, and some of them with speed histories that graced our shores were the Flying Cloud, Young America, Sea Witch, Flying Fish and Trade Wind. Sovereign of the Seas made a speed in 1852 of 425 nautical miles in 24 hours. But the clipper Lightning made a run of 436 nautical miles in one day. Even modern cargo steam vessels can hardly top that.

The Great Republic was the largest clipper ever built, 4,555 tons with a crew of 130. The Flying Cloud on her California trips got the most publicity. She could carry 60,000 hides in her hold, but she met a tragic death. She was burned in Halifax in 1875.

In researching old files, the author ran across an unsigned poem describing in touching lines the clippers on the San Pedro run. It has the tang of seasalt and the exuberant strength of ocean winds.

"The old clipper days were jolly when we sailed the seven seas.
And the house-flags of our merchant-ships were whipped by every breeze.
It was goodbye to your mother and the pretty girls on shore.
For we're off around the howling Horn, bound for San Pedro to Singapore.
We romped the rushing tradewinds and we raced the big monsoon:
We carried relling royals from Manilla to Rangoon;
We were chased by Malay pirates from Fiji to Penang,
And we drove her scuppers under to outsail the cut-throat gang.
We went rolling in the doldrums till the tar oozed from our seams;
We went pushing through the icepack till the pressure cracked our beams.
Those were the days to be remembered, when our good ship sailed away,
From the Boston port behind us to San Pedro, Calcutta or Bombay.
It was bundle out, my bullies, and give the sheet a pull;
It was ease her off a little, till the topsails stand rap full.
It was scrub the deck, my buddies, and we'll take the sun at noon;
It was Sou-sou-west, my boy, beneath the southern moon.
Then 'twas home again, my bullies, with our bow knee deep in foam,
To the mother that was waiting and the happy ones at home;
It was home from old Calcutta, San Pedro or from Bombay,
To the land we loved to think of when our hearts were far away.
The old clipper days are over and the white winged fleet's no more.
With their snowy sails unfolded, fly along the ocean floor;
And it's goodbye mother, once for all, and goodbye girls on shore,
And it's goodbye old clipper-ship that sailed the seas no more."

20
Cow Hide Guerdon

It was Los Angeles hide shipments that made Boston famous as a leather and shoe manufacturing center.

IT IS SAID THAT every age has its identifying vices and virtues. The vices are quickly recognized, the virtues take longer to discover. This writer is essentially concerned with the life and history of Phineas Banning and others who contributed to the early development of the Los Angeles Harbor complex, and of their influence in the progress of the old pueblo, now known as Los Angeles, and of Southern California as a whole.

While Phineas Banning may not have been the whole bowl of cherries, he definitely had his finger dangling in the bowl in the area's economic, political, military, and social development. We find Banning had many heretofore unpublished virtues.

Almost from the very first day he landed in San Pedro in 1851 from his native Wilmington, Del., Banning became an important fixture in the life of our community. His first venture was the establishment of a lighterage and barge business, unloading and loading cargo from the ships anchored in San Pedro Bay and bringing the goods to warehouse facilities which he built.

Then he entered into a passenger stage coach and freight transport business from the port to the village where Olvera Street is located in Los Angeles; his wagon train and coachlines soon extended throughout the Pacific Southwest, into Arizona, New Mexico, Utah, and Nevada.

In 1851, there were three ranch houses, the Sepulveda corrals, and a large hide and tallow warehouse near Pt. Fermin. Here hides and tallow were stored waiting for cargo space aboard clipper and other ships to take this precious, if smelly, cargo to Boston and New England ports. It was solely from the hide economy of Los Angeles County that Boston got its toe-hold in shoe and leather manufacturing.

During this period, L.A. county was about three times as large as it is now. Orange County was carved out in 1889, and some of Riverside, San Bernardino, Ventura, and San Diego counties took large real estate pieces from L.A. County.

It was inevitable that Banning would meet Don Jose Sepulveda at the wharf when Banning's ship Humbolt arrived in San Pedro. Don Jose and his bachelor brother, Diego, owned San Pedro by special land grant issued by the fleeing Mexican Governor Pio Pico, in 1946, giving them lordship over 31,629 acres embracing most of the Palos Verdes Peninsula.

The Dominguez family protested vigorously and this land grant episode lingered for years in land grant courts litigations. The Dominguez family claimed the Sepulvedas were squatters, but the Land Grant Commission sustained the Sepulvedas in 1852, two years after California was admitted to statehood. The Sepulvedas and the Dominguez family began to intermarry but teeth gnashing between the two pioneer families continued for decades.

James H. Dodson, Sr., married Rudecinda Sepulveda. His mother was a Dominguez. Both families contributed greatly in the development of the harbor area.

California was admitted as the 31st State in 1850 due principally to the gold mining influx of thousands of people, and the great rancheros who maintained the basic cattle economy.

The Sepulveda and the Dominguez families produced cowhides by the thousands. Hides meant ready cash in those days. One writer quipped: "Only its weight and odor prevented this commodity from becoming a personal medium of exchange!" Cowhides were known as California Bank Notes and were worth about $2.00 each.

21
California Became a State in 1850

The framers of the state constitution in 1849 consisted of San Pedro leaders. The State Legislature has been active and imaginative to 1979.

OF ALL THE states in the Union, California was the only one to elect senators and representatives to Washington, D.C., before it actually became a state.

The United States Congress had long established guidelines and procedures for all territories seeking statehood. First, according to the rules, the citizens of those areas needed to organize and function as territories of the United States and then, when ready, petition for full statehood. But California was different.

During the war with Mexico there was an American military rule in California from July 7, 1846, to September 6, 1849, consisting of Commodores John D. Sloat, and Robert F. Stockton; Lt. Colonel John C. Fremont, and Generals Stephen W. Kearny, Richard B. Mason, and Robert Riley. Each one acted as governor of California, some even before the Treaty of Guadalupe Hidalgo was signed on Sept. 3, 1848, ending the Mexican-American War.

California was never a territory of the United States. It worked itself out of such an awkward connotation when, on September 9, 1849, Riley called for a constitutional convention consisting of 48 citizen delegates—15 of them from

Southern California and 33 delegates from Northern California—to meet at Monterey to write a state constitution. They met, debated, and dickered for six weeks, finally pounding out a governmental framework, similar, and in some respects superior, to those of other states.

Despite all the sectional bickering between the delegates their constitution of 1849 served California well until May 7, 1879, when a new constitution was moderately rewritten with modifications of the old one.

"When the 1949 delegates finally overcame their political and sectional differences they wrote," according to Attorney General Evelle Younger, "a constitution that has stood the test of time, with few changes and amendments, through many generations to 1978."

Some of the citizen delegates from our district in 1849 were: Manuel Dominguez, Jose Sepulveda, Antonio Lugo, Andreas Pico, Don Jose Bandini, Jose Antonio Carillo, and Dr. John Brinckerhoff. And they were among those who petitioned Congress for statehood. California became the 31st state of the Union on September 9, 1850. John Charles Fremont was appointed the first United States Senator from California.

During its lifetime California has had six capitals. During the Spanish and Mexican period it was located at Monterey. For a short time before war started between Mexico and the United States, Pio Pico moved the capital to Los Angeles. The U.S. military governors moved it to San Jose until 1851. The capital was at Vallejo from 1852 to 1853, then moved to Benicia until 1854. The Capital of California has been at Sacramento from 1855 to the present date.

The Capitol Building at Sacramento was laid with full Masonic ceremonies on May 15, 1861, but the structure was not occupied until 1870. It is still being used but in recent years it has been deemed unsafe in case of a serious earthquake.

According to former Assemblyman Vincent Thomas, a new Capitol building has been planned near the present site. In the meantime new supports and other structural improvements are being installed to assure the safety of the building and the dome. The Capitol park consists of more than 40 acres, with 4,000 varieties of trees, shrubs and flowers.

The late George Hjelke, former head of the Los Angeles Recreation and Parks Department, told Ehrne Ehrke and this writer that he remembered when some rare species of plants were sent to the state Capitol grounds from our town Averill Park in San Pedro.

The State Legislature enacted into law that the poppy shall be the official state flower; the golden trout the official state fish; the redwood the official state tree; the desert tortoise the official state reptile; the valley quail the state bird; the grizzly bear the state animal, and the blue and gold the official state colors. And on March 23, 1966, it was enacted that Charles B. Garrigus of

Reedley, formerly of San Pedro, be state poet laureate. (With enthusiastic local approval, Councilman John S. Gibson, appointed local history buff Dick Wolfe, the local poet laureate in 1978.)

In 1911 the Legislature adopted the Bear Flag as the official State Flag, and in 1951, due in large part to the urging of the state Kiwanis Clubs, the song "I Love You, California" was adopted as the state song. It is a song the local Kiwanis Club sings at all their luncheon meetings.

But it was the original 48 constitutional delegates who drew the design and adopted the state seal on October 2, 1849, with the symbolic grizzly bear and the goddess Minerva seated majestically in the oval. The Greek motto "Eureka, I have found it," is indicative of a promised land.

Obviously it was a talented and sophisticated group of California citizens who debated on the merits of a constitution, in a cold damp room at Monterey in October of 1849.

To top it off the California Legislature enacted into law in 1973, that the dog-face large winged butterfly be the official state insect.

22
Banning's Early Inventory Comes to Light

Early estimate of Phineas Banning's wealth in 1858. Also some scathing remarks by Chamber of Commerce leader, Charles Dwight Willard, on biographical "Mug" book promotors.

SOMETIMES SIGNIFICANT tidbits of harbor history that has lain dormant for many decades come to light through unusual channels. Recently George M. Ponce, Wilmington longshoreman, gave the author a four-page written document dated June 18, 1858, which he found folded in an old history book.

It was written by an unsigned and unknown observer about Phineas Banning's business holdings, his inventory, and the estimated worth of Banning's varied enterprises as of 1858, the year Banning moved from San Pedro and founded a town which he first named New San Pedro. He later renamed it Wilmington in honor of his home in Delaware. Each page is faded with age.

It reads; "San Pedro is of very little consequence now except as a depot for passengers in transit. It has no charm except as a fine water view presents. All the fresh water used at the port is brought in tanks from the Sepulveda Palos Verdes Rancho three miles distant. The lack of fresh water in San Pedro is a serious defect and will always prevent the port from becoming a large place. It is a defect that has induced several efforts heretofore to make a settlement at a new landing for ships, now it has come about at New San Pedro (Wilmington) five miles nearer to Los Angeles.

"The real good business carried on now at San Pedro is farming. Nearly all the immense shipping business passes through the hands of one man, Phineas Banning, whose establishment is a curiosity in itself. In extent and value, it is probably not equalled by any other man in the state. To give an idea of this one-man institution, owned and directed by one man, I set down the following (estimated) figures:

"8-12 mule wagons – capable of carrying 10 tons each, total $40.00. 20-10 mule wagons – $2,000 each total $40,000. 20-6 horse wagons, total $30,000. 5-6 horse stage $4,000 each, total $20,000. 4-6 horse stage $2500 each, total $10,000. 2-6 horse stage deluxe $5,000 each, total $10,000. 6-6 horse stage $2500 each, total $15,000. 8 large lighters $6,000 each, total $48,000. The small boat Medora $2,000. Wharf & Bulkheads total $15,000. Several misc boats and barges total $8,000. Warehouse in San Pedro, New San Pedro, & Los Angeles, total $12,000."

The total value calculated by our unknown estimator represents a 1858 capital investment of $250 thousand dollars. But if calculated in terms of our 1977 dollars it would total well over $1 million dollars. No doubt, the total value of Banning's inventory estimated by this unknown evaluator may be highly exaggerated. It does provide, however, an approximation of the enormity of Banning's establishment and gives a new insight on Banning's economic resourcefulness.

The report concludes; "Mr. Banning has a contract for hauling freight to the different military posts, to Fort Yuma on the Colorado, to Fort Tejon on the north, and he exercises general supervision over his whole territory, often visiting the extreme points of his labors. I have seen those wagon trains scattered over many parts of California. Each covered wagon looks like a small house moving along on wheels."

The book in which the above written record was found, is titled; *History of Los Angeles City*, by Charles Dwight Willard, published in 1901. This is the same Willard that became the first secretary of the Los Angeles Chamber of Commerce, member of the Free Harbor League, and its publicity chairman. Willard was always in the forefront fighting for the port of San Pedro.

In the preface of his book Willard berated the "mug" book writers of his time with these scathing remarks: "The career of a city contains as much good material, out of which an entertaining history may be constructed, as does the life of an individual, or the development of a nation, but, for some reason, it has come to pass in America that the preparation of a city, or local history has usually fallen into the hands of schemers who exploit for a price the prominent citizen for his biography, and throw in something of a narrative, merely as an apology for the book's existence."

"The volume thus produced is a huge unwieldy affair, that circulates among the victims, and is not read even by them, except as to the pages where each one finds the story of his life set forth in a flamboyant and patronizing style."

23
Wyatt Earp's First Job

An interesting episode in the early life of Wyatt Earp. His first job was driving a stage coach in the employe of Phineas Banning.

PHINEAS BANNING never regretted having hired 17-year-old Wyatt Earp in 1865 to drive his six-horse stage coach from San Bernardino to the pueblo of Los Angeles.

Banning's regular driver broke his leg and was unable to take the reins for at least four months. He highly recommended young Earp to Banning, saying, "Wyatt Earp can handle this run, and what's more, the animals won't be ruined when I take them over again."

This was 16 years before the famous gun fight at the O.K. Corral at Tombstone, Arizona. For seven days a week for over four months Earp drove the stage coach. He had a few skirmishes with ambuscades set by highwaymen. At the trial of one of the bandits, Banning testified that Earp was never late and never lost a passenger, a horse, or an ounce of mail.

Banning was proud of Earp and wanted to keep him on. But Frank Binkley, a former Banning employee, offered Earp a profit incentive to drive a 10-animal team from San Pedro and Wilmington to Prescott, where commodities were sky-high because no merchandise had reached there for many months over the Santa Fe Trail from the east. The train consisted of 10 mules or horses per wagon. The route was through the burning sands of the Salton Sink, over and down hazardous mountain passes, across wide stretches of dry desert, the route was over rock and dirt roads the whole distance.

Wagons with trailers carried 1,000 pounds of freight to the animal, plus 500 pounds of fodder and water for each team. The schedule allowed 25 days for the 450-mile journey. Indians and renegade white bandits attacked the wagons, adding extra risks, but the long, hard haul paid handsome profits. After a year with Binkley, Earp transferred back to Banning for the Salt Lake City run on a profit basis. Freight rates from the harbor to Salt Lake was 16 cents a pound, which netted about $2500 for the trip.

On one trip Earp learned that the route from Julesburg, Colo., to Salt Lake was 20 cents a pound. Earp made a round trip on this run and quit before snowfall blocked the roads. In 1868 Earp was head of all work animals in a large Union Pacific Railroad grading camp 50 miles ahead of rail laying during the Union Pacific Railroad push through Wyoming.

Earp was a Missourian. In 1864 he and his family left their home and migrated by covered wagon to San Bernardino. The train numbered 40 wagons and about 180 people. Some of the wagons were pulled by oxen. Wyatt's father, Nicholas, was captain of the trek, and Wyatt was directed to keep at least 25 people in fresh meat all the way.

By the time the wagon train reached California, Wyatt had gone through two Sioux Indian raids, some hand-to-hand fighting, and experienced the loss of some cattle. Along the way in Wyoming, Wyatt met Jim Bridger, noted frontiersman of the early West. They became good friends and for a week hunted and fished together, swapping yarns that Wyatt in later years used to good advantage.

The experiences of Wyatt Earp ran the gamut from freighting and driving for Phineas Banning to buffalo hunting and scouting, to becoming a fearless peace officer in several frontier towns, including the sensational affair at the O.K. Corral in Tombstone, in 1881, where several people were killed. Earp also had the distinction of serving as marshal at Dodge City, Kansas. The Earp family lived most of their lives in California. Wyatt's father died in Colton in 1907, his brother Jim at Los Angeles in 1926, and his half-brother Newton at Sacramento in 1928. Wyatt died peacefully at his Los Angeles home in 1929 at age 80. There is a small community named for the family, Earp, California, near the Colorado River.

Wyatt was referee at the Fitzsimmons-Sharkey fight at San Francisco in 1896. Bat Masterson, Wyatt's contemporary and co-peace officer, said of him, "Wyatt could scrap with his fists; I doubt there was a man in the West who could whip him in a rough and tumble fight. He was the most courageous man I have known. No man could have a more loyal friend than Wyatt Earp, nor a more dangerous enemy."

Records show that Phineas Banning and Wyatt Earp met briefly at a horse auction in a corral near the Pico House in Los Angeles in 1882. It is reported that the usual friendly courtesies were exchanged, but it is believed this was the last time the two men saw each other.

24
Wyatt Earp Questioned

Some interesting quotes from Phineas Banning's grandson, George Hugh Banning, who wanted more details about Wyatt Earp's connection with Phineas.

THE AUTHOR has had several inquiries about Wyatt Earp including one from an expert on staging, George Hugh Banning, grandson of Phineas Banning. George Hugh and his brother, Hancock Banning Jr., are the two oldest living relatives of Phineas Banning. George Hugh wrote a best seller in 1930 titled *Six Horses,* published by the Century Co., and he certainly knows whereof he speaks.

Quoting from his letter: "John Reynolds was still the general's pride and joy as a stage driver at about that time. In Phineas' long, hot competition with the J.J. Tomlison drivers, it seems the general well knew the differences between ordinarily good drivers and reinsmen and had good reason to know. It is possible for a 17-year-old lad to be a driver of sorts, to the sorrow perhaps of horses over any long drive; but my only thought is that Phineas must have been rather hard-pressed for drivers if he were casual about hiring one Wyatt Earp! Can you give me your source in this case?"

The source is primarily, but not altogether, the book by Stuart N. Lake titled *Wyatt Earp: Frontier Marshal.* As of 1931, the publishers, Houghton Mifflin Co., noted on the front page that this book was in its 10th edition.

Lane's foreword states that he had done considerable research on the Earp family and personally talked with and interviewed Wyatt Earp for many years up to his death in Los Angeles on January 13, 1929. The book has other information on the Earp family such as: "In the summer after Wyatt turned 17, Banning's regular driver broke his leg. 'Who'll take your place?' Banning asked. 'You've got bad horses and bad men to handle on that run and young Wyatt Earp can handle both, and what's more, the animals won't be ruined when I take them over again.' This seemed to settle it and Earp was hired temporarily."

George Hugh Banning's letter also had this paragraph: "I mean drivers don't just occur. Apparently it was Wyatt Earp's good fortune to be an almost natural-born reinsman. One in several thousand perhaps."

George Hugh's apprehension is readily understandable about any lad of 17 being given the responsibility of driving six horses 60 miles over rough roads upon reading a few passages in *Six Horses.* In the chapter titled "Commentaries of a Stage Driver" he wrote: "Where the mountains were loftiest and most rugged, where the roads were most narrow and threatening, there, above all places, was the greatest demand for the 'whip' who had learned to rein. The driver who had mastered the most difficult of modes of driving was strictly a triplex power plant of duplex units operating on 24 hooves; and if, by means of his six lines and his brake and whip, he could exact from all its parts and potentialities a maximum degree of efficiency at all times, then he was a master of masters. He was one in a thousand."

Another point is that J.J. Reynolds did not start to work for Banning's Stage Lines until September 1866. Quoting an interview Ben Truman wrote about Reynolds in 1866: "One day, while riding with the remarkable Reynolds, I asked him how he happened to get a job with Banning," Truman wrote. "It was this way," Reynolds said. "I saw the biggest lot of prairie schooners start out for Arizona from Wilmington: I asked someone who they belonged to, and he replied, 'General Banning.' "Who runs the stage lines?" asked another. 'General Banning,' he replied.

"I saw herds of cattle, horses, and sheep between Wilmington and Los Angeles and I was told they belonged to Banning. I soon learned that Banning owned three steamers at Wilmington, he owned the wheelwright and blacksmith shops, sawmills, boat building, trip hammers, warehouses, and storehouses without number. I then concluded that General Banning owned nearly everything and everybody in the country, and being a professional 'whip,' I determined to add myself to his outfit.

"Banning asked me 'Can you drive a stage?' 'Yes,' I said. 'Do you like to work?' 'Yes.' 'Do you drink whisky?' 'No.' 'You're engaged!' "

And that was how John Reynolds got his job. He remained with Banning long after Banning's railroad from Los Angeles to Wilmington was completed in 1869. Banning was delighted with Reynolds' expertise with the reins, but warned Reynolds "not to exercise himself too solid with the fair sex, as he (Banning) claimed some privileges in those premises that must not be infringed upon by subordinates!"

25

Banning's Love of Labor

The Utopian and easy approach to labor was taboo in Banning. He gave rewards to the most deserving.

A RECENT LETTER ASKED ABOUT the kind of labor-management relations Phineas Banning experienced during his business life in the harbor. At one time, he had about 500 employees in his wagon and carriage factory, blacksmith shop, mule skinners, wagon drivers and passenger coach experts. Banning was a keen observer. He was most concerned in affording a better standard of living for his employees.

Banning could, and often did, ponder over the cyclical nature of his help. He enjoyed a most cordial and friendly relationship with his office, field, factory, and domestic workers and he paid them more than the going wage. He maintained an employment office, but no one of importance was officially hired and put on the payroll without first being personally interviewed. He had 50 wagons each carrying 10 tons and 70 drivers. His freight wagons were driven by expert drivers whose virtuosity in profanity seemed to be an important part of the trade, but Banning frowned on cursing and profanity.

One day Banning saw a copy of Fred Engels, *Communist Manifesto,* printed in 1848, and a copy of Karl Marx's *Das Kapital,* first published in 1867. These books were in the captain's cabin of a ship that had sailed from Europe. Banning read the books and froze in disgust. "In all creative arts," Banning said, "there may arise a difference of opinion, but these books are not art, they represent spiritual and economic blasphemy." Banning knew that one could not be a Christian and a Communist, that he could not have the one and enjoy the other. Banning was a devout Christian, and nothing could sway him from his faith in God. At this very time, both Engels and Marx were living it up in London and Paris in a concerted effort to uproot the status quo of world labor-management tranquility.

Banning's library at his Wilmington mansion was filled with well-balanced books embracing every phase of civilized thought. He had no hate books such as the radical concepts of Karl Marx and Fred Engels. He did have, however, one of the great masterpieces in the realm of social and economic behavior in Adam Smith's *An Inquiry into the Nature and Causes of the Wealth of Nations.* This book has been a reference text in the classrooms of most every university since 1777. But in most of the nineteenth century, capital was static and labor was frustrated.

Because of the radical influence of Karl Marx and Fred Engels, many early socialized, Utopian-type cooperative commonwealth societies sprang up in California. One of them was the 500-member group that organized the Keweah Cooperative Colony which intended to take over the Sequoia forest and sell its timber. This ambitious project was nipped in the bud just in time, when the federal government nationalized the area into the Sequoia National Park.

There were Utopian colonies in other states, but they all fizzled out because of the lack of economic and social stability. Phineas Banning was well versed about the inroads radical leaders were attempting in California; and when he was a state senator representing the harbor district in 1865, he was instrumental in enlisting other legislators to prevent radical encroachment in California. Banning was a subscriber to English magazines and looked forward to the arrival of ships from England and Europe bringing new books, magazines, and pamphlets, besides the regular mail pouches.

When Banning received and read a pamphlet from a textile factory in London in 1858 titled *Office Staff Practices,* he knew it was inevitable that labor laws would have to be enacted to protect conditions and working hours of women and minors in American industry.

It read: "The firm has reduced the hours of work, and the clerical staff now will be present between 7 a.m. and 6 p.m. Daily prayers will be held each morning in the main office. The craving for tobacco, wines, or spirits is a human weakness, and, as such, is forbidden to all members of the clerical staff. A stove is provided for the benefit of the staff. It is recommended that each member of the staff bring four pounds of coal each day during cold weather. You will provide your own quill pens. No member of the staff may leave the room without permission from Mr. Rogers. The calls of nature are permitted. All boys and juniors will report to Mr. Rogers 40 minutes before prayers and will remain after closing hours for cleaning up work." Phineas Banning was amazed at such labor-management regulations.

In his own labor-management discipline, Banning himself was a hard worker. This seemed to instill a high regard for him, thus inspiring his employees to keep the business going and not slip into a recession—and for them—fewer jobs.

26
Razor Sharp on Law

Banning and Timms could not agree on shipping techniques in San Pedro, so Banning moved to Wilmington.

PHINEAS BANNING WAS as sharp as a newly-honed razor on contract law and was quite proficient on Blackstone's Commentaries. He learned this phase of the lawyer's art while studying in his brother's law office in Philadelphia before coming to San Pedro in 1851.

Banning went to fiscal court 11 times between 1851 and 1865. During this period of controversy and confusion, most all business dealings were based upon contracts involving some question that often had to be settled in the courts.

Three of Banning's cases, Numbers 486, 489, and 525, were against his chief competitor, Augustus W. Timms, and concerned landing rights at the Sepulveda wharf.

Banning testified that Timms was cagey and bought the Sepulveda landing before he could say "scat." It was a location Banning swore the Sepulvedas had promised him.

Timms quickly renamed the facility Timms' Landing. It was at the foot of where Fourteenth Street is now located and the safest and most convenient place where goods to and from ships could be loaded and handled by lighters with some semblance of success.

Banning figured he had prior rights to this choice spot and took Timms to court with case No. 486. Banning lost. But Banning caught Timms off base and won the other two suits over payment of the lighters. Banning said Timms was "unbearable and hard to get along with even with my best patience and diplomacy."

It was obvious that their opinions and temperament were not conducive to any working arrangement, so Banning started dredging the estuary for a deeper channel to what is now Wilmington.

Banning felt correctly that Rattlesnake Island, now Terminal Island, would afford protection from wind and waves.

"Timms," said Banning, "could remain in San Pedro and froth at the mouth all alone at the incoming, unprotected tide when lighters often would be battered against the rocky cliffs on Dead Man's Island and the boulders on the hidden ledges. Let him pay the damages when valuable shipments would get soaked or lost."

Court case No. 587 was against his friend José Diego Sepulveda, who attempted to block Banning's move up the estuary to Wilmington. Banning won this case and forced the Dominguez heirs to recognize their contract to sell 2,400 acres to him and his partner, Don Benito Wilson, for $1.10 per acre.

Thus the town of Wilmington was begun, becoming an important entity in 1858. However, Banning knew that Wilmington could not become a successful port of call without a breakwater protecting San Pedro.

Banning urged Congress to appropriate the necessary funds for the breakwater and for the Point Fermin lighthouse, without which there could be no port of entry.

Banning moved his home from San Pedro to a house he built on Canal Boulevard, now Avalon Boulevard, in Wilmington. And he began the design and landscape for his famous 30-room mansion, completed in 1864, which is now the centerpiece of Banning Park.

Banning provided himself with one of the finest private libraries in California and was an ardent reader of history.

A few years ago, while doing research in one of the homes of the Banning heirs, the author found a note which Phineas wrote about the Magna Carta.

"When King John in 1215 A.D. signed the Magna Carta," Banning said, "which became the greatest law document of all time, individual freedom and contracts between people, verbal or written, became synonymous."

Banning knew the frailties of human nature. Even in his day many people could not read or write, often consummating contracts with an "X" on a document.

One of Banning's observations on contract law is most significant. He wrote, "A letter writer or scrivener's services were required to write the documents. When any question arose as to the contract or document, the scrivener had to be called upon to identify or read the instrument.

"This method, however, was not satisfactory to illiterates who doubted and were suspicious of wrongdoing, so it was agreed generally that only one copy of any written document should be made; this was torn or split lengthwise; one half was given to each contracting party, thus giving them an ocular demonstration of the identity of the document and completely satisfying them."

Phineas Banning pointed out that from this operation all written instruments thus became known as indentures, a name still used in all formal agreements, although its original historical significance has long since disappeared.

27
Mitigating Circumstances

Banning went to fiscal court many times against his close friends, including Gov. J.G. Downey, José Diego Sepulveda, and others just to prove a point.

LOS ANGELES COUNTY court records show that Phineas Banning went to fiscal court 12 times between 1865 and 1880, taking on some of the most sophisticated individuals and business firms in the country. Banning was the plaintiff in all but two of the actions and was the victor nearly every time.

In one of the two suits in which Banning found himself being sued, John Temple, a banker and large landowner, was seeking $5,831.60 for an overdue note and interest. At the trial sat a good friend of Banning's, an equally prominent and affluent businessman by the name of Harris Newmark. When Temple would not give Banning an extension on the note, Newmark loaned Banning $6,000 to pay off the note, not even asking for a signature. The transaction was based solely on reputation and honor.

Banning repaid Newmark within six months, and Newmark wouldn't accept any interest on the loan, although prevailing interest rates at the time were as high as 10 per cent per month.

The other hotly contested case where Banning was the defendant, he won from his aggressive hauling competitor, J.J. Tomlinson. Tomlinson was attempting to collect $7,000, claiming Banning owed on a contract for the rental of certain hauling equipment.

Tomlinson's partner, John Goller, was the owner of the largest and best-equipped blacksmith business in the country, and both these gentlemen became thorns in the side of Banning and his well-established freight and passenger hauling business. They attempted to embarrass Banning in every way they could.

Tomlinson especially became a bitter enemy over the profitable government contract enjoyed by Banning from San Pedro and the harbor to Fort Tejon, Fort Mojave, and Fort Yuma, and other outlying government posts in Arizona, New Mexico, and Utah.

In 1859, while Tomlinson was on a freighting trip to Salt Lake City, John Goller leased their equipment to Banning for six months, for which Banning was to pay one-third of his profits made from the rental. When Tomlinson returned, he filed suit against Banning for the $7,000, alleging that Banning had made large sums but had refused to pay for the equipment rental.

In his answer before the court, Banning testified that in October 1859 Los Angeles County Sheriff Sanchez, urged by Goller, took the property, thereby breaking the contract with Tomlinson. Banning also said he had paid Goller $5,000 and returned the equipment. Banning won. A short time later, a Judge Hayes decided that Tomlinson and his partner, Goller, must pay $700 to Banning for interference.

Goller refused to shoe any more horses or mules for Banning after that. Banning then established the largest blacksmith and light iron works in Southern California near Fries Avenue in Wilmington, employing 50 new workers. At this time, Banning owned about 500 horses and about 1,000 mules and more than 100 prairie schooners (covered wagons). This ended the lawsuits between Tomlinson-Goller and Banning.

The *Los Angeles Star* commented: "We are glad that all matters between Phineas Banning and J.J. Tomlinson have been amicably settled." Although these business rivals stopped suing each other, their business competition continued until Tomlinson's death in 1866.

Court case No. 897 filed in 1865 was aginst J.G. Downey, who was governor of California from 1860 to 1862. While governor, Downey appointed Banning a brigadier general in the National Guard. Banning served at Drum Barracks during the Civil War.

The suit was brought on behalf of the Pioneer Oil Company board of directors to force Downey to pay for his 100 shares of the stock he bought at $300 per share. Downey's neglect was holding up the operations, and the board made Banning file suit. Banning was president of the company and guaranteed payment. Downey paid up and remained good friends with Banning.

Another case was against John G. Nichols, who had been mayor of Los Angeles for two terms, 1852 to 1853 and 1856 to 1859. The suit was over title to some property which Banning purchased in Los Angeles. Banning won again. Nichols was fearless and reputed to be an honest man. He resigned in 1853 from his mayorship to head a lynch posse in a band of vigilantes.

Nichols lived in the first brick house built in Los Angeles, and his son was the first American child born in Los Angeles. He took the lead in presenting the city's claim to its land as a Spanish pueblo before the U.S. Land Commission, and gained title to four square leagues of land for the City of Los Angeles. He and Phineas Banning remained good friends all during their lifetimes.

28

Civil War Drum Barracks Established

The Fort MacArthur site was first considered for the Civil War barracks but decided in favor of Wilmington due to its abundance of fresh water.

PRESIDENT GROVER CLEVELAND, by executive order September 14, 1888, set aside a strip of land adjacent to the newly incorporated city of San Pedro, to be used as a military reservation.

James Buchanan, president of the United States from 1856 to 1860, had nothing to do with it, although some writers sometime mention Buchanan's name in connection with the action.

The property did not become identified as Fort MacArthur until January 10, 1914. It was named for Lt. General Arthur MacArthur, father of Gen. Douglas MacArthur. The Fort became an important facility during World War I with a large recruitment depot where several thousand soldiers were trained for war duty.

The author saw service there for a few weeks before being transferred to Camp Lewis. Dick Wolfe remembers selling papers to the author at that time on the Upper Reservation of Fort MacArthur.

A few years ago, the Chambers of Commerce of San Pedro and Wilmington passed resolutions to petition Congress to make Fort MacArthur a permanent installation.

Although called a fort, it was actually a camp. The petition was ignored and the Defense Department has curtailed the facility and served notice that it intends to close all of Fort MacArthur. This is mentioned because of its early connection with Drum Barracks, established in Wilmington in 1862.

When Spanish Governor Fagas gave Juan Jose Dominguez the 75,000-acre land grant in 1784 known as Rancho San Pedro, it was supposed to take in all the land along the Pacific including Palos Verdes and all of what is now Redondo Beach.

During the intervening years, however, controversy over control of Palos Verdes and San Pedro became a hot political and legal fight between the

Dominguez and Sepulveda heirs. Where Fort MacArthur now stands became a part of this land squabble.

Mexican Governor Pio Pico in 1846 decided in favor of the Sepulvedas, who in turn became lords over this property, including the town of San Pedro.

The following clause is apropos: "They shall leave free at San Pedro, 500 varas square to the cardinal points, where houses may be built by persons obtaining permission. None, however, can prevent the use of pasture by those engaged in traffic of horse to the port."

This clause later proved to be the legal cornerstone for the U.S. government reservation decision upon which President Cleveland's order was based in 1888.

This area became an important shipping and loading center, including the hide house, up to the Civil War in 1861, when Wilmington took over. The U.S. Army considered establishing a barracks on this side in San Pedro, but decided against it principally because of the lack of fresh water and being too far to build a viaduct to bring water from the San Gabriel River (which they did in Wilmington). They also thought Wilmington was a safer port for unloading war commodities for the outlying posts such as Ft. Yuma, Ft. Mojave, and Ft. Tejon.

Even before the army gave the Fort MacArthur site a thought, Phineas Banning was urging President Lincoln to establish a barracks in Wilmington supported by many troops to quell the recurrent uprisings and Indian depredations against the Northern cause.

When Banning offered the army of the West all the land they would need for one dollar, they plotted 60 acres, and Drum Barracks was built in 1862 in Wilmington, instead of San Pedro.

29

Dirt Road to Fort Tejon

The army facilities of Ft. Tejon were merged with Drum Barracks, including camels, in 1862. Some of their artifacts will be displayed when Drum Barracks is open to the public sometime in 1979, as a Civil War Museum.

THE 115-YEAR-OLD Civil War Drum Barracks, 1053 Cary St., in Wilmington, is expected to be fully renovated and reconstructed, and opened to the public in 1979, according to Joan Lorenzen, president of the Society for the Preservation of Drum Barracks.

The Drum Barracks renovation project has been hanging fire since 1967, when the California Legislature under the leadership of Assemblyman Vincent Thomas, D-San Pedro, and Sen. Ralph Dills, D-Gardena, had a bill passed appropriating $125,000 to re-establish Drum Barracks.

Very little was done by the state, and in early 1975 it was urged by Councilman John S. Gibson, with the cooperation of both Thomas and Dills, to turn the project over to the Los Angeles City Department of Recreation and Parks. The City got the project and what was left ($83,000) of the original grant.

The Barracks now needs contributions of Civil War memorabilia, period furniture, beds, desks, lamps, discharge papers or anything pertaining to the Civil War period. It is expected that a letter from President Abraham Lincoln, dated Jan. 15, 1865, to Gen. Phineas Banning, thanking him for saving California during the war through Drum Barracks will be on display after the barracks is open.

Recently Ed Hauck of Gibson's staff, and this writer hired a pickup truck and drove to Fort Tejon State Historic Park, near Lebeck, to bring back a donated wagon wheel from the first wagon Banning drove in 1854, opening the first road to Ft. Tejon. This wheel, together with other artifacts from Ft. Tejon, will be on display when the barracks is opened.

Ft. Tejon, in Grapevine Canyon on Highway 99, is 87 miles north of San Pedro. The highway runs through the original area of the old fort, constructed in 1854. The fort was an important Army post with patrols traveling as far east as the Colorado River. They penetrated unexplored regions of Owens Valley. The troopers protected Indians, guarded miners, chased bandits and offered protection to the southern part of California.

Fort Tejon became one of the largest settlements in Southern California. In 1858 a Butterfield overland mail station was established there on the line from St. Louis to San Francisco. Banning's wagon trains and mail served the area for the southern part of the state.

Fifteen commissioned officers who served at Ft. Tejon during its active periods later achieved the rank of general in the Civil War, eight of them with the North and seven with the South.

Under the direction of U.S. Secretary of War Jefferson Davis, camels were first imported in 1856 for transporting supplies to isolated posts in the arid Southwest.

Lt. Edward F. Beal headed a brigade that drove 35 camels to Ft. Tejon in 1857 from Texas. For a while camels were used to pack supplies from San Pedro and Los Angeles to Ft. Yuma via Ft. Tejon. Beal's reports mentioned that one camel was more valuable than four of the best mules. We quote:

"The camels carried water for the mules; they traversed stretches of country covered with the sharpest volcanic rock without injury to their feet, they even plunged into rivers without hesitation and swam with ease."

With the outbreak of the War between the States, most of these camels were moved to various posts, some of them to Drum Barracks in 1862, some sold to zoos and carnivals, some to miners in Nevada, Arizona, and New Mexico.

Fort Tejon was dismantled in 1862 and much of the personnel and equipment were transferred to Drum Barracks where Banning was a brigadier general. It was Banning who recommended that the barracks be named for Major Richard Coulter Drum, whom Banning helped gain promotion to brigadier general to be.

After the Army abandoned Ft. Tejon, the land became part of General Beal's Tejon Ranch which now embraces more than 100,000 acres and is one of the largest ranches in California.

But most of the old Army buildings and the paradeground is still intact. There are two old artillery pieces on display.

In one corner of the parade ground is the Peter le Beck Oak. First mention of the tree is in a report of 1853, by R.S. Williamson. He wrote that one of the oaks in Grapevine Canyon (future site of the fort) had an inscription cut deeply into the wood. It read:

"Peter le Beck, killed by a X bear, October 17, 1837."

30
Post-Civil War Period

This chapter contains a most prophetic letter written by U.S. Naval Admiral, W.K. Thatcher, in 1879, about the future of San Pedro Bay.

STARTING WITH THE Civil War period, Wilmington became the main port in San Pedro Bay. More ships and more cargo were loaded and unloaded in Wilmington than in any other port south of San Francisco, and even today it is still larger than San Pedro in terms of cargo handled.

Just as the Bella Union Hotel in Los Angeles was the main meeting place and the terminal for stage coach lines, the Wilmington Exchange Hotel was the chief meeting place in the harbor.

San Pedro's first city attorney, W.H. Savage, who later became a state legislator and judge, wrote impressions in 1866 of his first visit, accompanied with two friends, to the Wilmington Exchange:

"We registered, washed, and approached the bar that advertised that it was well supplied with a full line of ales, wines, liquors, cigars and tobacco. On the back bar was a wooden mallet, known as the Bum Starter, to be used in sustaining order when customers became too noisy or rowdy.

"Large mirrors and loud pictures covered the walls. In the corner stood a double-barrelled gun, and an old musket within convenient reach, also two large Colts of the army pattern. The bar evidently was not to be taken by surprise.

"A tubercular looking man was playing the piano. A sign was over his head bearing the following legend: *Please do not shoot our musician. He is doing his level best.* Phineas Banning, the transportation mogul, owned the hotel and tavern. He came in and smiled all over, slapping people on their backs."

During these tense years Banning had considerable difficulty in his quarrel with San Francisco port officials who were opposed to any improvement of the San Pedro Bay facilities.

A few weeks ago Frederick Heim, president of the Los Angeles Harbor Commission, and himself an ardent student of harbor history, suggested that the author research for a significant letter written by a former admiral of the U.S. Naval Squadron of the Pacific who served from 1866 to 1868.

The author recently found a letter in Sarah Bixby Smith's book *Adobe Days,* published in 1931. The letter was written to her grandfather, Rev. George W. Hathaway, by Adm. Henry Knox Thatcher. Hathaway's four daughters married three Bixby brothers; Sarah to Llewelyn Bixby, Margaret to Jotham Bixby, and Susan to John W. Bixby. After the death of Sarah, Llewelyn married her sister, Mary Hathaway.

This letter, written by Thatcher Sept. 25, 1879, dwells in good perspective on conditions in those days and shows how far the San Pedro Bay has progressed under the present system of harbor commissioners and administrators. It reads:

"My dear friend Hathaway, . . . During my various visits to the Port of San Pedro I observed the facility with which that Bay could be made a perfectly safe harbor for ships in all weather by simply building a mole of stone (breakwater) with which the shore is lined for miles. And then blasting Dead Man's Island close at hand for the foundation of said mole and using the millions of smaller rocks to be found all along the shore for the filling in.

"At present the anchorage of San Pedro is perfectly safe so long as the wind remains north, but when from the south no ship could escape destruction at that anchorage unless supplied with steam power.

"I foresaw that San Francisco would strongly oppose any attempt to make San Pedro a Port of entry because it would deprive them of the power of plundering San Pedro and that fair and fertile portion of California as they now do. And all the products of that best portion of the state must now be carried at great cost to the only exporting custom house in San Francisco, whereas if they could be shipped directly from San Pedro the producers would save tens of thousands annually even now.

"But now is as nothing, for the day is not far distant when Los Angeles and adjoining counties will become the greatest producing area on the face of the globe; everything points to it, a soil of unsurpassed fertility, and a climate as perfect as is to be found upon earth. It is but for the people themselves to wake up and insist upon aid from the government to accomplish this noble work.

"With my feeble efforts I did what I could to bring this about during my command of the Pacific Squadron and had great hopes, but my successor felt no interest in the matter and the few producers at that time appeared quite indifferent except Mr. Banning who seemed to be a man of enlarged views and exerting considerable influence.

"But I think the San Francisco element was too strong for him to contend with. Yet I am satisfied that this scheme will one day be accomplished, though I may not live to see it . . . of course the railroad will aid in developing that lower section of California but it will be found a very expensive mode of transportation compared with the floating process" . . . Affectionate friend, H.K. Thatcher.

These were prophetic words indeed. Thatcher was the grandson of General Henry Knox, President George Washington's first Secretary of War.

31
FIRST OIL WILDCATS

In 1865 Phineas Banning organized the first oil company in California. It failed. Banning neglected to test his own property for oil. Wilmington later became one of the most prolific oil producers in the world.

IN THE REAR OF THE 117-year-old Civil War Drum Barracks, 1053 Cary Street, Wilmington, is a water well with an old oaken bucket hanging from a rod surrounded by ivy.

It was a deep well, and the water was fresh from 1862 to 1868 before it was fouled up by seepage of brea and crude oil. The water was unfit to drink; the well was cemented and capped. Barracks' officers were enraged by "this awful-smelling devil's tar that ruined our water well."

This was a real petroleum discovery, but nothing was done about it until the Ranger Oil Corp. brought in its Watson No. 2, January 26, 1932, and opened up the Wilmington oil field in a big way.

Since that time, according to the *California Oil Journal,* 1,681,810,000 barrels of oil have been produced in the Wilmington field. According to Joe Mike McKinney, Exxon manager, his company plans to produce another 75 million barrels of oil through its pressurization process now in operation.

"There are 1,500 Wilmington landowners getting monthly oil royalties which adds considerably to the economy and well-being of the Harbor Area," McKinney said.

In comparison, the touted Elk Hills Naval Reserve near Taft has a potential much less than the Wilmington field, according to C.C. Albright, petroleum expert.

Phineas Banning organized the first oil company in California in January, 1865, known as "The Pioneer Oil Company." At the time, Banning was a state senator in Sacramento. Capitalization was $1.5 million. Shares sold for $300.

Its officers and directors were leaders in the Harbor area: Phineas Banning, president; Charles Ducommun, founder of Ducommun Steel and Hardware Co., treasurer; Patrick Downey, secretary. Others on the board were: J.G. Downey, former California governor; Don Benito Wilson, former L.A. mayor and owner of San Pasqual Rancho, the land that now comprises most of Pasadena; Matthew Keller, owner of Rancho Malibu and real estate developer; Gen. Winfield Scott Hancock, former Drum Barracks Quartermaster and second in command with Gen. U.S. Grant in the Civil War; Dr. John Griffin, medical officer at Drum Barracks and personal physician of the Banning family; Dr. J.B. Winston, M.D., in 1865, one of the six practitioners in L.A., Volney Edwards, George Hansen, and Richard Heath, prominent businessmen.

Bannings's company was seeking petroleum for axle grease, lubricants for tools, and kerosene for lamps. They wanted to substitute something to take the place of whale oil which reeked with distasteful odors.

The Pioneer Oil executives were well informed about John D. Rockefeller's Standard Oil Company, incorporated in Ohio, and its first oil well in Titusville, Pennsylvania, in 1859. However, Banning's company had no oil geologist nor efficient drilling tools. It had only reels of heavy hawser rope, 20-foot, 12-inch diameter steel bits, and walking beams powered by steam boilers. Drilling on the Palos Verdes Peninsula found only salt water. In the Pasadena area, there were dry holes. In the San Fernando Valley, oil was struck at 325-foot depth, considered a remarkable achievement for that period. A few barrels of this oil were refined before it petered out.

The Pioneer Oil Company ran into too many problems and folded in 1868. Unfortunately, it did not occur to Banning to drill on his own land in Wilmington, which incidentally became one of the most prolific oil finds in history.

The Banning heirs, however, are large royalty owners in the field, and Wilmington resident Frank Alexander also is one of the largest benefactors in this oil jackpot.

It was the advent of the discovery of the internal-combustion engine, and the manufacturing of automobiles that started the boom in the oil industry.

In 1885, Gottlieb Daimler and Karl Benz of Germany were the ones who introduced gasoline engines of the type used in today's cars. In 1894, the Duryea brothers built the first successful American gasoline-powered car. In 1896, Henry Ford, Eli Olds, and Alexander Winton first introduced their cars.

The first mass production of automobiles was the Oldsmobile in 1901, followed by Ford a few years later. Gasoline is now the prime energy product in oil refineries.

But crude oil was actually discovered in 1818 by Marcus Huling in the remote wooded hills of Wayne County, Kentucky. Huling was drilling for salt brine from which he could distill and sell salt, a scarce and expensive commodity on the frontier. His operation was slow. At 200-foot depth, he struck a pocket of heavy black oil which overflowed into the Cumberland River and killed all the fish and most of the ducks—in fact, all waterfowl.

Huling was threatened by irate farmers and moonshiners. He almost lost his life trying to float a few barrels across the river. He eventually packed it out by mule and sold it to patent medicine manufacturers throughout the South.

In 1820, due to legal battles and pot shots, Huling abandoned the well and moved on into the Appalachian Mountains, still searching for salt brine—and peace.

If this last bit of information is a digression, it is meant to be. This writer was raised within yodeling distance of this well, and, growing up, visited the spot several times. Moonshiners are still there. The well is plugged, and on it is a plaque from the Kentucky Historical Society attesting to the authenticity of the first oil well in America.

32
The Board Chairman Speaks

Loquacious Boards: The History of the Civil War Drum Barracks, when it was built, and how it was named.

ON A QUIET EVENING in late October as the purple and gray of dusk trailed the pinks and golds of a beautiful sunset into the west, I was walking near the old Civil War Drum Barracks in Wilmington and the lonely Officer's Quarters. It was a moment of mystery and suspense, as though something spectral and eerie were about to take place.

I could almost hear the careful clatter of arms being stacked and the easy murmur of voices in light banter at the end of a wearing day. It was a charmed moment of ghostly recall in these abandoned quarters.

The only sound was the chirping of a colony of mocking birds saying their vespers before nestling in for the night. I sat down on the worn, weathered floor of one of the four remaining porches that gave a forlorn welcome to the occasional passerby.

As I reflected upon the glory of a long-gone era in California history, a quavering but gruff and distinct voice suddenly spoke out of the darkness, "I'm the Board Chairman of these barracks," the voice declared. "I and these other old boards don't have many visitors these days, but we insist on being heard whenever anybody comes. We've got plenty to complain about, so don't expect just idle chatter."

The voice stopped suddenly as if distressed.

"Wait a minute!" came the rasping sound. "Come closer, young fella! Why, sure enough, you're the one they sent to Sacramento to get us a reprieve and an appropriation from the Legislature that would save us from oblivion. You're a special friend of ours. Smart, too. You saw the right people and the proper committee."

"Yep, you came back in June 1967, announcing all over the place that Governor Ronald Reagan, with the urging of Assemblyman Vincent Thomas and Senator Ralph Dills, signed into law a bill for $125,000 which was enough to straighten our stanchions, firm up our foundation, even up our floors and secure our walls . . . to paint us, refurnish us, and make us more presentable as a Civil War Museum.

"But what have they done for us? Just plain nothing, that's what they've done! Your society, under the leadership of Mrs. Fred Lorenzen, known as The Society For The Preservation of Drum Barracks, had better get on the ball! Otherwise you may lose us. We're getting tired, and frustrated, and not just a little bit angry!"

I had been so taken back by this astonishing encounter that I couldn't marshall my thoughts, even if the Board Chairman had stopped long enough in his tirade to let me speak. But now I broke in lamely with, "What's this? A talking building?"

"And why not a talking building?" the gruff voice retorted. "There's talking birds, talking dogs, talking horses, talking trees. Well, we're just more mature—and far more experienced and wise than any of them. Anyway, why should you be surprised when we're just a short ride from Walt Disney's place, where they've got more talking wood than . . . than you can shake a stick at." And I thought I heard a soft chuckle.

There was a dry rustle as of chafing limbs among wintering elms brushing each other in the wind. Clearly, the other boards in the barracks were voicing their approval of his discourse.

The Board Chairman continued: "Phineas Banning, father of the Los Angeles Harbor, helped put us together and donated 60 acres of land, after our long voyage from the East Coast and we're two years older than his mansion, which was completed in 1864."

"Please don't forget that, being an army barracks, we were conceived by the U.S. Congress and rededicated by Abraham Lincoln in his Gettysburg address. Although a continent apart, we were on his team, and he had us in mind when he said 'of the people, by the people, and for the people.'

The Chairman was vibrant, his voice clear and forceful.

"The community experienced hard times after Lincoln was shot. The harbor was rough, tough, and crude. Real estate sold for almost nothing, and property went on the auction block for delinquent taxes."

"Before you write a report about us," the Chairman asked, "let us tell you that we were named in honor of Adjutant General Richard Coulter Drum, who had been head of the U.S. Army of the West for many years and saw exemplary service in New Mexico and Arizona."

"During Drum's pioneering days he had hiked the mountains and walked the plains with Kit Carson and John Charles Fremont, whom he consulted frequently about the Western Frontier.

"Within these walls we have known many secrets and heard the voices of many soldiers who became famous . . . Gen. Philip Henry Sheridan, Gen. Winfield Scott Hancock, Gen. George Stoneman, Gen. Cave J. Coutts, and, of course, General Phineas Banning, not to mention Lt. Fitzgerald Beal of Fort Tejon fame and his camel caravan.

"Phineas Banning, bless his soul," the Board Chairman continued, "he was so loyal to the Union cause that he lost, for a time, most of his hauling business to his aggressive competitor, J.J. Tomlinson, who was, along with most of the other merchants of Los Angeles and Southern California, sympathetic to the Confederacy and antagonistic to Phineas Banning.

"The dissidents and mercenaries met at the old Bella Union Hotel in Los Angeles, where they ate, drank and conspired against the Union."

"I want a specific story from you," I interrupted. "For example, with your great knowledge and wisdom you can tell me what Christmas was like, say, in 1865."

"Very well, but first let's finish what I was going to tell you about Gen. Phineas Banning. He was such a dedicated Unionist that he gambled his all against overwhelming odds for Lincoln and the Federal Cause. The General persevered, and he won out with lasting glory."

"Tell me more," I pleaded.

"Very well! In 1865, the general was elected to the California State Senate. Talk about Christmas! That was the most joyful Christmas in our history, except maybe when we were young sprouts growing up in the Mohawk Valley of New York, but that's another story."

"On Christmas Day, 1865, General Banning invited his close friends and their friends to be his guests at his 30-room mansion, and they came virtually in caravans, most with horse-and-buggy. But some came on foot, some on horseback.

"My, I can still hear the mellow strains of Christmas music and lovely carol singing from the mansion, which is, as you know, just yodeling distance away. We have never heard so many popping corks and warm toasts."

"They were celebrating the occasion and making the occasion a celebration. First, to General U.S. Grant's complete victory at Appomattox, then to Banning's clean sweep at the polls. It was a super-duper lallapaloozer, if you will pardon my slang. You could hear the clip-clock of spirited horses coming and going all day and all night long."

"How could we forget? Many of our barracks officers were honored guests, all coming back to their quarters pledging renewed faith in the Union. General Banning was a maestro in patriotism as well as of the minuet, quadrilles, waltzes, schottisches, and mazurkas."

"When the hilarity was at its height, the general asked everyone to stand at attention and drink a special toast: 'To our loyal and staunch friend, whom we all admire and love, that hero of Antietam and Gettysburg, Drum Barracks' pride and joy. An officer who left our barracks early in the war and became, for a time, second in command to General U.S. Grant. Let us drink to our own wonderful Quartermaster, General Winfield Scott Hancock!"

"You know," the Board Chairman said knowingly, "many years ago when the Quartermaster first came to the barracks and put his 'Hancock' on all those lucrative government contracts for Phineas Banning to haul army ordnance, soldiers and supplies, to Fort Yuma, Fort Tejon, Fort Mojave, and other outlying centers all the way from the wharves of San Pedro and Wilmington, Banning beamed with grateful appreciation and vowed that as long as the Banning family survived there would be a Hancock Banning named in honor of General Winfield Scott Hancock, and so it is to this day.

"In October, 1866, Phineas Banning named a son Hancock, who bore a son named Hancock, who also bore a son named Hancock. They have all been prominent in the economic and social life in California. The first Mrs. Hancock Banning, with Mrs. Ada Edwards Laughlin, were the founders of the prestigious Assistance League of California, an organization doing a fine service in worthy causes."

"Tell me," I coaxed, "about being young sprouts growing up in the Valley of the Mohawks."

The Board Chairman was elated. "All of us, including Banning's mansion," he began, boastfully, "came around the Horn, and all of us claim kin to the clipper family that went to sea."

"But our greatest ambition was to grow up and become barracks to shelter and protect the military in the service of our nation. Some of us made it, and some of us grew up and became famous flag staffs, mast booms, wooden Indians, toys, and some, God forbid, became low-down ax handles. But we are most proud that each year millions of our family bring great joy and happiness as Christmas trees to warm the hearts of a million homes.

"My father and many of our uncles and cousins went to college. We have ancestors at Harvard, Yale, Princeton, Columbia, and West Point. Some of them are still there, not because they are dumb, although, some are blockheads. They're there to give support to the ivy that curls and winds itself around our kin. It symbolizes the college image, and they love us."

"Bravo, keep going," I demanded.

"Many of us," the Board said sadly, "were tramped-on by the marching feet of Gen. George Washington's soldiers. For weeks in 1776 they bivouacked near us, where they planned for their victory at strategic Trenton. When news of this victory spread, even the Mohawks became friendly."

"Now, let's talk more about Drum Barracks," I interrupted, so we could get back on the main track. "Just how strategic were you during the Civil War?"

"Well, we know we were a powerful bulwark against the encroachment of rebel enemies, and they were legion in California and Arizona. Secessionist elements were prominent throughout the West, and political pharisees urged marauders and culprits to flagrant acts of depredation.

"Our cavalry pursued these desperadoes through miles of mountains and sand, eventually bringing them to the stockade and to justice. Our Battery A Light Artillery was sent to Catalina and other off-shore islands, coming back heroes after subduing the rebel pirates who were harassing the important clipper ships from San Francisco, loaded with the Comstock gold and silver sorely needed by the federal government.

"At one time we had over 7,000 troops stationed here at Drum Barracks," the Board Chairman went on. Without them—and without us to keep body and soul together—California would surely have been lost to the Union cause and now look at us. Who cares what we have done in the past? Look at those leaning stanchions and those warped boards! Look at our beams and our siding!"

It was time for a little sympathy and reassurance. "You have certainly served your country well to have provided sustenance and shelter for so many at a crucial time in our history," I said. "What a shame to become decrepit after such glorious service." But the Board Chairman needed to get his mind off his present plight.

"By the way, with as little care as you have had, how do you keep termites from devouring you?" The ploy worked beautifully.

"Those critters!", the Board Chairman fairly yelled. "Why, we play games with them, and the crazy mites never learn."

"How's that?" I asked, with genuine curiosity.

"Those of us who came from the Valley of the Mohawks exude an infinitesimal granule of noxious oxide that spells taps for all who attack. The only happy taps that ever rang out from the barracks. It's a sort of a time bomb that takes no time at all, a tricky kind of sugar plum. When they touch us they subside into a terminal moraine.

"But we're running out of time. We need fixing up. Please hurry and help us. Go see Vincent Thomas and Ralph Dills again, but hurry."

Thus the gruff old Guard concluded his narrative about Drum Barracks. I left the quarters with renewed hope that this patriotic Civil War building would soon be rescued. As a Civil War museum, it would be the only one west of West Point in a building erected specifically for Civil War service.

Then the immortal poem rang in my ears:

"I think that I shall never see
A poem as lovely as a tree.
A tree that looks at God all day
And lifts her leafy arms to pray.
Poems are made by fools like me,
But only God can make a tree."

And as I finished ruminating upon our incredible conversation and upon Joyce Kilmer's great tribute to the living thing without which none of us could live, I thought I heard the gruff Chairman clear his throat once more.

"Amen," was the last word that came out of the dark, lonely barracks.

33
Mormon Island Does Not Mourn

The U.S. Borax Company with its 350 employes adds greatly to the economic prosperity of Wilmington and to the harbor area.

THIS STORY HAS to do with Mormon Island and the U.S. Borax Corporation that occupies it. The question of how the island was named has recently come to light.

There was a group of Mormon volunteers skilled in carpentry and building techniques stationed at nearby Drum Barracks. General Richard Coulter Drum assigned these volunteers in 1862 to build needed barges, tugs, and lighters, sorely needed in the war effort.

The Mormons lived on the 30-acre island, now connected to Wilmington by Fries Avenue. The site was on the old Banning Shipyard complex, from which many ships have been launched. The U.S. Borax Company has occupied much of the island for 50 years. It is the only privately owned land in L.A. Harbor not subject to rentals.

At the close of World War I, the Pacific Coast Borax Company (predecessor of U.S. Borax) had mines in Death Valley and refineries in Alameda and Bayonne, New Jersey. When cheaper water transportation became available via the Panama Canal, the company moved its Alameda refinery to Mormon Island. Operations began there in 1924. The first cargo left the harbor November 1, 1924, aboard the S.S. Santa Paula for New York.

In 1957, the Borax Company opened its plant at Boron, California, and, according to Joe V. Kern, public relations manager, the Borax Company is now a conglomerate of 10 specialty plants ranging in daily production of five tons of boric acid to 44 other products in 175 different packages. Over 350 people are employed in the Wilmington plant.

On November 28, 1963, the 20,000-ton M.S. Johann Schulte departed the harbor with the first shipload of bulk borate products. It was consigned to Holland. In 1973, the 30,000-long ton class M.S. Strassburg sailed with 36,001 tons for Rotterdam, which established a new record. When one sees Dutch Cleanser on cans, it is safe to say that it originally came in bulk from the Borax company in Wilmington. In Wilmington, Borax also manufactures industrial chemistry products, agricultural and industrial herbicides, plant foods, fertilizer, weed killers, soap, and dispenser items. Some of its household products are 20 Mule Team, Borateem, and Boraxo.

Actually, much of the world's industry depends on borates. Boric acid, borax, and other compounds of boron are used in almost every major industry, and are essential to modern agriculture. Fibreglas, porcelain enamel, ceramics, soap and detergents, flameproofing, pharmaceuticals and photographic chemicals all contain the same basic ingredient—borax and boron.

Like gold and silver, borax has been known for thousands of years. Sixteen centuries ago, borax glazes were used in China. Specimens of this pottery are in museums, the glazes still brilliant and beautiful.

F.M. "Borax" Smith, founder of the Pacific Coast Borax Company in 1881, made history but had no time to write it. He was the archetype of those romantic exiles who were unsuccessful in gold digging. Smith became convinced California's future was in borax, as its past had been in gold. He became so addicted to uncovering borax deposits in Death Valley that, it is said, he experienced painful withdrawal symptoms when he left for a few days' vacation.

How to get borax out of Death Valley was a problem until the advent of the 150-foot-long, 20-mule team to haul it across 165 barren miles of desert to the railroad junction at Mojave. These wagons, built in Mojave, had rear wheels seven feet high, front wheels five feet high, each with eight-inch-wide steel tires, one inch thick. The hubs were 18 inches in diameter and 22 inches in length. The spokes of split oak were 3½ inches square. The wagon beds were 16 feet long, four feet wide, and six feet deep. When loaded with borax and 12,000 gallon water tank, it totaled 36½ tons. Much of the raw material for these wagons was brought from the Banning Shipyard on Mormon Island.

Kern said there is a great dynamic growth potential in boron chemistry, even in space flights and atomic reactors.

One of "Borax" Smith's early booklets recommended borax for digestion, for keeping milk sweet, for the complexion, for removal of dandruff, and for the bath; also, it was said to be good for washing carriages and curing epilepsy and bunions.

Presently, the U.S. Borax combine is contributing greatly to America's needed cash balance in the export economy.

34

A Mexican President and His Camel Roots

A brief history of the Drum Barracks Camel Corps, and their herders.

PLUTARCO ELIAS CALLES, president of Mexico from 1924 to 1930, was the son of "El Turco" Elias, one of the three camel drivers who were stationed for a brief time in 1863 at Civil War Drum Barracks in Wilmington.

When Elias left Wilmington he moved to New Mexico, then into Sonora, became a Mexican citizen, added Calles to his name, married a Yaqui Indian girl, did some ranching, and raised a family. One of the sons of that marraige was Plutarco Elias Calles.

As a youngster, young Calles was known as "El Turco." Even as president of Mexico, Calles often reminisced about his childhood and about his father's herding camels for the U.S. Army in California and the American Southwest.

One of the other two camel drivers was known as "Greek George," who in 1867 was naturalized as an American citizen with the name of George Allen. He lived in a modest adobe house on Santa Monica Boulevard in Hollywood.

There, in 1903, he was visited by the late Charles F. Lummis, founder of the Southwest Museum in Pasadena, who described Greek George as a modest, well-mannered, sturdy man with a Homeric beard and a rich thatch of hair, both so dense as to seem bullet-proof.

Lummis said that since Greek George left Smyrna in 1855 he had forgotten his Greek and had learned no English but could speak Spanish very well. Greek George died at Mission Viejo on September. 2, 1913, and is buried in Whittier.

The other driver of the trio was Hadji Ali, who became known as Hi Jolly. He was buried in 1902 in Quartzsite, Arizona, in a pyramidal tombstone 15 feet high topped with a metal camel. The monument has become an important tourist attraction.

The Camel Corps idea started on March 3, 1855, at the urging of Secretary of

War Jefferson Davis, to get Congress to appropriate $30,000 to import camels on an experimental basis to aid western army camps and forts in transporting goods and supplies through the desert.

By 1857, about 100 dromedaries were unloaded at the port of Indianola, Texas, to be driven westward, some of them to Ft. Tejon, California; others to Camp Verde and Camp Hudson; some went over the Mojave Desert to Fort Yuma for supplies, later to Los Angeles and San Pedro, and finally to Drum Barracks.

Lt. Edward Fitzgerald Beal, in charge of the first trek of the camels from Texas to California, gave glowing reports in his journal of October 18, 1857:

"My admiration for the camels increases daily. The harder the test the more fully they seem to justify all that can be said of them. They pack water for the mules for days and never get a drop; they pack a heavy burden of corn and oats for months and never get a grain; and on bitter greasewood, cactus, and other worthless shrubs not only subsist but keep fat; withal, they are so perfectly docile and so admirably contented . . . I look forward to the day when every mail route across the continent will be conducted altogether with this economical and noble brute."

Beal's wave of enthusiasm was published in the October 1857 issue of *Harper's Monthly*, was read by King Monghut of Siam, who later was romanticized in a stage play and movie, "The King and I."

On February 14, 1861, the king wrote a letter to President Abraham Lincoln:

" . . . Though formerly there were no camels on the America continent, you have sought for and purchased them, some from Arabia, some from Egypt. Camels propagate their race and are serviceable and of benefit to the country, and are already numerous in America, and having heard this it has occurred to me that, if on the continent of America there should be several pairs of young male and female elephants turned loose in a forest where there is an abundance of water and grass under the Sun's declination both North and South . . . we are of the opinion that after a while they will increase till there be large herds . . . we shall be kind to send you a few pair . . ."

President Lincoln answered in a letter dated February 3, 1862:

". . . Our political jurisdiction does not reach a latitude so low as to favor multiplication of the elephant. Steam on land, as well as on water, has been our best and most efficient agent of transportation in (our) internal commerce . . ."

Coincidentally, President Lincoln, a Republican, dampened the idea of importing working elephants, and President Grover Cleveland, a Democrat, frowned on further importation of working pack camels, preferring the donkey instead.

35
S.S. Ada Hancock Blows Up

Phineas Banning's first steamers; a vigilante hanging of a killer on his way to San Quentin aboard the S.S. Crickett; and the tragedy of 26 deaths when the Hancock blew up.

IT'S A FAR CRY from the modern steamers docked in the Los Angeles Harbor now back to the old sailing vessels and side-wheel steamers that called at San Pedro Bay when it was an open roadstead without a breakwater.

There also is a sharp contrast between present activity at the local shipyards, including Bethlehem, Todd, and Al Larsen, and that day in 1831 when the first boat, named Guadelupe for the Patron Saint, was launched in the Los Angeles Harbor by Joseph Chapman.

Chapman was a sailor, and on a voyage from Boston to the Sandwich Islands, he was shanghaied by the cutthroat pirate, Bouchard. Later Chapman was captured while on one of Bouchard's raids near Santa Barbara. He was sent under guard to the San Gabriel Mission where he was put to work on a 100-ton duplicate of the Guadelupe, a vessel wrecked in San Pedro harbor in 1828.

Passengers disembarking in San Pedro descended a rope ladder onto a lighter to be rowed ashore. After 1851, Phineas Banning built a fleet of barges and small steamers to lighter travelers and freight. After Banning moved his dock facilities in 1858 to Wilmington, his line of stages carried the visitors to Los Angeles. A few years later he took them all the way to Fort Yuma and the Pacific Southwest.

Banning's first steamer was the little Medora; then he added the Crickett, the Clara, the Los Angeles, and the Ada Hancock. The latter was named for the daughter of General Winfield Scott Hancock, who had befriended Banning when he was Quartermaster at Fort Tejon and Drum Barracks by giving Banning profitable contracts to haul ordnance as well as to transport soldiers to outlying sections of California and Arizona.

The 100-foot Crickett, built in San Francisco, was slim, low-draft vessel that drew only two and one-half feet of water. It easily could get over the sandbar in the channel.

This little sharp-nosed Crickett played an important role in bay shipping. It carried many celebrities, United States Senators, Army officers, governors, and railroad moguls such as Collis P. Huntington, Leland Stanford, Mark Hopkins, and Charles Crocker, ship captains and other big brass who happened to be in the harbor.

There was great excitement on the Crickett one day when a prisoner named Cerradel, who had murdered a prominent rancher, was hanged. The judge gave Cerradel a light sentence of about 10 years at San Quentin. When the sheriff put his prisoner aboard the Crickett to be taken down the channel to the S.S. Senator anchored about where Angeles Gate is now located, vigilantes forcibly took prisoner Cerradel from the sheriff, hanged him to the flagstaff, and dropped his stone-weighted body into the bay between San Pedro and Wilmington.

At about 5 p.m. April 27, 1863, the loaded S.S. Ada Hancock left Wilmington for the S.S. Senator, five miles out in the anchorage. About a mile from Wilmington, a violent squall arose. The boat careened in the sudden gale; water engulfed the boiler, and it exploded.

Twenty-six people were killed outright. With the miraculous exception of Phineas Banning and Rebecca, everyone at the front of the steamer was killed. The dead included some prominent people: Captain William Seeley, skipper of the Senator, William Sanford, Rebecca's brother, Tom Workman, Banning's general manager. Only seven of the 60 aboard escaped injury. Banning and Rebecca were injured but recovered.

In the confusion and terror, four hours passed before word got to Los Angeles. Its four doctors went to Wilmington at once.

The tragedy weighed heavily on Banning. The Coroner's inquest completely exonerated Banning, but he insisted on paying the expenses of all those injured, and the families of those killed. It hurt, but Banning met the emergency, borrowing heavily to do it.

Banning's Mormon Island Shipyard became more active than ever. His first steamer, the Los Angeles, launched in 1869, was much larger than the Crickett or the Ada Hancock. The Banning ships carried passengers and freight to the off-shore islands.

Since the stage route to San Francisco was a rough one, most Southern Californians preferred to travel by steamer. Of all the ships on the run, the S.S. Senator was the most popular. Built on the East Coast, she had traveled around the Horn and for many years plied the Sacramento River during the gold rush days.

The Senator advertised large and airy rooms, a ladies' salon, and a bridal suite. Eastern visitors often mentioned trips on the Senator. When Richard Henry Dana revisited San Pedro in 1859 he traveled on the Senator to San Francisco. It was Dana's first trip to San Pedro since 1835 when he was a sailor aboard the Pilgrim. Dana spoke highly of the S.S. Senator.

36

Charlie Lim Yong—Major-Domo

The romantic story of a grateful Oriental who crossed the seas to China to bring back the most exotic wisteria seeds for Banning's garden.

THE ANCIENT WISTERIA of Charlie Lim Yong, Phineas Banning's expert cook of 15 years, has bloomed in profusion for the benefit of the thousands of guests who attend the Annual Wisteria Festival in Wilmington. The festivities are at Banning Park in Wilmington and usually begin with an artillery Civil War skirmish between the Blue and the Gray.

Charlie was the one who brought the wisteria shoots to the Banning garden in 1881. Charlie Lim Yong was the product of the early migration of Chinese to California in the 1860s spurred by railroad recruiting stations in Chinese towns, principally along the Pearl River Delta. Canton was the main source of recruits.

Charlie became an indentured worker under bond to the Central Pacific Railroad. Soon after arriving, he was assigned to laying rails and clearing the right-of-way. Charlie aspired to the lofty station of cook, but there was much pick-and-shovel work before he could hope to gain a toehold in the camp galley. Then one day it happened.

The camp boss gave Charlie a job peeling spuds and scouring pans. He soon became a favorite and was promoted to chief cook. In the rugged terrain of mountains and deserts, engineers plotted a steady sunup-to-sundown workday. After a few months, Charlie's courtesies and manners were noticed by a railroad executive who had a mansion atop Knob Hill in San Francisco. He had Charlie transferred to his home.

The decade of the 1860s was a tense period in California history. It was a time of hope and despair when gold seekers and adventurers from all parts of the world descended upon California's shores. In covered wagons and clipper ships, they kept coming. An acute labor problem was inevitable. Teeth-gnashing rivalry sprung up with recurrent race riots against the Chinese. Charlie had to endure the bitterness of an inhospitable urban citizenry. Even the marketplaces were not safe for him. He had no covered wagon.

In time, Charlie found his way into the Hollister home in Santa Barbara, where a combination of favorable environments began to unfold for him, beginning February 14, 1870, when Gen. Phineas Banning married the socially prominent Mary Hollister. She asked Phineas to send for Charlie and interview him for the major-domo job for the 24-servant household at the mansion.

Charlie was sent for; he arrived wearing a new blue-and-gold quilted pajama coat, behind which his freshly braided queue dangled. After about 60 tick tocks from the old grandfather clock, Charlie was hired as the kitchen major-domo.

In the spring of 1880, after 10 years in the Banning house, Charlie asked the general if he could make a trip to his native Canton. He wanted to visit the land of his ancestors, to see again the quaint locality of his forefathers. Charlie had nostalgic visions of his beloved Pearl River Delta—a horizon of rice paddies peopled by his cousins, of water buffalo, peacocks, eagles, tigers and dragons. He wished to see again the good earth of his childhood.

Banning bought Charlie a roundtrip ticket to China. Before the China Clipper from Philadelphia, loaded with steel drums filled with oil to light the lamps of China, sailed from Wilmington, Banning asked Charlie to be sure and bring back some wisteria shoots, which he wanted for his 20-acre garden.

Two months after leaving Wilmington, Charlie arrived in Hong Kong and continued his journey via sampan up the Pearl River to Canton, the home he had left 15 years earlier.

Charlie extolled the virtues of the Banning family who lived far across the western seas in a land called California. His kin were radiant with blessings for this great family who had befriended their cousin, and they vowed to go far, if need be even to the Yangtze Valley in Szechwan Province (a month journey overland) to find the most perfect wisteria seedlings for Charlie to present to the general.

But Charlie was in no great rush. He had many people to see and new recipes to collect. People came from far places to talk with this remarkable kinsman, boss of 24 servants in a wealthy far-off land across the seas.

Since Charlie was an indentured worker, now under bond with Phineas Banning, it was necessary that he continue to wear his queue, or pigtail, and dress only in Chinese attire. Charlie did not resent this. To him, it was not a mark of indignity. Rather, his queue, he felt, gave him as much notice and distinction as the long beards and fuzzy whiskers worn by some of Banning's guests, such as Collis P. Huntington, Leland Stanford, Charles Crocker, Mark Hopkins and U.S. Grant.

Charlie arrived back in Wilmington in March 1881, on the Eastern Merchant, with the finest wisteria seedlings in all of China. Banning was grateful. He and his wife and two daughters, Mary and Lucy, planted the shoots near the carriage house. It is likely that these same vines are still there. After Phineas Banning died March 8, 1885, Charlie returned to China. His body lies in a Kubla Khan bamboo cemetery, 10 kilometers from Canton along the Pearl River Valley—in the land of his ancestors, his temples, and his gods.

37

Alonzo Horton Visited the Harbor

In 1867 Horton bought most of San Diego for $100 cash. He first consulted Phineas Banning about possibilities there.

THE MORE WE SEARCH archives, screen reports, study letters, and read books about Phineas Banning, the more we are amazed and impressed by the complexities of his time and the facets of his life.

At his mansion in Wilmington he entertained the great and near great. One of them was Alonzo Erastus Horton.

Horton left an indelible imprint on the history of Southern California, and in 1967 San Diego celebrated "Father Horton Centennial Year," an affair that should make every resident cognizant of the importance and benefits of the American Free enterprise system, and make them even more proud of their government and their historical heritage.

Nowhere in the world except America could a man, even as late as 1867, buy a plot of ideally located land the size of San Diego for a mere $100 and have the deed withstand all litigation in American courts since that date. It was a district already long established as the Pueblo of San Diego.

Horton was born in Ohio in 1813. Early in life he started a freighting business on Lake Erie, later moving to Wisconsin, where he became a land speculator. His doctor told him he had tuberculosis and probably wouldn't live over six months. He advised Horton to go west.

Horton came to California and became involved unsuccessfully in mining ventures. In San Francisco he heard a lecturer extol the virtues and speculative potential of harbor land all the way from Seattle to San Diego.

Horton was especially enchanted by the description of the "Beautiful Landlocked Harbor" of San Diego. He knew about the ambitions of Phineas Banning and what Banning was doing for San Pedro and the harbor of Los Angeles.

Before going to San Diego to investigate the possibilities there, he would first have a talk and get advice from Phineas Banning.

After Horton bought the land which is now downtown San Diego—the old Pueblo was three miles north—he returned to San Francisco and sold lots in his San Diego holdings. A boom for the lots started when Horton told them what Banning had said about a railroad that would surely be built to San Diego.

When ground was broken in 1870 for the Horton House in San Diego, Horton invited Banning to be with him. This is the place where the U.S. Grant Hotel now stands. Banning was there, then rushed back to be present at a gala opening of the Pico House in Los Angeles.

Alonzo Erastus Horton died in 1909, but he lived to see his "heaven on Earth" plot of land blossom and prosper. Today it is an industrial and shipping complex boasting over 850,000 population, becoming the second largest city in California.

38

La Brea Tar Caulked Our Ships

Banning made brea (tar) famous for caulking clipper ships and for roofing. Quartermaster Winfield Scott Hancock, who befriended Phineas Banning, became a famous general in the Civil War. U.S. Grant accolade to Hancock.

OF ALL THE RANCHOS in which Phineas Banning had an equity, or business connection, the Rancho La Brea held for him a deep-rooted affection, due principally to Banning's high regard for the Hancock family who owned the property.

The original La Brea land grant was given to Antonio Jose Rocha by the Alcalde (mayor), Jose Antonio Carrillo, in 1828. Carrillo was the great-great grandfather of the late Leo Carrillo, the actor and comedian. The land grant consisted of one square league of land, a unit equal to three statute miles, and it was specified that all inhabitants of the pueblo of Los Angeles would have riparian rights to carry away as much of the brea, or tar, as they might need for their adobes. The Rocha family became prosperous and had a landmark home on Plaza Square on Olvera Street. The city bought this house in 1855; for many years it was used by the City and County of Los Angeles for council meetings and courthouse. The jail was built in the rear.

The Rocha heirs sold Rancho La Brea to John Hancock in 1860, and they gave Banning the privilege of hauling tar from the pits for ship caulking and other needs for the L.A. harbor.

Banning's large blacksmith and wagon factory in Wilmington constructed a special wagon for this purpose, and some of this brea was used in the construction of Drum Barracks, which by 1864 consisted of 26 buildings. Much of this tar also was used in San Pedro home buildings and for roofing. And ships in the port were grateful for barrels of this good consistency and high-quality grade of tar.

La Brea has been, and still is, a famous geological landmark because of its strange tar pits, which have preserved animal skeletons of prehistoric ages.

Today, it is in the center of the exclusive Wilshire District of Los Angeles. The John Hancock (not to be confused with the John Hancock who signed the Declaration of Independence in 1776) family built an oil empire from these holdings and became one of the wealthiest families in California.

They contributed greatly to the University of Southern California, where monuments have been erected in their honor. Former U.S. Senator Cornelius Cole of California received 500 acres of land as legal fees for representing the John Hancock interests. These acres are now a good part of Hollywood.

Also let us not confuse the John Hancock name with Winfield Scott Hancock of Ft. Tejon and Civil War fame. Banning first met Quartermaster Hancock on the docks of San Pedro in the 1850s. Quartermaster Hancock suffered with problems of communication and getting freight to his Ft. Tejon outpost. He even imported camels for the project, but this proved a dismal failure.

Banning came to his rescue, built a wagon road to Ft. Tejon, and Quartermaster Hancock became deeply impressed with Banning's ability and character, whereupon Banning received valuable contracts from the army to haul soldiers and equipment to Ft. Yuma and other Pacific Southwest sections.

In October 1866, a new son was born to Phineas and Rebecca Banning. They named him Hancock Banning in honor of Quartermaster Hancock, and to this day the name Hancock is attached to a Banning. The first Hancock Banning married beautiful and talented Anne Smith, who founded the Assistance League of California, an organization still doing an excellent job in worthy causes.

Almost at the outset of the Civil War, Quartermaster Hancock was in the thick of the campaigns. He became a general, and in U.S. Grant's *Personal Memoirs,* Vol. 11, Grant gives Hancock the greatest accolade of all his generals. Grant wrote: "Hancock stands the most conspicuous figure of all the general officers. He commanded a corps longer than any other one, and his name was never mentioned as having committed in battle a blunder for which he was responsible . . . Tall, well-formed, and at the time of which I now write (1885), young and fresh looking, he presented an appearance that would attract the attention of an army as he passed. His genial disposition made him friends, and his personal courage and his presence with his command in the thickest of the fight won for him the confidence of troops serving under him . . . no matter how hard the fight . . . their commander was looking after them."

Winfield Scott Hancock ran for President of the United States in 1880, was defeated by James A. Garfield by only a few votes—the narrowest margin of any campaign for the office before or since.

39

TRAGEDY OF JAMES WILDES: GOOD HEARTS AT THE BIDDING

A happy ending to a sad start. Sentiment ran high. The widow at Searsport will get it all.

IT IS SAID THAT history turns on small hinges, and so do people's lives. The aftermath of a beautiful love story took place aboard the clipper ship Down East in San Pedro Harbor on July 15, 1852.

In the personal memorabilia of Phineas Banning the author found the story:

During the California gold rush, James Wildes left his home in Searsport, Maine, in 1849 working his way as a sailor for California. After arriving at San Francisco, he left the ship for the rich diggings at Hangtown, determined that he would find a stake sufficient to ease the dire circumstances of the wife and children whom he left behind.

Wildes was a powerfully built man, not afraid to use his fists if necessary. He was serious at his work on his assigned plot of ground. He became bronzed, bearded, and weathered. During the three years he was there he sifted and panned many tons of dirt and sand looking for the glittering dust of gold.

He bought a good rifle and kept himself supplied with wild game. He did not gamble or drink. He was lonely for his wife and children, and in 1852, by frugal living he had saved what he thought was a small fortune—anyway enough to call it quits and return with his money to his wife and children.

When the Hangtown stage arrived over the plank roadway at Sacramento, he missed the last boat connection with San Francisco by an hour. He was bewildered and afraid to stay overnight loaded with his gold. Then his eye caught a bank across the street from the stage depot. The bank was open.

Wildes entered and saw a vault. He saw piles of gold upon the floor. In the middle of the counter was a pair of tall scales on which gold nuggets and dust were weighed.

A young clerk asked the stranger what he could do for him. Wildes said: "I've missed my boat for San Francisco. Here's my fix; I'm going back home to Maine. I have about $5,000 in gold stowed away, I don't know a person in Sacramento, and I might get knifed before morning. I'd like to deposit this hoard with you and pick it up tomorrow morning in time to meet the first boat."

The miner was dressed in a faded woolen shirt, pantaloons secured at the hips by a belt. Tucked loosely in his high boots were many pounds of gold dust and nuggets. In his leather jacket dangling from his shoulders were pockets loaded with the precious metal. After divesting himself of every ounce of gold, he was issued a certificate testifying that he had on deposit with the Mutual Confidence and Trust Company, the equivalent of $5,000.

"Thanks mister," Wildes said, "I can eat and sleep now."

But while Jim slept soundly, his destiny was being fulfilled. The officials closed the bank and absconded during the night.

When Jim read the words "Bank Closed" he was despondent, but still was determined to return to his wife and children. Some kind souls paid his passage to San Francisco, where he joined the crew of the clipper "Down East," bound for Boston with about 50 passengers.

Jim was heartsick with an agonizing feeling of shame of going home broke after writing to Jane of his wealth. He could not stand the thought of going on. The night before the ship anchored in San Pedro Bay to take on a cargo of 10,000 hides, Jim jumped overboard and drowned.

At eight bells the next morning after anchoring, the ship's captain assembled all the crew and passengers around him, saying, "Our drowned mate left in his kit a daguerreotype of two blooming children hand in hand, a few articles of clothing, a bank certificate, and a recent letter from his wife. It's an old sea custom to sell by auction the kit of a shipmate who dies on a voyage. I've found out that he had been fleeced out of his money in Sacramento, and it strikes me right here that he found it too heavy for him. God knows. But it's more to the point that he left a wife and two children, whose sole support he was. Gentlemen and mates, take off your hats while I read you this letter."

The letter, which bore evidence of having been read over and over, said:

"Oh, James! and are you really coming home, and with such a lot of money too? How happy we shall be once more. It makes me feel just like a young girl again when we used to roam in the berry pastures hand in hand, and never coveted anything in the world but to be together. Do come quick. Surely God has helped me to wait all this long, weary time, but now it seems as if I couldn't bear it another day. And the little boy James, just your image; it's all he can say, 'Papa, come home.' "

The captain then read the fatal certificate of deposit, holding it up that all might see.

"When we get to Panama," he said, "I'm going to write a letter to the widow and dispatch it by steamer. It's for you to say what kind of letter it shall be. That's why I asked you here. Now, purser, put up the certificate of deposit. How much am I offered?"

The sale went on, each buyer putting the certificate up for sale again and again. "Stop it, purser," said Capt. Williams, "here comes Phineas Banning and Able Stearns on the lighter to arrange for the loading of the hides."

When Banning and Stearns read the letter, they began the bidding all over again. In a short while Capt. Williams counted the money and, with a shout, announced, "That will do. The sale is over! Here are $5,000 dollars. The certificate of deposit is redeemed. The widow and children will get it all."

40
ICE AND SNOW IN SAN PEDRO

Research items reveal hot times and cold times. Herein are early weather reports and a party where Phineas Banning recites poetry.

HISTORY IS A great teacher. It teaches us that life is divided into three parts: that which was, that which is, and that which will be. We learn from the past to profit by the present and from the present to live better in the future.

Take the weather, for instance. Mark Twain wrote, "Everybody talks about the weather, but nobody does anything about it." In his research on local history, the author has come across various periods of unusual weather conditions.

You may be surprised to know that ice one-half inch thick formed on ponds, lakes, and all still waters during the 1865 Christmas holiday season in San Pedro. Several inches of snow fell on our local communities that year.

"Snowflakes fell throughout Christmas Day," reported the *Los Angeles News*, "and all the inhabitants indulged in the novel pastime of snowballing."

This moisture was in great contrast to the terrible drought years of 1862 and 1864, which forced most of the cattle ranches into total bankruptcy. It is said that during this time one could almost walk for miles on cattle carcasses.

During these drought years people wondered where the rain went. They were amazed to learn that while their sky was cloudless, in Cherrapunji, Assam, all rainfall records were broken with an average rainfall of 610 inches per year during 1862-64. It is still the wettest place in the world, while the normal yearly average for Los Angeles is around 16 inches of rain.

Reporter H.D. Barrows wrote in the *San Francisco Bulletin* on Jan. 10, 1865: "After several seasons of severe drought and cattle disasters, we look forward that the coming season will be one of bounty and plenty."

Rain began to fall in abundance during December 1864, and it is recorded that churches were crowded with prayerful rejoicing.

The *Los Angeles News* wrote on Feb. 7, 1865: "A severe windstorm swept over the valleys all the way to the sea. Many houses and trees were uprooted, awnings and signs blown down. The large barn and harness warehouse of Banning & Co., situated on Front Street (Los Angeles), was blown entirely down, not even a stick was standing . . . the wind was a record and had hurricane force. Several homeowners were compelled to lash down the roofs of their houses; some of the workers were blown off and sustained injuries."

The newspapers reveal that during Christmas and New Year's 100 years ago most people in Los Angeles and the Harbor Area celebrated the holidays with bullfights, bell-ringing, fiestas, firecrackers, and fandangoes. But it was different at Banning Mansion.

People often ask how Phineas Banning celebrated the Christmas holidays and the kind of books he liked.

Banning relished history and biography, contract law, verse, newspapers, and magazines. His favorite writer was Lewis Carroll, and Banning delighted in mixing absurdity with serious reading. His favorites were Carroll's *Mad Hatter, The March Hare, The Red Queen,* and *Alice in Wonderland,* which he often read to his children.

During the Christmas holidays of 1878 a clipper ship captain from far-off places moored his ship to Banning's dock at Wilmington.

Banning, always eager for world news, met the captain with open arms, took him and his crew to the mansion for refreshments and a well-prepared dinner.

Mrs. Banning accompanied on the piano a house guest who played the violin. After carols were sung, led by Banning, the entire crew joined in singing.

Near the close of the evening, Banning recited one of Lewis Carroll's poems:

"The time has come," the Walrus said.
To talk of many things.
Of cabbages and kings,
And why the sea is boiling hot,
And whether pigs have wings."

41

Ben Truman— A Deciding Factor

Truman was Secretary to President Andrew Johnson and helped him enact the Homestead Law in 1862. Truman came to visit Phineas Banning in 1867, liked what he saw and became publisher of the Los Angeles Star *in 1873.*

BEN TRUMAN IS A name that all local history buffs and scholars should know.

Ben Truman, distantly related to President Harry Truman, played an unusual and important role in American history, plus his contributions to the early history of San Pedro and the Harbor Area. Truman was Phineas Banning's first chronicler and recorded that Banning was indeed the first person to appear before Congress with the original bill urging appropriations for harbor improvements.

When Andrew Johnson was sworn in as president April 15, 1865, after the assassination of President Abraham Lincoln, Truman became Johnson's personal secretary. Truman also acted as a liaison press relations officer and had full run of the White House for over a year when he was appointed a special representative for the U.S. Post Office. In 1867 Truman made his first trip to California.

But it was at the White House that Truman first met Phineas Banning. Truman's chronicle records this incident: "For be it known that Phineas Banning was the first person who placed before Congress the original bill asking for harbor appropriations; and it was my extreme good fortune to assist this man in June 1866, in getting the matter in the hands of California Senator Cornelius Cole and Congressman Sargent of San Pedro."

Truman was a close follower of Andrew Johnson from the start, and in 1857 when Johnson became a senator from Tennessee, Truman headed a committee to submit all the evidence and public sentiment he could dig up to help Johnson enact the Homestead Act, a program that Johnson first proposed when he was a congressman in 1843 to 1853. It became law in 1862, and it is said that Truman was one of the greatest factors in aiding this legislation, which granted 160 acres of land to each settler with guaranteed deed free from tax.

In 1867 when Truman came to San Pedro and Wilmington to meet with Banning, Truman brought up the payment of retroactive compensation for the years of Banning's stage coach mail handling and delivery.

"You've been carrying the mails for a long time, General Banning," Truman said, "but you've never sent Uncle Sam a bill. What kind of a way of doing business do you call that?"

Banning replied: "It's my way. There has never been any regularly established mail routes here. Letters mean a lot to our people, so I took the responsibility of getting mail where it belongs. I was going that way anyway, and I don't want any pay."

And that's the way it stood. Banning never received any payment in his lifetime for the delivery of mail, although his wagon and coach lines covered all of Los Angeles, the whole harbor complex, and the entire Pacific Southwest, including trips to Denver and Salt Lake City.

Truman became fascinated with Banning. During Truman's stay as a guest of Banning at the Wilmington mansion they often discussed the harbor problems. Truman became convinced that a protected harbor at San Pedro was imperative, and lost no time in reporting his views to the right people in Washington, which in the long run enabled Banning's plans for a breakwater.

In 1865 Banning bought the *Los Angeles Star.* It was during the time he was a candidate for the state Senate. He renamed it *The Wilmington Journal.* A few years later the *Star* reappeared. In June 1873, Truman bought the *Star* and headed it for many years.

By this time Los Angeles leaders were in agreement that Truman's forceful pen and loyal support for harbor improvements became increasingly important in Washington circles.

Truman made several trips to Washington from Los Angeles. He was with Banning in 1873 when they were entertained at the White House by President U.S. Grant.

Of course, Sen. and Mrs. Cole were also guests at this formal dinner party. Truman wrote a piece about it, published Feb. 12, 1873.

"Mrs. Cole, attired in ashes of roses silk, gracefully trimmed with blue satin; hair in the prevailing fashion. She looked beautiful and completely captured our military General Banning by the graceful way she excused him for not appearing in uniform."

A P.S. was attached to the communication on Banning's state of mind:

"General Banning failed to receive a letter from his home this morning and consequently is laid up with the epizootic."

42

San Pedro—Leading Lumber Port

San Pedro grows from a mere 300 and develops a volunteer fire department, a transportation system, and thriving lumber business.

LOS ANGELES HAS BEEN an amazing success story almost since Phineas Banning arrived on the scene in 1851, when the population of San Pedro was a mere 300 people.

At the turn of the century, it had grown to around 3,000 souls, and within a few short years after 1900, the population increased rapidly due to the construction employment on the breakwater project. People throughout California became conscious of the importance of San Pedro and began to flock to her shores looking for jobs and business opportunities.

By 1905 San Pedro became the leading lumber port of the Pacific and was the main source of commerce with five large lumber companies that owned their own wharves. There were two large planingmills with a capacity of six million feet per month, which, according to the records, was the largest in the United States.

The lumber industry, with its interest in ships that brought logs and cut lumber from Eureka and the Pacific Northwest, required considerable financing. As a consequence, San Pedro had four banks—the First National, the Bank of San Pedro, the Citizens' Savings Bank, and the State Bank. Los Angeles City had eight banks.

Also in 1905 construction had begun for the new high school and the new library. There were only two elementary schools at the time—Fifteenth Street School and Fifth Street School. This also was a period of considerable real estate activity and home building, with sub-divisions by George Peck and his associates.

The payroll on the wharves and public works in San Pedro in 1905 averaged about $200,000 per month. The permanent payroll was more than $150,000 per month and steadily increasing. Two electric railroads came to San Pedro and Wilmington, California Pacific and Pacific Electric, both providing half-hourly transportation service to Los Angeles and making the trip in 45 minutes.

Both of these lines were owned and controlled by Henry E. Huntington, heir and nephew of the late Collis P. Huntington, architect of the Southern Pacific Railroad.

At this time the San Pedro and Salt Lake Railroad Co., a subsidiary of the Union Pacific Railroad, was operating smoothly along with the Southern Pacific, and both roads enjoyed terminal facilities with their own wharves in San Pedro. But both railroad companies fought the encroachment of the Santa Fe Railroad for many years with every legal technicality known to them.

When the Santa Fe and Terminal Island Railroad won the battle, Collis P. Huntington made an expensive but abortive attempt to have the San Pedro and Wilmington port of entry closed down and moved to the milelong pier at Santa Monica. He lost by a close vote of the U.S. Senate in 1899. Huntington died in 1900, leaving an estate of over $100 million.

In 1904 steamship companies berthed 1,002 of their vessels in San Pedro and Wilmington, plus 372 coastwise sailing ships, 10 foreign ships. There were three yacht clubs, three fish canneries, a U.S. Marine Hospital, and a busy U.S. Custom House. San Pedro became the headquarters in the fishing and canning industry.

In 1905, San Pedro had electric lights, a gas and water company, and a completed sewage system with outfall outside the breakwater line. The Point Fermin Lighthouse was in full operation. But Dead Man's Island was still a menace to safe navigation and finally was removed in 1928 with its rock and dirt dumped near Observation Point on Terminal Island.

In 1905, San Pedro had a large and active volunteer fire department with impressive uniforms and the letters SPFD sewed onto their jackets. More than 50 merchants and citizens were numbered among this proud group, among them the late Wilbur F. Wood, the first man to make a success of canning tuna. The methods developed by him are standard practice today.

W.A. Gilmore compiled and published a history of the San Pedro Fire Department in 1905. A copy of this 80-page case-bound book was loaned to the author by Helen Cole, daughter of Wilbur F. Wood.

In his introduction to the book Gilmore wrote: "A word should be said of the brave, but modest, men who protect our homes from devastation and ruin, and who are as indispensable to us as the guardians of the peace, or the doctors who bring us back to health from the verge of the grave."

The citizens of the Harbor Area still salute the courage and stamina of firemen who hasten where danger awaits.

43

Hassel at Fort MacArthur

It is hoped that through the dedicated efforts of Congressman Glenn Anderson and John Sonneborn, the lower reservation can be saved. The grounds of the Fort have been the center of significant local history.

THE LAND AREA now known as Fort MacArthur was the center of the early shipping activity of the harbor. In 1796, Father Fermin Lasuen built an adobe shelter where the present post engineers building now stands.

When Father Fermin left in 1797 to build the San Fernando Mission, the adobe was extended and used for a storehouse for supplies of provisions and hardware for a transshipment to Los Angeles.

The Fort MacArthur land was in dispute and in litigation for many years. The quarrel that ensued was mitigated for a time by intermarriage between the Sepulveda and Dominguez family, but later it became boiling hot.

The U.S. Land Grant Commission sustained the Sepulvedas in 1852. San Pedro was then owned lock, stock, and barrel by the Sepulveda family.

It was Jose Diego Sepulveda who first met Phineas Banning when he arrived at the port in 1851. It was reported, but not officially confirmed, that the Sepulvedas charged a landing fee from all new arrivals.

During the Mexican-American war, 1845-1847, Commodore Robert F. Stockton used some of this area for storage of ordnance and supplies for his advance on Los Angeles, also as a training ground for Marines and Army troops in cooperation with Gen. Stephen W. Kearny.

It was on these grounds where a famous dispute arose in 1847 between Kearny and Stockton, as to who should be in command. Also, it is said, but not substantiated, it was here Gen. Kearny ordered Lt. Col. John C. Fremont to be courtmartialed for insubordination.

Army officials in Washington, D.C. sustained Kearny, but Kearny died in

1848. Commodore Stockton resigned from the U.S. Navy to run for the U.S. Senate. Elected in 1851, he brought pressure to rescind the Fremont court-martial. At this time Fremont had help from two other U.S. Senators, one of them being Fremont himself, the other Thomas Hart Benton, a "show-me" senator from Missouri, father-in-law of Fremont.

The court-martial act was unprecedented, whereby an admiral came to the rescue of a colonel over the heated objections of a U.S. general.

While Col. Sal Rizza was commandant of Fort MacArthur from 1969 to 1970, he assigned his deputy, Col. Clark Trainer, to give the author full access to all historical records kept at the engineer's office. These records have since been transferred to Fort Leavenworth archives.

Until the breakwater was completed in 1910, even to 1928, a 42-acre land mass known as Dead Man's Island, about 1,500 feet from Fort MacArthur, was considered a serious hazard to navigation.

In the author's research, he found three letters written to Fort MacArthur by three U.S. Presidents: one from Ulysees S. Grant, one from Grover Cleveland, who commissioned the area as a military reservation in 1888, and one from Woodrow Wilson.

They were all concerned over the proximity of Dead Man's Island to the fort. The island was completely removed in 1928. The early supervision of Dead Man's Island was under the U.S. Treasury Department in Washington, D.C., and records mention in complimentary terms the part the Coast Guard played in the early development of the Fort MacArthur complex.

However, we feel no running narrative of this area can be historically recorded without the name of Phineas Banning looming up from almost every perspective. From 1851 until 1858 Banning used the old adobe buildings near the location where the post engineer's building now stands.

It served as the terminus for his freight and stage line between the Port and Los Angeles. Moreover, it was at the foot of where Fort MacArthur is now located that Banning in the 1850s sent his lighters out to where sailing vessels were anchored in the bay.

From this vantage point Banning could see the urgent necessity for a protective breakwater. He enlisted help from Congress for an engineer's survey. In 1872 congress also set aside $5,000 for the Point Fermin Lighthouse.

This famous lighthouse, completed in 1874, was the citadel for safe navigation of ships entering and leaving San Pedro and Wilmington until World War II, when radar was installed on the San Pedro hills.

There was a centennial celebration in 1974 headed by John Olguin and his committee in which more than 10,000 people were joyously entertained by the large group of talent toasting this old lighthouse, standing majestically atop the treacherous bluffs of San Pedro, where once it radiated its powerful lightbeams seaward.

The observatory still stands, clothed in simple beauty and dignified modesty. Without it, historians feel, Fort MacArthur, named for Gen. Arthur MacArthur in 1914, could not have been selected in the first place.

We have faith that Fort MacArthur's lower reservation will be retained, thanks to the dedication of Congressman Glenn M. Anderson, John Sonneborn, and Col. Robert Freeland.

Five-star General Omar Bradley told this writer at a reception in the officers' club in 1974 that if they closed it, he would have no place south of San Francisco or Fort Ord to hang his hat in any army installation. Perhaps history yet to be written will assure General Bradley and all who follow a place to hang their hats in San Pedro.

44

Local Shipwrecks Found

Local archaeologists with advanced equipment are finding most of the old sunken ships lost along our coast.

THE WATERS OFF San Pedro and the Palos Verdes Peninsula and between the harbor and Santa Catalina Island are dotted with wrecks of sailing ships, some believed to date back to pre-Columbian days.

Larry Pierson and Patrick Gibson, nautical archaeologists and underwater experts on sunken ships, have a list of more than 450 sunken vessels between Point Concepcion and the Mexican border.

They have, individually or together, personally surveyed the sites of many shipwrecked vessels along our local shore. Among the notable wrecks in the waters off Palos Verdes that Pierson and Gibson have found are:

SS Star of France—a companion ship of the Star of India which has been restored as a museum ship in San Diego. Both ships sailed in the early part of the 20th Century in the Alaska Packers fleet out of San Francisco.

Melrose—a former San Francisco ferryboat that had been converted into a posh fishing barge, said to be the finest ever to sail off the coast of California.

SS Avalon—the ship purchased by William Wrigley in 1920 from Lake Michigan that ran for many years from Wilmington to Santa Catalina Island.

SS Cricket—A small walking beam sidewheel vessel built in the 1850s in San Francisco as a boarding vessel afterward refitted. It was a Phineas Banning ship that in 1878 was refitted as a luxury fishing yacht and was lost around 1900. They found pottery at the wreck site that was dated 1893, indicating the vessel was in service after that year.

Another fascinating wreck is one believed to be that of pre-Columbian times that may have engaged in Pacific Ocean trade on a regular run between ancient China and the Indian empires of Mexico and South America.

Near this wreck, Pierson and Gibson found several 250-pound hard, oval sandstone rocks with holes in the center. These are thought to be Chinese anchors, some speculating that they may have been used as ballast. We can find no record of ballast weighing more than large cobblestones and large bricks which the clipper ships out of Boston used and unloaded in San Pedro. Sam Bolstad of San Pedro has more than a hundred of them. But ballast the size of the rocks would have been too difficult to remove from the hold of the ship.

The wreck sites, according to Gibson and Pierson, are suitable for use as underwater classrooms for field training for future archaeologists. It is now a requirement that all marine archaeologists have training in underwater work, Gibson says, and they are preserving most of these wrecked sites for future scientific study.

Marine environment has become an important adjunct in ocean science education, and many hundreds of students are now enrolled in underwater marine programs.

Both Pierson and Gibson are trustees of the new Los Angeles Maritime History Museum. Other graduate marine specialists serving as trustees are Jim Bacon, Jim Shuttleworth, and Bob Crowther. All these men have made many purposeful dives off the Palos Verdes shore and have recovered numerous artifacts and other treasures which they intend to donate to exhibit at the museum which will be in the old San Pedro ferry building at the foot of Sixth Street.

Other displays planned for the museum are the history of San Pedro Bay, including the development of the main channel; the Indian period, pre-1542; pioneers of the past; the story of the breakwater and the lighthouse; sport and commercial fishing industries; evolution of West Coast ships; the story of the annual Hawaii yacht race; early sea explorers; a marine art gallery; shipping methods of the past, present, and future; artifact displays from the sea; and Navy and Coast Guard history in the port.

It is planned that the museum will be compatible with the planned new Cabrillo Marine Museum, which will feature marine biology and the story of the living sea.

The author has obtained records of nearly all the early ships that anchored in this harbor, including the Spanish galleon San Carlos, which arrived in San Pedro on July 12, 1774, bringing supplies for Gaspar de Portola and Fr. Junipero Serra; and, the Spanish men-o-war Princesa and Favorita, which came in 1779 carrying material for the building of the praesidio of Santa Barbara.

In 1794, 17 ships entered San Pedro; in 1834, 31 ships came. Some of these vessels were lost off our coast. Perhaps Pierson and Gibson will find them.

45
Wilbur Wood—First Tuna Canner

San Pedro's leading industry, canning tuna, was founded by the dedication of Wilbur Wood in discovering how to prevent spoilage by properly venting the cans.

THE LATE WILBUR F. WOOD, who died in San Pedro, November 8, 1975, at the age of 96, was the first man to make a success of canning tuna, and the methods he developed are standard practice in all fish canneries today, according to a Van Camp executive.

Wood's first job was making tin cans for the Southern California Fish Company in 1895. They were packers of mackerel, sardines, salmon, and various other fish, but not tuna. Wood became superintendent of the company in 1909, and started experimenting with albacore tuna, plentiful in the San Pedro and Catalina waters, but generally unwanted. At first Wood canned them raw in 1-lb cans, but this proved unsatisfactory.

In 1911 Wilbur Wood began to pre-cook them with heads, tails, and dark meat eliminated. He injected steam, then cooked the tuna in cans, but that pack would not keep. Wood finally hit on the idea of venting the cans from both the top and the bottom. Before this, a shoemaker's awl was used to vent the cans only from the top for the escape of gases. The hole was then soldered, but venting the bottom as well as the top did the trick by permitting all the gas to escape. Single venting permitted only half of the gas to escape.

In 1912 Wood resigned from the Southern California Fish Company, and formed the California Tunny Canning Company in San Pedro. This was the first successful tuna canning factory in America.

In 1915 Wood sold his cannery to the Van Camp Sea Food Co., after Frank Van Camp, and his son, Gilbert, Sr., transferred their business to San Pedro from Indianapolis. Wilbur Wood stayed with them as production manager until September 17, 1917. The factory was located near the end of Fisherman's Slip in San Pedro, near the old Timms' Landing Wharf. The plant was removed to Terminal Island after World War I.

Records from the *Pacific Fisherman,* a monthly magazine, in 1902, reveal that experiments to can tuna had been started as early as 1903 with albacore cuts in chunks, steeped in brine, and canned in olive oil after the Mediterranean manner. The pack was generally unsuccessful, although it did find a good market with the Italians in New York and Brooklyn; much larger acceptance was needed.

In 1918 Wilbur Wood, Bismarck Houssels, A.J. Cohn, Wiley Ambrose, and others started the International Packing Corporation at Terminal Island, taking over the Premier Fish Co., and the Pacific Fish Company plants at San Diego; three tuna canneries were in operation. In the 1920s depression came, and the entire tuna industry became financially troubled, until the Van Camp engineered an amalgamation comprising the International Packing companies and several other smaller canneries. By so doing, it became the largest tuna canning company in the nation under their new albacore "Chicken of the Sea" label.

During the time Wilbur Wood operated the California Tunny Canning Company, he allowed others to use his plant for private labels. For instance, C.E. Pierce introduced "Pierce Brand" tuna to the Midwest. Wood sent A.B. Seal, his sales manager, all over the nation on a goodwill tour to popularize the taste for canned tuna, which at the time was sold under the label "White Star Brand" tuna. Seal's orders kept the San Pedro factory humming. Cannery workers were put on three shifts, night and day, with overtime allowed.

Wood was also the innovator of a new quirk in merchandising. In 1912 he sent two attractive girls from his San Pedro plant to the People's Store in Los Angeles, now the May Company, with some canned tuna. The cans were opened and customers were served samples on tooth-picks.

This idea of sampling food in market places served from tooth-picks originated in San Pedro and soon became world-wide as a new technique in merchandising. A steady demand for tuna and albacore packed in one-half-lb tins followed rapidly; from this start popular national demand developed for San Pedro's most important and profitable industry, thanks to the foresight and guiding genius of pioneer Wilbur F. Wood.

The citizens of San Pedro can be heartened by the recent decision that the Van Camp division of the Ralston Purina Co., of St. Louis, will not leave San Pedro after all. However, they still intend to maintain a canning facility in San Diego.

46

Catalina Island an "Ugly Wart"

Covarrubias miscalculated, and his heirs lost millions of dollars when Catalina was called an "ugly wart," the greatest wart mistake in history.

WHEN DON JOSE COVARRUBIAS, a Santa Barbara rancher, sold the 48,438-acre Catalina Island to Albert Packard for $1,000 in 1853, he could not have even dreamed how strategic and economically important this island would become within a few decades.

Covarrubias dubbed Catalina an ugly wart on San Pedro Bay. But in modern times we see Catalina Island anchored majestically 21 miles offshore, often fog-shrouded and windswept, where now more than 2,000 people live. It is mountain-serrated in a sapphire sea and enjoys a sunny interior. Catalina Island is, in fact, a small world of its own with a romantic history of adventurers and explorers, buccaneers and smugglers. It is also a storehouse of geological, archaeological, and botanical treasures.

Moreover, the island has experienced active mining and real estate booms, game-fishing tournaments and yachting forays, and has become an acknowledged world-renowned resort.

Santa Catalina also enjoys a fascinating history of scientific "firsts." Here Dr. Lee deForest in 1904 and 1905 first worked on the development of his famous audion vacuum tube. He patented it in 1907, and it was hailed worldwide as the greatest scientific breakthrough of the twentieth century. It is basic to long-distance radio and television communication, without which we could not tune in on our radio or TV. DeForest staged the first radio broadcast in New York in 1910.

DeForest in 1911 moved back to Catalina, where he worked on sound pictures and diathermy, and methods for photographing sound waves on motion picture films. His inventions made talking motion pictures possible. DeForest studios and laboratories were centered in 1911 at Two Harbors, near where Joseph Brent Banning lived. During this period William, Joseph Brent, and Hancock Banning owned Catalina Island, and all three brothers aided and encouraged DeForest in his research. They remained steadfast friends during their lifetime. DeForest, a Yale graduate, class of 1896, died in 1961.

Another scientific first has to do with the world's first commercial wireless telegraph station, built on Catalina in 1902. It was known as the "Pacific Wireless Telegraph." The Banning brothers built a telephone line from Avalon to Two Harbors in 1903, and the first wireless telephone was inaugurated from Pebble Beach in July, 1919.

In 1922, Lawrence Gordon Mott, short-wave radio pioneer, started in Catalina Island with a broadcasting station with little more than a crystal set, yet he kept in contact with the McMillan Expedition at the North Pole. It was the only contact with the outside world the expedition had for at least a month. His call station, 6XAD, was in existence until recently, when it was changed to KFWO.

In May of 1946, about the time John Sonneborn, San Pedro general manager of Pacific Telephone Co., went to work for them, another first in communications was the installation of the Microwave Radiophone at Pebble Beach. The microwave system was a well-guarded secret and was used to great benefit during the Second World War. On Catalina it added eight circuits to their 15 submarine cable circuits. Presently it is centered on the summit of Catalina Island in order to facilitate added telephone service to the other offshore islands served by the San Pedro office of the Pacific Telephone Co.

Catalina boasts an unusual TV station known as KBIG. It has only 10,000 watts of power, but its elevation at "The Airport in the Sky" more than doubles its effective power. The station operates only during the daylight hours with broadcasts of news, music, weather, and fishing activities.

The Wrigley interests, owners of the island, stated recently they are well cognizant of silver, lead, and gold veins that criss-cross through much of the island, but they will open it up for commercial mining only when the proper time comes, if ever.

47

Catalina Island Hovers Like a Super Nova

Like a football, Catalina passed from one player to another for 73 years. The Bannings passed it to William Wrigley in 1919.

UNTIL THE WRIGLEY FAMILY bought Santa Catalina Island 60 years ago, the 48,438 acres were passed around quite a bit.

The passing game started in earnest during the heat of the Mexican-American War. Pio Pico, the last Mexican governor of California, gave Capt. Thomas M. Robbins the 75-square-mile island with the last stroke of his almost worn-out land-granting quill pen on July 4, 1846.

On the northwest slope of the island, near Two Harbors, is July Fourth Cove, named for the event. The deal is said to be in payment for certain favors Pico owed Robbins, a native-born American. To do it, Pico had to naturalize Robbins into a Mexican citizen because, in those days, only citizens of Mexico could own land in California.

The area was 16,438 more acres than Pico gave the Sepulveda family in granting them the deed to Rancho Palos Verdes on June 3, 1846.

Pico, whose brother Gen. Andreas Pico was in charge of the Mexican troops during the war, obviously had some insight as to how things were going—that Mexico would lose the war and that California would soon be a territory of the United States. Pico's vision was cactus-sharp. On September 9, 1850, California became the 31st state in the union.

The Guadalupe Hidalgo Treaty officially ended the Mexican-American War just two days short of 19 months after Pico had granted Catalina Island to Robbins. This treaty gave the United States all of California, the off-shore islands, Nevada and Utah, most of New Mexico and Arizona, and parts of Colorado and Wyoming.

The American Land Grant Commission sustained Pico's grants to Robbins and the Sepulvedas in 1852.

That same year, Robbins sold the land, which set off passage of the island from hand-to-hand almost like a football scrimmage until it ended up in the Wrigley family 69 years later.

The play went Pico to Robbins to Covarrubias to Packard to Ray to Sullivan to Hauzhurst to Hitchcock to Lick to Shatto to Banning to Wrigley.

Some made money—a few quite a bit—and some lost during the many transactions involving the island.

Don Jose Covarrubias was born in France, became a citizen of Mexico and got a large land grant near Santa Barbara. He paid Robbins $10,000 for the island in 1850.

Three years later he sold the island to Albert Packard for $1,000, or two cents an acre. Covarrubias was quoted in the August 10, 1853, *Los Angeles Star* as saying that Catalina Island was an "ugly wart off the shores of San Pedro" and not suitable for cattle grazing and inaccessible for proper supervision.

Covarrubias was equally unkind to San Pedro in that article, saying it was unable to shelter ships and was fit only for small lighters like those of Phineas Banning to transport freight and passengers to shore from ships anchored in a "treacherous wind-swept bay."

Packard kept the island for 10 years and in 1863 made a tidy profit when he sold it to James Ray for $12,000.

Ray sort of subdivided the island when he sold parts of it to Eugene Sullivan Charles Hitchcock and Walter Hauzhurst. It was the only time the island has not been held by a single owner or family.

It came back under single ownership nine years later when James Lick, famous for his contributions to the Lick Astronomical Observatory near San Jose, bought the entire island for $23,000 in 1872.

When Lick died, George Shatto bought the island from the Lick trustees for $200,000 in 1887.

The heirs of Phineas Banning purchased the island seven years later from Shatto for $128,740. They included Banning's three sons, William, Joseph, and Hancock, and their half-sisters, Mary and Lucy Holister Banning, daughters of Banning's second wife.

The Bannings held on to the island for 25 years before selling it to the Wrigley family in 1919 for $3 million.

The Wrigley family, of course, has owned the island since, with only the one-square mile town of Avalon owned by anybody else. The $3 million investment is worth far more today, although most all the island is under the protective control of the Conservancy of Santa Catalina Island.

The Island of Santa Catalina that passed through many hands so quickly during the late part of the 19th Century is now one of the few unspoiled refuges around where wildlife and flora and fauna abound. The Wrigley family will not sell it.

48
Catalina's Abortive Gold Rush

During the Civil War promoters reaped a harvest in selling gold shares of fake mines on Catalina. However, there are gold veins which Wrigley may open up in the future.

THE SOUTHERN CALIFORNIA rancheros suffered some trying years in 1862 through 1864 because of a prolonged drought.

Cattle died by the thousands in the fields throughout Southern California. Rancho owners were frantic about how to save their land and money.

They had been warned years before that they should not depend wholly upon their cattle hides and tallow. But they did not heed the warnings that crops of grain, hay, fruits and vegetables should be planted and cultivated, and they continued to rely solely on the cattle economy.

The prolonged drought of 1862-64 left the ranchero owners ripe for a group of gold stock swindlers who swooped down upon them promising instant riches and a perfect chance to recoup their cattle losses.

It all began when George Yount and Samuel Prentiss, a couple of sea otter hunters, were holed up in a cave near Two Harbors on Santa Catalina Island. There they found rich out-croppings of ore that assayed as high as $1,000 a ton. The word quickly spread that Catalina was a veritable island of gold.

The swindlers used the Young-Prentiss samples in selling their gold certificates to the unsuspecting ranchero owners on the mainland.

Nearly all the ranchero owners were victimized, including many of the most prominent—Don Benito Wilson, Don Juan Bandini, Don Diego Sepulveda, and Don Manual Dominguez.

Perhaps the man who suffered most, however, was Damien Marchessault, mayor of Los Angeles from 1861 to 65. He invested heavily in the gold stocks in his attempt to recoup his losses in a system of transporting water for irrigation with wooden pipes.

Marchessault received much criticism from that venture, and now from his loss in Catalina gold stocks. He found things unbearable and committed suicide at City Hall in 1868.

The Catalina gold stocks were not all failures. There was gold on the island, and there still is.

But they are in outcroppings, with no central source. And then, too, the Civil war took part in the ruination of many ranchero owners.

During the Civil War suspicion and hatred ran rampant throughout the nation, and California was no exception.

Orders were issued by the War Department to wipe out the Secessionists who, intelligence informed them, were using Catalina Island as a rendezvous for pirates menacing ships carrying gold and silver from the Comstock and Mother Lode mines which President Lincoln urgely needed for the Union cause.

Ironically, it was Brig. Gen. Phineas Banning, whose large land holdings centered around Wilmington, who was sent over to eject all but a few legitimate citizens from Catalina.

Banning also lost considerable money during the drought, but he did not invest in the Catalina gold stocks.

Banning was fortunate. He eventually got his money back, plus a lot more, that he had lost during the drought years. But it wasn't Catalina gold, it was from the gold mining boom in the Owens River Valley.

We quote from *Port Admiral:*

"One circumstance that helped Phineas Banning get back on his financial feet was the opening of a considerable mining industry in the Owens River Valley. He started a system of wagon trains from Wilmington to the mines. Each wagon carried food and mining supplies to the Owens River diggings; on the return trip they brought ore that would be shipped by boat from the Port of Wilmington to San Francisco for smelting."

Hauling the loads both ways was very profitable and helped Banning discharge the heavy obligations he had assumed in the expansion of his shipyards in Wilmington.

After the Wrigley family purchased Catalina Island, some mining was begun again. In 1923, a floatation mill was built on the island to process ore into concentrates which were being shipped to smelters in Belgium and to Selby, near San Francisco.

More than $100,000 worth of silver, zinc, and lead ore was shipped in 1924. But, according to the book, *Catalina Story,* just as the operations got into high gear, the price of metals dropped until it was no longer profitable and also because some of the larger veins had petered out.

The mining project was finally abandoned in 1927. But the Wrigleys haven't forgotten completely.

"When the time comes," said William and Phillip Wrigley, "that we need to mine, we know where it is."

49

AUGUSTUS TIMMS DONATES BURIAL GROUNDS

The oldest cemetery in the harbor area, where many of our local pioneers are buried, is a historic landmark of great significance.

HARBOR VIEW MEMORIAL PARK at 2411 S. Grand Avenue in San Pedro is sacred ground to hundreds in our community who have kin buried there. Here lie the bodies of more than 2,000 people.

This land of four acres was donated by August William Timms in 1878. There are 275 buried in a space known as Potters Field, and another plot if set aside for children. The first infant burial was that of Jennie Crittenden, age 2, 1879. There are 21 infant burials "Known Only to God."

In this list of unknowns many a dark mystery has remained unsolved, as the tombstone read: "Man found dead in Watson's Lake," "Unknown man picked up in gulch near Center Street." "Unknown man found dead in San Pedro Hills." "Two men killed off breakwater." "Three skeletons uncovered on Dead Man's Island." "Unknown man drowned in Harbor."

The author's visit was one of reflection and reading names on markers. He reasoned that if these dead could only talk one could write of harbor heritage in living prose. Some headstones stand out above the others, but the majority are level with the ground. The carpet of grass and flowers covers all alike.

Some of these dead lived in the harbor in the days of the "Golden Cornucopia," when there was no smog and little fog—more sun and maybe more fun. They could observe the clipper and other sailing ships leaving the harbor agleam from stern to bow with fresh waterproof caulking. Even the gallies with their heavy cabinets and massive coal and wood-burning stoves got extra attention, and all provided by Phineas Banning from the La Brea tar pits.

In its early heyday, San Pedro Bay lured adventurers, explorers, and settlers from all over the world; fishermen, fur traders, miners, missionaries, loggers, seamen, cattlemen, steamship and railroad people. Some of them are buried here. One of them was "Crawfish George," who wrote a verse for his own headstone: "Now the only ships that got into this port were fur-traders, hide-droghers and whalers. Where Crawfish George was plying his trade, for the benefit of all the other sailors."

One of the most impressive monuments is in memory of 10 sailors killed aboard the Battleship U.S.S. Tennessee during an explosion in June 1908, in San Pedro harbor while the Great White Fleet was anchored in the harbor. It reads: "These men died heroically at their stations in line of duty."

One of the saddest is a marble stone inscribed; "Our Darlings, Clara, Alfred, and Violet, children of C. and A.L. Foster, who almost hand in hand went to Jesus, March 1887."

San Pedro retiree, Captain Vincent Di Rocco, who served 29 years as port pilot, showed the author eight graves of the Di Rocco family. Vincent's father, Francesco, and his uncle, Frank Di Rocco, were among the first Italians in the San Pedro fishing industry with their boat Two Brothers.

Monuments list three of the Timms family. Augustus died in 1888; his nephew, August Gottlieb Timms, in 1946; and Emile Timms, in 1907. At the entrance to the cemetery is the Rudecinda Chapel, a mausoleum containing the bodies of most of the early-day Sepulvedas, and the Dodsons, including Rudecinda, and her husband, James Dodson, Sr.

Snuggled on the far side of the cemetery is the old St. Peter's Episcopal Church. It was moved there by the 30-Year Club many years ago to save it from the jaws of the hated bulldozer. There is now a high note radiating almost every Sunday from pews filled with visitors to hear the operatic talents of Shirlee Sawers and Frank Politeo. Councilman John S. Gibson, Jr., is the sponsor with his local staff, Tony Di Rocco, Tom Coulter, Bernie Evans, Beryl Goss, Susan Pritchard, Yvette Kovary, Anthony Pescetti, Kurt Muller, Richard Garcia, Marie Trevino, and Ed Hauck, participating.

While strolling around the buried dead, the author began to think about his own past, and to wonder about his future, and decided then and there to resign from his position of 10 years as curator-historian, a work of love—at the Banning Mansion and Museum as of Oct. 15, 1975, and devote the sunset years of his life to more writing and lecturing, and to get the *Harbor Heritage* book published.

Then, with a panoramic view of these four acres of dead bodies, the author silently asked: Where have they gone? A good answer was found in Victor Hugo, who wrote near the end of his life these prophetic and consoling words:

"Winter is on my head, but eternal spring is in my heart. The nearer I approach the end, the plainer I hear around me the immortal symphonies of the world to come. For half a century I have been writing my thoughts in prose and verse, but I feel I have not said a thousandth part of what is in me. When I have gone down to the grave, I shall have ended my day's work, but another day will begin the next morning. Life closes with twilight but opens with the dawn."

50
San Pedro's First High School

San Pedro can be proud of its high school, and the thousands of graduates who have peopled the world with their genius in the professions and in business. Daniels Field took its name from a principal.

SAN PEDRO HIGH SCHOOL is the focal point of happy days and nostalgic memories in the minds of many graduates. No one expresses this more fervently than five local graduates, Louis Sepulveda, Al Atchison, Vincent Thomas, John Olguin and Harry Fairall, each representing a different class year.

From these five knowledgeable men, the author ran into many interesting historical tid-bits, not only about school athletics, but how the high school itself got off to a running start through years of bureaucratic scrimmage and blocking.

There was no high school in San Pedro until 1903, when two rooms were reluctantly set aside for it in the old Fifteenth Street Elementary School. It started with an enrollment of 23 students and two teachers; only one student was graduated. From 1903 to 1907 it taught the four high school grades. The seventh and eighth grades were added in 1907, but in 1919 the seventh grade was dropped.

In 1905, after a hard fight at the polling booths, headed by Joseph Atchison, Al's father and a school board member, a high school was built on Gaffey Street, between Twelfth and Thirteenth Streets, where the Safeway store now stands. In 1909 the school became a part of the Los Angeles Unified School District. In 1912, Ralph C. Daniels, became principal.

In the 1913 *Black and Gold* yearbook, high tribute was paid to Daniels:

"In the few months since he took charge of San Pedro High, Mr. Daniels has won a strong place in the heart of every student. He has taken a personal interest in each and every one of us and is always ready to help us out of our difficulties. We greatly appreciate the interest he has taken in all our activities and feel that our future cannot help but be successful with Mr. Daniels at the helm."

During his tenure Daniels provided incentives to the faculty and to the students. Many innovations took place in the classroom and on the athletic field.

Until 1915, only rugby was allowed. Football was considered too rough and was declared off-limits by the Board of Education. Daniels, in cooperation with other school principals, persuaded the board that good old American football was favored throughout the country. The school board then rescinded their taboo.

Unfortunately, Daniels died in 1918 from the Spanish flu, a disease that claimed many casualties in the high school during World War I.

Shortly after Daniel's death, the school board purchased the 3.6 acres for the athletic field and named it in honor of Daniels. In 1945 the Los Angeles Department of Recreation and Parks purchased the field from the Board of education. The property is still under the control of the Department of Recreation and Parks.

The old school was dismantled, and a new high school was built in 1937 at Fifteenth and Meyler streets, on the property once owned by James and Rudecinda Dodson.

Louis Sepulveda, class of 1912, put baseball on the map for San Pedro High School and made it a popular sport when scouts saw him as an outstanding catcher and signed him into the Northwest League at Vancouver in 1912. Later the San Francisco Seals bought him, and Louis was their star catcher until 1917, when he enlisted in the U.S. Navy at the start of World War I.

After his honorable discharge, Sepulveda returned to San Pedro and became the fiscal agent of his family's large land holdings. Both Vincent Thomas and John Olguin are proud graduates. They contributed memorabilia for this chapter.

Harry Fairall was class president in 1916, another amateur baseball star, and prominent in dramatics and the glee club. The 1916 *Black and Gold* yearbook said of him:

"Captain Fairall has been playing a fast game behind the plate and has fooled many an opposing runner by his perfect peg to second. His graduation next June will be a great loss to the team."

Harry told the author that Louis Sepulveda taught him the techniques of being both a good catcher and a good hitter, and how to catch base stealers.

Al Atchison of the class of 1918 made the varsity in track and field and won the school tennis championship. He was active in student affairs and became "Josh Editor." His horoscope was mentioned in the 1916 *Black and Gold* as being a flirt and melancholy in appearance.

Another student who made good in San Pedro and was mentioned in the 1914 *Black and Gold* was John Gaudino, 1913 class president, a baseball athlete who worked his way through school as bookkeeper in the State Bank. Gaudino later became a vice president of Bank of America, Tenth and Pacific branch.

The author was intrigued by an editorial in the 1915 yearbook by Virginia Smith:

"The freshmen know that they don't know. The sophomores don't know that they don't know. The juniors don't know that they know. The seniors know that they know.

"In short, it takes three years to find out that we know we don't know."

51
San Pedro Hospital Gets Toe-Hold

The San Pedro Peninsula Hospital is one of the finest and most modern in America, staffed by highly trained technicians and researchers.

THE FIRST HOSPITAL in the Harbor Area was a two-story structure on top of Knob Hill, First and Front Streets in San Pedro. It was the site of the luxurious Clarence Hotel, the largest and finest in the community.

In 1909, while the Los Angeles city government was taking over the Harbor Area, Dr. Lillian B. Mullen, not only an M.D. but a graduate nurse from the Bellevue Hospital in New York, discovered the Clarence Hotel property and grabbed it. She was searching for a suitable hospital location, and she lost no time in transferring every room into an ideal sanitarium.

Dr. Mullen was well experienced in establishing rest centers for the ill and infirm.

The San Francisco fire and earthquake in 1906 destroyed her "ideal sanitarium" there. She then established another in Santa Monica, but this building was sold by the owners to a hotel developer; Dr. Mullen moved to San Pedro, where she turned the Clarence Hotel into the San Pedro Hospital.

She remodeled the hotel premises so the patients could have an excellent view of the harbor with its activity of sailing ships from foreign ports always arriving or departing.

A gracious lady, Mrs. Matties Edens Melberg, still active and alert, was one of the first nurses at the new hospital in 1909 and became for many years an aide to Dr. Mullen.

Mrs. Melberg met a patient at the hospital who was in for an operation on an injured leg. She married him a year later. It is said other romances started at this first hospital, most of them leading to marriage.

The second hospital in San Pedro was established in 1915 in a new building at Gaffey and San Cruz streets. It was in charge of Mrs. Constance Christian, a registered nurse.

Dr. Mullen was doing major surgery at her hospital, and the U.S. War Department ordered her to move the facility to a safer place during World War I.

The first units of the present San Pedro and Peninsula Hospital, built on West Sixth Street and Patton Avenue, were opened in 1925. At that time, Mrs. Christian closed down her hospital at Santa Cruz and Gaffey and donated what equipment she could to the new facility and then became head nurse there.

The present San Pedro and Peninsula Hospital has come a long way from the modest red brick building that was dedicated on June 14, 1925. In 1924, a group of doctors and local businessmen incorporated a hospital known as the San Pedro General Hospital Association, which operated as a private stock corporation.

Today, the hospital is owned and controlled by the people of the community as a non-profit facility. There are 850 employes.

Leslie Smith resigned an important job with Los Angeles County to become the hospital's administrator. An administrator with his skill and dedication and his courteous and enthusiastic staff lightens the burden of all who enter as patients.

The San Pedro and Peninsula Hospital has a board of directors who are community leaders and who volunteer their time and efforts to the advancement of the facility.

The current officers are Melvin L. Rowan, D.D.S., chairman; Harold Fogle, M.D., vice chairman; JoAnne Jordan, secretary; Tom Papadakis, treasurer; Leslie R. Smith, executive director and president; and Robert LeSage, M.D., chief of staff. Directors include Richard Franklin, Alvin Goldenson, M.D., Jim Groth, Foster James, Donald Jortner, Ph.D., Louis Kanister, Ray Martin, Eugene A. Pimental, Robert A. Smith, M.D., John Sonneborn, and Irving Welsh, Jr.

The word "hospital" comes from the Latin *hospitium,* which means an institution for guests where one is treated hospitably. No institution expresses this more truly than our own San Pedro and Peninsula Hospital, staffed by highly trained technicians and leaders in medical research.

52

First San Pedro Lighthouse

Phineas Banning was the first to get appropriations from Congress for the construction of the Point Fermin Lighthouse and for the Breakwater.

THE STORY OF THE old Point Fermin Lighthouse with its famous observation platform is an integral part of the history of this harbor. Phineas Banning, father of the San Pedro harbor development and breakwater, was ever confronted with conflicts, crises and collisions.

Banning was the first to petition Congress for an appropriation sufficient to start preliminary work on a much needed breakwater and for a lighthouse atop Point Fermin. Banning asked for $100,000, Congress voted $30,000.

The lighthouse was built and opened in 1874. It became the citadel for safe navigation for almost 100 years, standing majestically atop the treacherous bluffs of San Pedro, radiating its powerful 10,000-candlepower beams seaward.

The building still stands, clothed in simple beauty and dignified modesty. The facility is now a part of the Los Angeles Department of Recreation and Parks, where it poses for cameras and commands the awe of tourists. Its service has been replaced by radar and other electronic devices to warn mariners that danger is still near if they come too close to the rocky cliffs.

In earlier years when night fell on ship and shore, the shining light beams from the lighthouse led thousands of sailing and steam vessels to safe harbors. Although Congress allocated the funds in 1858, there was considerable skullduggery for more than a decade before the lighthouse was completed but not before several lumber barges, tugs and other ships were pounded to pieces on the inhospitable rocks off Point Fermin.

Banning called it a political scandal and went about devising the best possible plans to make Congress conscious of the importance of appropriating large sums for the immediate construction of a breakwater.

It is said that the old Point Fermin Lighthouse was the scene of many social parties in the late 70s to which Banning invited friends. The location was named for Father Fermin Lasuen, a contemporary of Father Junipero Serra; together they carved the route and road from San Diego along the coast in 1769 which they named El Camino Real (The King's Highway).

Although Lasuen belonged to the Franciscan Order, their property on Western Avenue in South Shores, now a home for the aged, is under the Order of Oblates of Mary Immaculate.

"It makes no difference," Monsignor George Scott said. "We all stand, under God, for the same thing."

The Point Fermin site was under consideration for a mission, but Father Lasuen decided on San Fernando instead, because, the report states, "The San Fernando area is nearer the Pueblo of Los Angeles, and our sister mission of San Gabriel; besides, fresh water is more plentiful there and there are more Indians to convert."

Maybe the old lighthouse is just a shell now, useless in the onward surge of modern progress. Nevertheless, it stands in honorable retirement, majestic in its old age, and proud of its windswept lattices. And when one looks closely, one thinks of vanished ships and forgotten men, gone in the fog-shrouded mists and overpowering waves—courageous mariners, they, who struggled heroically for safety, unknown and unheralded.

53
Horses are Heroes

The horse was not known to the early American Indians. There are more horses now than ever before, but automobiles and trucks do most of the work.

THERE ARE SEVERAL RECORDS of early-day horse races, but the greatest took place July 4, 1852, between Don Jose Diego Sepulveda's Black Swan and Pio Pico's Sarco. The horses were well matched. It was a gala affair during a holiday of festivities featuring hundreds of caballeros in fancy costumes, riding in silver saddles worth a king's ransom.

The festivities were attended by thousands, from San Diego to San Francisco. The event was of such importance that over $50,000 in gold was bet, plus several hundred horses, hundreds of cattle, leagues of land, and a fortune in jewelry.

According to Harris Newmark's *Sixty Years in Southern California:* "Senora Sepulveda was there with a fortune in gold slugs wrapped in a large handkerchief. She opened her purse and distributed the shining fifty-dollar pieces to her many servants with instructions they find bettors against Black Swan and wager it all."

It was a nine-mile race, commencing on San Pedro Street, Los Angeles, and running south four and a half miles, then turning back for another four and a half miles to the starting place. Black Swan won.

Sepulveda imported Black Swan from Australia for the race. Pico's Sarco was California bred.

When Sepulveda's horse arrived in San Francisco, he went there to receive his consignment in person, then he committed the thoroughbred into the keeping of Bill Brady, his trainer, who rode the horse to Los Angeles.

Black Swan ran a few more races, winning all of them. She ate the finest clover and oats that the Palos Verdes could offer. Sepulveda was proud of his Black Swan, and referred to his horse as a person "with great strength of character, courage, fidelity and endurance, unflinching and unchangeable."

The horse has been one of man's most useful animals for thousands of years, and the West certainly could not have been won without the faithful dobbin. The Assyrians, 800 B.C., hunted lions in chariots drawn by two horses. Museum tapestries show early Persians playing a kind of polo. The early Greeks and Romans became expert horsemen. Palos Verdes riding academies still follow their principles.

The first European colonists found no horses in North America. The American Indians never saw one until the Spanish conquistadores came in 1519.

The Indian tribes of the western plains began to use horses about the year 1600 in hunting buffalo and in battles.

There are some famous horses in history and in legend. For instance the horse Cincinnati carried Gen. U.S. Grant during the Civil War. Comanche, a cavalry horse, was the only survivor of Custer's Last Stand in 1876. The horse Copenhagen carried the Duke of Wellington to victory at Waterloo in 1815, and Marengo, a white stallion, was ridden by Napoleon in his defeat.

The horse population is now at its highest peak in the United States. A record 18 million horses inhabit this country according to estimates from the American Horse Council in Washington, D.C., and the number is increasing rapidly. The horse population has more than doubled since 1960. In fact, according to the reports, there are more horses now in the United States than before the birth of the automobile, when horses were used as a primary source of transportation and power.

According to Grace Hoxworth, Weymouth Science Center 4H community leader, "There are over 2,000 4H members in the Horse Project in L.A. County alone. We estimate U.S. equine events drew over 105 million spectators in 1974. Moreover, at the end of 1974, the 4H Club had 320,767 members in horse projects, compared with 160,846 in beef cattle and 106,526 in swine. Los Angeles County leads them all in 4H projects."

The draft horses were the most popular in the 1800s. They were the strongest, heaviest, and tallest group of California horses. They supplied much of the power needed for jobs that heavy trucks and tractors do today.

They pulled plows on farms and hauled freight wagons from town to town. Draft horse breeds include the Shire, Clydesdale, Belgian, Percheron, and Suffolk. The work horse breeds are not now in demand, and are not increasing. But they built our country and they did it well. Their work is done.

54
That Sleepy Cow Town Won't Amount to "Nothin'!"

When the Southern Pacific Railroad started building its tracks from Sacramento south in the 1870s through the San Joaquin Valley and over the Tehachapi Pass to Mojave, it did not intend to build to Los Angeles.

WHEN ASKED ABOUT IT, the stock reply was, "No, that sleepy cow town won't amount to nothin'. We're going to El Paso and to New Orleans. Besides, it would cost too much to dig the San Fernando tunnel."

But the Railroad did come to Los Angeles. On Sunday, Sept. 5, 1976, the author was a guest of the Pacific Railway Historical Society, to help celebrate the centennial of the completion of the 7,000-foot San Fernando Tunnel near the old Lang Station.

It was due principally to the efforts of Phineas Banning and Judge Robert M. Widney in 1874 that Los Angeles voters approved a large subsidy for the Southern Pacific to build the San Fernando tunnel, which required about 3,000 Chinese laborers almost two years to complete.

Another demand by the railroad officials was that Banning and his associates sell their railroad, completed in 1869, to Southern Pacific. Banning sold and the new owners extended the rails to San Pedro from Wilmington. Banning had not brought his railroad to San Pedro during the seven years he controlled the railway, although the line carried the name San Pedro.

The *Los Angeles Star* of Sept. 6, 1876, said that the completion of the San Pedro Railroad into Los Angeles attracted promoters and settlers and, a few years later, competing railroads, including the Santa Fe and the Salt Lake & San Pedro Railroad (subsidiary of the Union Pacific).

These latter companies were prevented from building their railroads into San Pedro proper under protest from Collis P. Huntington, Leland Stanford, Mark Hopkins, and Charles Crocker, and had to make their terminal on Rattlesnake Island, a name disliked by them. They had the name changed to Terminal Island.

But even so, competition became so unbearable to the Southern Pacific that Huntington and his colleagues made an abortive attempt in 1899 to make Santa Monica the legal port of entry to Los Angeles and close down the ports of San Pedro and Wilmington. They lost a close vote in the U.S. Senate, principally because of the efforts of California Sen. Stephen M. White.

The *Daily Star* mentioned that the excursion train that left Los Angeles at 9 a.m. Sept. 5, 1876, for the dedication arrived at the tunnel within an hour.

The engine and five passenger cars included prominent community leaders, among them Gov. William Irwin, Mayor Prudent Beaudry, Banning, Judge Widney, Ex. Gov. J.D. Downey, B.D. Wilson, Charles Ducommun, Harris Newmark, Matthew Keller, and Gen. Winfield Scott Hancock. It took 10 minutes to go through the tunnel. The ceremonies were at Newhall.

"A glance out of the windows could not fail to bring forcibly to mind the days of stage coaching," the *Daily Star* said. The spot selected for the ceremonies was on a broad and beautiful plain, surrounded by undulating hills, rugged peaks and deep gorges of the San Fernando Mountains. The scene was worthy of the painter's brush, but, by some strange oversight, no photographer was present."

Records show that the San Francisco train arrived at about 1 p.m. and was the signal for hearty cheering, handshaking, and congratulations.

Downey, the master of ceremonies, introduced L.W. Thatcher, a local goldsmith, to Charles Crocker, who was presented with a gold spike and a silver hammer which would be used in the ceremonies. Crocker thanked Thatcher for the gift and promised the railroad company would treasure them in its archives as souvenirs of the event.

Downey introduced Crocker, who said, "It has been deemed best on this occasion that the last spike to be driven should be of gold, that most precious of metals, as indicative of the great wealth which should flow into the coffers of both Los Angeles and San Francisco when this connection is made; and is no mean token of the importance of this grand artery of commerce which we are about to unite with this last spike.

"The wedding of Los Angeles and San Francisco is consecrated by the bands of steel." These ceremonial words pronounced the momentous consummation of a historic project.

Then reaching for the spike and the hammer, the founder of the Crocker Bank said, "I am no public speaker, but I can drive a (gold) spike."

55
The Railroad Builders

The Big Four, Huntington, Stanford, Hopkins and Crocker, started in business by selling pots, picks, and pans from their stores in Sacramento.

THE STATE OF CALIFORNIA was greatly benefited in 1857 when Andrew Johnson, elected to the U.S. Senate from Tennessee, put through the Homestead Act which became the most important factor in building the West.

Johnson also supported legislation after he became President in 1865, granting a charter to Collis P. Huntington, Leland Stanford, Charles Crocker, and Mark Hopkins to build the Central Pacific Railroad, completed on May 19, 1869.

Who were these Sacramento businessmen who sold shovels, pots, picks, and pans to the early gold miners, and founded a railroad empire that in 1881 touched San Pedro?

Collis P. Huntington was born in Litchfield, Connecticut, October 22, 1821. In school, Huntington excelled in geography and was noted for feats of memory. At 14, he was over six feet tall and muscular. He left home to shift for himself. He earned $84.00 his first year, plus room, board and clothing, working on a farm and saving every penny of it.

In 1849, he came to California via Panama, where he was delayed three months with other 49'ers waiting for a northbound ship. While most of the men in the group sat and drank, or did nothing, Huntington walked up and down the

Isthmus 24 times buying, trading, and selling trinkets or merchandise. He left the East Coast with $1,200 and landed in Sacramento with over $5,000.

Huntington did not try his luck at mining. He started a store in a small tent. Shortly afterward he hired Mark Hopkins as a clerk and bookkeeper, who later became a junior partner.

It was at the Huntington & Hopkins Store on K Street in Sacramento where they first met engineer-surveyor Theodore Judah, who had a complete file of blueprints and surveys over the Sierra Nevadas, without which a railroad could not be built.

Before Huntington died in 1900, leaving a legacy of almost $100 million, he had controlling interest in the Chesapeake and Ohio Railroad and the Southern Pacific Railroad, and owned the Occidental and Orient Steamship Co., whose ships used to dock in our harbor.

His nephew, Henry Huntington (1850-1927), headed the Pacific Electric Railroad System with the old red street cars that came to San Pedro. Henry founded the Huntington Library and married his uncle's widow, Arabella. There are about 40 communities named for the Huntington clan, including Huntington, West Virginia, and Huntington Park and Huntington Beach, California.

Mark Hopkins was born in September 1, 1813, at Henderson, New York. He came to Sacramento in 1849. Hopkins was the oldest of the Big Four. According to Stuart Daggett, in his *Southern Pacific,* Hopkins was neither dynamic nor colorful. Hopkins came into Huntington's store to buy some shovels and picks and pans to try his luck at panning gold. He joined Huntington as a junior partner in 1855. Hopkins died on March 29, 1878, at a Yuma, Arizona, railroad siding in his private Pullman. He stretched out on a couch for a nap and never woke up.

Collis P. Huntington paid him this tribute, "I never thought anything was finished until Hopkins looked at it. He was my most loyal friend and partner." The Mark Hopkins Hotel atop Nob Hill in San Francisco is named for him. In fact, all of the Big Four partners once had elaborate mansions on Nob Hill.

Leland Stanford was born in New York State in 1824. He was a bright student, but frail. He went to Wisconsin for his health and studied law. He came to California in 1852 and opened a store on K Street in Sacramento, one block from the Huntington store.

He also sold shovels, pots, pans, and picks to the miners. He met Charles Crocker, who became a junior partner. In 1861, Stanford was elected Governor of California, and Charles Crocker won a seat in the legislature.

Stanford got the State of California in the mood for subsidies for his railroad partners. He went to Washington, D.C., and helped Huntington get the charter for the Central Pacific Railroad. Stanford founded Stanford University in 1885, in honor of his late son, who died in his teens.

Stanford was U.S. Senator from California from 1885 until his death in 1893. Stuart Daggett said in his book, "No she-lion defending her whelps or a bear her cubs would make more savage a fight than did Stanford in defense of his material interests and the Southern Pacific Railroad."

Charles Crocker was born September 16, 1822, in Troy, New York, crossed the plains in 1850 and mined gold for two years. He joined Stanford as a junior partner in his store. He was a powerfully built man of 275 pounds and became head of the construction part of the railroad project. Crocker started many enterprises, one of them being the Crocker Bank. He died in Monterey on August 14, 1888.

Crocker told U.S. Senator Frye that he would go to China and enlist coolies to help build the railroad across the mountains. Frye commented that the Chinese are little people who "eat rice, and couldn't possibly be strong enough to build a railroad." Crocker quipped, "Well, they built the Chinese Wall, didn't they?"

56 GET RICH QUICK RAILROADERS

Cornelius Vanderbilt was the most cunning of the railroad builders. He laid traps for investors, explaining, "He who sells what isn't his'n, must buy it back or go to prison."

NO CALIFORNIA HISTORY hits with a greater economic and moral impact than the period during and after the Civil War—a period of frantic railroad building and the millionaires it created.

Looking back over a century, we can see the structures it built and the growth and progress it made, punctuated by sporadic intervals of war and speculative excesses, followed by depressions and panics.

The giant of all railroads became known as the Southern Pacific. Theodore Judah, born in Bridgeport, Connecticut, April 4, 1826, was the sparkplug who ignited the fire in Collis P. Huntington, Leland Stanford, Mark Hopkins, and Charles Crocker—the Big Four railroad builders.

Judah was a surveyor and geological engineer who in 1858 and 1859 had mapped the rugged terrain and winding canyons for a possible railroad route over the Sierra Nevada Mountains. In 1862, Huntington sent Judah to lobby in Washington, D.C.

In Panama, Judah caught yellow fever and died at the age of 37. His widow sued the Big Four for an accounting, but she received very little. They left Theodore Judah unknown, and almost forgotten.

The start of the Civil War in 1861 assured success in getting a charter for the building of a transcontinental railroad. In April, 1862, Huntington telegraphed Stanford: "We have drawn the elephant."

Eventually, the U.S. government gave 158 million acres to these four promoters—every other section of land along the right-of-way on either side of the tracks, with right of public domain. They received enormous sections of valuable forests, mineral rights, gold, silver, oil, copper and iron. Oil royalties from Wilmington, Terminal Island, and the whole L.A. Harbor Area are still pouring into the coffers of the Southern Pacific. Its land and mineral department has always been the most profitable adjunct of its enterprises. This also is true of the Santa Fe and the Union Pacific Railroad.

Who were the other millionaires created in part by the Civil War? They included Jay Gould, Jay Cooke, J.P. Morgan, John D. Rockefeller, Andrew Carnegie, Thomas Mellon, Jim Fisk, Daniel Drew, James Hill, Cornelius Vanderbilt, John Jacob Astor, O.D. Mills, Henry Frick, August Belmont, George Hearst, Anthony J. Drexel, E.H. Harriman, Cyrus Field, James G. Fair, Philip D. Armour (meat packing), Abraham Overholt (rye whiskey), and many more.

John Jacob Astor was known as the landlord of New York City. He founded Astoria, Oregon, in 1811, the first American settlement west of the Rocky Mountains. It was a fur trading center, and the terminus of the Lewis and Clark Expedition in 1805.

Matthew Josephson, in his book, *The Robber Barons,* says Collis P. Huntington hired several Civil War generals who had been trained as engineers, mostly graduates of West Point. One of them was General David Colton, who got a town named for himself, but that's about all. "Colton became an important adjunct, so he thought, with the Big Four," Josephson said.

"One day, he wrote this note to Huntington: 'I have learned one thing. We have got no true friends outside of us five. We cannot depend on a human soul outside of ourselves, and hence we must all be good-natured together, and keep our own counsels.' Huntington wanted to know where Colton got that WE stuff, and fired Colton."

It is said that of all the railroad builders, Huntington, Jay Gould, Cornelius Vanderbilt, and J.P. Morgan were the most shady. Up to 1895, no governor of California was nominated except by the wish of Huntington and the Southern Pacific. The police commissioner, harbor police, and judges of two federal courts were appointed at the urging of Leland Stanford, who became a senator in 1885. They maintained an army of political retainers.

By 1890, Huntington was in cahoots with Vanderbilt, Jay Gould, Rockefeller and Andrew Carnegie, from whom Huntington bought his steel rails. Josephson said these millionaires acted as though the Civil War was fought and won for them. "They were masters of all they surveyed. They carried on an economic revolution in the midst of the war, and even in the hour of danger and confusion, they alone were prepared. They had a whole continent to plunder and they did, by promoting, manipulating, and watered stock—millions and millions of it. Deliberately running business and industry down and building them up again to suit their own advantage—rebates and drawbacks."

Here is an old angle of the modern "pigeon drop":

Vanderbilt had a monopoly on the Erie Railroad and kept this stock in his vault. He went into the New York Bankers Club, which was frequented by speculators and brokers all out to break him. Vanderbilt let fall a piece of paper which he paid a waiter to pick up and give to his enemies. It was filled with notes to buy Erie stock for some large investors. His enemies bought many thousands of shares from their brokers. Vanderbilt had shot it up a few days before to over $300 a share. His enemies were caught. They couldn't deliver the stock. Vanderbilt wouldn't sell. He is quoted as saying: "He who sells what isn't his'n, must buy it back or go to prison."

57

Santa Monica's Awakening

A Comstock millionaire and the Southern Pacific Railroad, at different times, fought hard to make Santa Monica the Los Angeles Port of Entry.

DURING PHINEAS BANNING'S LIFETIME he was loved, hated, feared, suspected, praised, and condemned, but never ignored.

And no one feared Banning more consistently than Sen. John P. Jones, a comstock lode millionaire from Nevada who came to the Harbor Area in 1874 with the avowed purpose of wrecking San Pedro and Wilmington as the legal port of entry.

To accomplish this ambitious project Jones had to come to grips with Phineas Banning, which he did many times during this tense struggle over the merits of Santa Monica or San Pedro and Wilmington as the shipping center for Southern California.

Collis P. Huntington and the Southern Pacific Railroad tried again in 1899, 14 years after Banning's death, when San Pedro and Wilmington were saved by Sen. Stephen M. White from Huntington's abortive attempt to close the port.

Jones started out in 1874 by buying the 31,000-acre Rancho San Vicente Y Santa Monica. This grant was given to Col. Francisco Sepulveda, December 20, 1839, by order from Mexico directing Gov. Juan B. Alvarado to remember "Good old Francisco," who had fought well against numerous uprisings against the Mexican takeover in 1822 from the Spanish crown.

In 1872 Francisco's heirs, believing the rancho had reached its peak value, sold the land to Col. R.S. Baker for $2 an acre. This was prime land in the center of a hacienda known as "Shoo Fly," later to be known as Santa Monica.

For several years before 1872, Santa Monica Canyon had been used as a summer resort. Campers from Los Angeles enjoyed the sycamores and surf-bathing. Saturday night dances were held in a big tent. Bonfires blazed.

On the mesa itself, site of the unborn town of Santa Monica, an old Indian trail became Colorado Avenue. It was used by ox-teams that hauled brea from the tar pits to a little wharf that extended into the ocean, where ships took the brea to San Francisco. This was the only pier in 1874 when Jones bought most of the rancho from Baker for $162,500.

In April 1875, Jones completed a 1,700-foot wharf, and by October, he had built his contemplated Los Angeles and Independence Railroad from Santa Monica to Los Angeles.

By 1876, the year the Southern Pacific Railroad bought Banning's L.A. & S.P. Railroad, Santa Monica began to boom. A thousand people had bought lots; some built homes, others lived in tents.

Ocean steamers that formerly berthed at San Pedro and Wilmington were now docking at Santa Monica.

Banning's ire was up. He enlisted the help of Collis P. Huntington and his associates, including Leland Stanford, Mark Hopkins, and Charles Crocker, to put a stop to Jones' encroachment.

Many concessions were made to shippers to ignore Santa Monica. Freight and passenger rates from San Pedro and Wilmington were cut sharply and continuously for months. Jones began to lose so much money that he finally threw in the proverbial sponge. His Comstock riches could not compete indefinitely with Southern Pacific resources and Banning's influence.

But Jones still owned the Santa Monica Land Co., and he started to unload land and town lots in wholesale quantities by advertising land sale opportunities in Chicago and the east coast.

Jones offered special one-way railroad fares from Chicago for as low as $10 to attract people to Santa Monica. He used about every trick known to land promoters in advertising. It is doubtful that his copy would have met the modern standards of the Better Business Bureau.

Some of this copy in large bold type described Santa Monica as the "Zenith City by the Sunset Sea"; "the most delightful place on the Pacific Ocean"; "the most beautiful, thriving and fashionable seaside resort"; "the climate is perfect, never ranges below 60 degrees in winter, nor above 80 degrees in summer"; "water is abundant everywhere"; "the soil is inexhaustibly fertile—fruits and flowers can be grown almost without care"; "plenty of livery stables"; "throw up your shoes in the morning and knock down your breakfast"; "the resort of the tourist and the invalid."

Well, this last sentence in the advertising copy did it. People came by the hundreds, many of them overflowing into Los Angeles City, broke, no jobs and disillusioned.

Jones was later quoted as saying, "Too many people are out here from Chicago and the east with one dollar, one shirt, and one lung. They spend their dollar, and here they are."

"Something has got to be done about this mess," said Los Angeles Mayor Prudent Beaudry in 1876. It was left to Mayor James R. Toberman who, in 1878, started the first settlement project for the poor and indigent. On New Year's Eve, 1881, Toberman not only turned on the first electric lights in California, but opened the doors to the worthy indigent in a new 50-room Settlement House.

58

CONESTOGAS CONQUER THE WEST

General George Custer's father was a builder of Conestoga wagons in Ohio. Phineas Banning specialized in them.

WHILE CELEBRATING THE BICENTENNIAL in our community in 1976 this writer spoke at a large meeting in Los Angeles on the romantic Conestoga wagons with their four- and six-horse teams that transported thousands of immigrants along the Santa Fe and Indian Trail to California.

It was the produce of these early Californians and their heirs that made progress possible and gave impetus to the building of San Pedro Harbor.

The origin of the Conestoga wagon came from the rich farmland of southeastern Pennsylvania, where a breed of horse and type of wagon unique in American history were created. Both the horse and the wagon became known as Conestogas, a valley named for an Indian tribe that inhabited that area.

The wagon grew out of the needs of the farmers to haul their produce and goods to such cities as Philadelphia. The Conestoga dominated heavy freight hauling long before the event of canals and railroads.

Wood planks used in their construction were about an inch thick. The wagon beds were 16 feet long, four feet wide, and four feet deep. The wagon had a sag in the middle to help prevent the cargo from shifting. Up to 24 square feet of white canvas formed a canopy over wood hoops. The front wheels were three and a half feet high, and the rear wheels were another foot higher.

During his recent trip to the East the author saw a few Conestogas in museums, usually with a lecturer explaining the part they played in the Revolutionary War.

Such wagons required equally unique horses, and the Conestoga horse was bred specifically to pull these massive wagons, which carried six to 10 tons of freight.

The origin of these horses, according to one of the lecturers, goes back to three Flemish stallions which William Penn sent to the Conestoga Valley for breeding to Virginia mares. Docile in temper, the Conestoga was large, well-muscled and had long strides and endurance, capable of covering 15 to 20 miles a day. But the horse has disappeared, giving way to the mule and the Western-type draft horse.

After the Revolutionary War, covered wagons followed the old Boone Trail over the Alleghanies into the Mississippi Valley and finally to Independence, Missouri, the rendezvous for all western travelers and the origin of the Santa Fe Trail.

Between the Missouri River and the Pacific Ocean, the land was mostly waste and sterile, no better than the Sahara Desert and just as dangerous to cross. At Independence each family, providing its own wagon, horses, food, bedding, and arms, would be escorted along the trail by a covered-wagon train sometimes numbering 100 or more wagons. If necessary, the wheels could be removed from the wagons, and the wagons could be used as boats.

The Conestogas figured in many historical sidelights. They were the only wagons to be driven from the left side; thus, they set the pattern for what became the standard American method of driving vehicles.

Another characteristic of the wagons was the multi-toned sets of bells worn by each horse. It gave rise to the saying, "I'll be there with bells on." And if a wagoner slipped into town silently it was a sign he had found trouble along the way. It was the custom that the price of helping to pull a stalled Conestoga out of the mud and mire was the bells.

It took a hardy breed of man to drive the Conestoga. Many of them carried a pocketful of black cigars, which became known as stogies—a corruption of Conestoga.

After arriving at their destination most families would live in their wagons until they had settled permanently. At one time there were more than 100 acres set aside for these wagons and their attendant families in an area near San Pedro and Alameda Streets in Los Angeles.

When Benjamin Franklin saw the Conestoga in Philadelphia, he contracted for hundreds of them in support of the American cause in the Revolution. It was this wagon that carried most of the ordnance and supplies from camp to camp and aided Washington in his famous victory at Yorktown.

Many of the builders of the Conestoga were farmers and artisans whose names are largely unknown. But two are familiar. Phineas Banning had a Conestoga wagon factory near Wilmington. He also operated freight service with the wagons throughout California and the Southwest. Banning was contracted by Brigham Young in the 1860s to move a large colony of Mormons in the Conestogas from San Bernardino to Salt Lake City. The Sepulveda family of Palos Verdes bought the San Bernardino land when the Mormons left.

The other well-known Conestoga builder was Manuel Custer, who ran a factory in Ohio for many years. His son, Gen. George Armstrong Custer, made history with the U.S. Military Academy at West Point, and at Little Big Horn.

59
Booms and Brass Bands

In the 1880s the railroads cut their fares from Chicago and the Middlewest to as low as one dollar to Los Angeles. After arriving, it was free rides and free luncheons to the harbor. Long Beach was born.

REAL ESTATE AND BUILDING booms flare up occasionally in the Harbor Area. San Pedro, Wilmington, and Los Angeles have experienced several booms in their history. Presently, we are in another period of inflated real estate values and building activities. The boom seems to have a cyclical pattern.

The first boom of any economic consequence occurred in the 1880s when the Southern Pacific and Santa Fe Railroads started passenger rate wars from Chicago and the Midwest to Los Angeles. Fares dropped from $130 to $6. For a short time it was as low as $1.00 per head one way.

These low train fares prompted tens of thousands of families to leave their homes and come to California. Some of them were newly arrived immigrants from Europe seeking new homes in America. Records show that from 1886 to 1888 there was such a rush for passage that the Southern Pacific and the Santa Fe combined had an average of five to six trainloads of people arriving in Los Angeles daily. In a single year the Southern Pacific brought 120,000 people to California.

The newcomers, who had arrived and found suitable places to live, wrote glowing letters back East about the new paradise of California. It is reported in the *Los Angeles Times* that these newcomers surge up and down the streets meeting train arrivals bringing their relatives and friends, taking them in tow to outlying districts and communities to purchase lots.

Land promoters arranged for colorful brass bands, drum and trumpet corps to attract the new arrivals as they strolled off the train, or from hotels or boarding houses where some of them went to rest up from a jolting and tiresome five-day chair-car trip.

There were daily auctions with professional spielers all along the South Coast, from Santa Monica, Redondo Beach, San Pedro, and Wilmington. This was the period when Long Beach was born.

Many beautifully decorated horse-drawn carriages tempted the prospective buyer with large red block letters advertising a free ride and a free lunch. It is said that some of the visitors came to scoff, but many of them remained to invest their money and speculate. Some of them who bought land at that time built homes and had families; they became our pioneers and a good part of our heritage.

Another land and building boom started in 1899 when Congress gave the go-ahead for building the San Pedro harbor breakwater. During this tense period of land division activity, Harbor City came into being. A little later Lomita was created. (Separate chapters deal with these two municipalities elsewhere.) This breakwater building boom took on a new dimension in 1909 when Los Angeles annexed the Harbor Area and extended millions of dollars in loans for building new marine berths and warehouses. Palos Verdes began to blossom after 1915, when Frank Vanderlip took charge.

Possibly the greatest real estate building boom happened in Los Angeles and the harbor area in the 1920s following the end of World War I. As in all wars, building activity had been suppressed, but it was inevitable that the acute shortage of housing had to be overcome. At the close of the war there began a flood of new people coming to California from the southern states, comparable with the growth of Chicago immediately after the Civil War.

People were beginning to flock to the coastal areas where the big oil boom was taking place. During 1925 to 1929, almost a billion dollars worth of new construction was completed, according to City Hall records. Los Angeles was growing rapidly and, because of this boom, San Pedro and Wilmington became the largest lumber port in the world. Nearly every newcomer, then as now, was the seeker of a home. This resulted in a tremendous demand for, and a great speculation in, real estate.

Records show that in 1922 and 1923 alone, and within a 20-mile circle of Los Angeles, more than 2,000 new tracts were opened comprising approximately 200,000 lots and covering some 50,000 acres. Prices of all kinds of property, both close in and ultra-suburban, rose rapidly, and large profits on quick turnovers were made. This boom reached its greatest intensity during 1923.

By that time bankers and the more conservative businessmen felt that there were certain elements of gamble and inflation in the boom and the need for proceeding cautiously was apparent.

60

A Squatter's Paralogism

A romantic story of early Inglewood, a royal court, and one, Fernando Ayala.

PHINEAS BANNING lived through the hectic transition period of the old ranchero era of a cattle and hide economy, of pastoral simplicity, to one of agriculture, planting of citrus trees and grape culture. Banning aided the rancheros in the development of this new economy, which created another hue in California's rainbow.

Banning took more than a passing interest in all the old ranchos, and he noted that no rancho was kicked around with more abandon and indifference than the "Rancho Aguaje de la Centinela," now the City of Inglewood. In 1844, the Mexican governor granted this rancho of 2,000 acres to Ignacio Machado, who a year later traded the property to Bruno Avila for an adobe house on the plaza at the pueblo of Los Angeles. To bind the deal, Machado had to give Avila two barrels of brandy. Avila grazed the land with several hundred cattle for 10 years, then lost the deed due to his inability to repay a $900 loan, and the accrued interest of 6 per cent per month, or 72 per cent per year, which in those days was often the prevailing rate.

Hilliard P. Dorsey got the rancho for a bid of $1 per acre at a sheriff's sale on the city hall steps at the plaza. Three years later, Dorsey died and his widow, Civility, almost immediately sold the ranch for 35 cents an acre to Francis I. Carpenter, with a proviso that he must dispossess a squatter named Fernando Ayala.

When this was accomplished, the land trebled in value back to $1 an acre, whereupon Carpenter sold the acreage to Joseph Lancaster Brent. Brent was a Southern sympathizer, and when war broke out between the states in 1861, Brent went to New Orleans. In 1862, he became a general in the Confederate Army and an aide to General Robert E. Lee.

Banning had noticed that many prominent people in L.A. county were rooting for the South to win the war, long before Brent and others like him joined the Southern army. It was these intelligence reports that prompted Banning to write to Abraham Lincoln in 1861 to build a barracks in Wilmington staffed with enough soldiers and cavalry to put down the tenseness and uprisings. Drum Barracks was the result, with a maximum of 7,000 troops.

In the meantime, Brent sold the Centinela Rancho in 1862 to Sir Robert and Lady Burnett for $3,000. Burnett was a British Baronet, who immediately after arriving at the Centinela Rancho found squatter Ayala back on the premises. The Baron lost no time in kicking claim-jumper Ayala clean off the place.

This was the second time for poor Fernando, who learned his lesson, returned to the pueblo, got a job cooking tortillas and later returned to Sonora, Mexico.

Sir Robert and Lady Elizabeth put the land under cultivation, erected a windmill, and got enough water for vegetable gardening and grape culture. The Burnetts became social leaders and were generously entertained by the leading citizens of the time, including the Ducommuns, the Hellmans, the Bixbys, the Sepulvedas, and others.

The Burnetts simply adored the Banning Mansion and Phineas Banning's hospitality. He loved to look through Banning's telescope from the mansion cupola and scan the horizon. On the busy quay in Wilmington and San Pedro, he could see lumber barges unloading miles of redwood logs and ponderosa pine, and lumber freshly cut in the northern forests around Eureka—the lumber that would build a thousand homes in Inglewood.

In the Palos Verdes and the Dominguez Expanse, he saw Mexican-Spanish symbolism—dashing dons on horseback, cattle herds by the ten fold, hooves, horns and hides, adobes and corrals, and Spanish ox-drawn carettas loaded with hides to barter with sailing captains for needed items for the ranchos.

Daniel Freeman bought Burnett's property in 1885 for $140,000, and the Burnetts returned to England to live in their castle, where they could again meet and entertain their titled relatives and friends, and reminisce at royal gatherings about the far-away California prairie, Indians, and the 30-room Colonial-Victorian mansion of the Bannings. And one Fernando Ayala.

61
A Pirate's Legacy

A fascinating story, comparable to the Count of Monte Cristo, of an early California buccaneer who founded one of the most respected families in Los Angeles.

AN EXCITING EPISODE in San Pedro history occurred on Christmas Eve, 1828, when the brig Danube was dashed on the rocks near Dead Man's Island after being whipped around by a terrific Santa Ana wind.

The ship was a total loss, although her crew of 28 officers and men survived.

The southeastern wind that wrecked the Danube was the indirect cause of the building and launching of the first ship in San Pedro Bay.

The hull of the wrecked ship was purchased for $1,780 by a group connected with the San Gabriel Mission. The salvaged timbers and iron furnished material that heretofore had been impossible to obtain in California.

Other parts for a new ship were put together at the mission and hauled 30 miles on wooden-wheeled ox carts to San Pedro.

Alfred Robinson tells the story in his *Life in California:*

"Her builder was Joseph Chapman, and she was a schooner of about 60 tons that had been entirely framed at San Gabriel and fitted for subsequent completion at San Pedro.

"She was named Guadalupe in honor of the patron saint of Mexico. Many people were invited, and many came from far and near to witness her launching in 1831."

The construction and launching took place just above what was later to be known as Timms' Landing, about where Fifteenth Street is now.

Historians differ as to the tonnage of the ship, but estimate it as much as 99 tons.

Col. J.J. Warner, an early historian who came to California the year the Guadalupe was launched, said, "In 1831, the minister of San Gabriel, Father Sanchez, aided and encouraged by Samuel Prentice and George Yount (of Santa Catalina gold fame), William Wolfskill, Nathaniel Pryor, Richard Laughlin and Joseph Chapman, built a schooner in San Pedro which was employed in the hunting of sea otter."

After five years of sailing up and down the coast in quest of sea otter, the Guadalupe had a sad ending. She was wrecked in 1836 on the Mexican coast, and no record of her log or manifest has ever been found.

Joseph Chapman, the man most responsible for the ship, had an extraordinary life. The first American to arrive in California, he came as a hunted pirate in 1818.

He was on a pirate ship that opened fire on the fort at Monterey. When answering fire from the shore battery damaged the ship, it sailed away without attempting to land.

Two days later, the word had spread to the Ortega Ranch near Santa Barbara when the pirate ship again tried to land. Five men did come ashore but were captured by soldiers while plundering the ranch house. Joseph Chapman was among them.

The next day the pirates raided San Pedro, finding nothing worth stealing. It then plundered the mission at San Juan Capistrano, taking the church jewels and some art work, then sailed away and was never heard from again.

The commandant at Santa Barbara was kind to Chapman after finding out that his prisoner was a highly-skilled artisan, shipbuilder, blacksmith, carpenter and jack-of-all-trades.

The other prisoners were handcuffed and sent to Mexico for trial for piracy—a capital offense. Chapman was sent, under guard, to the San Gabriel fathers who urgently needed his talents to help build the Plaza Church on Olvera Street.

In a short time Chapman proved himself worthy and was set free. He joined the Catholic faith, was naturalized as a Mexican citizen and married the daughter of a prominent ranchero family, Guadalupe Ortega, who only a year before was an eye-witness to her husband's pillage of her home.

In those days courtship was done by the elders. The only privilege a senorita had was to say yes or no. She said yes and was given away by Don Antonio Lugo, a highly respected Mexican leader.

The marriage of Jose Chapman and Guadalupe Ortega was a happy one. Their children became lawyers, doctors, bankers, and real estate brokers. During the 1920s and 1930s, the Chapman Building at Broadway and Eighth Street in Los Angeles was the biggest building in the city. To this day the family ranks high in the economic and social life of Los Angeles.

Joseph Chapman died in 1849. By his clever discernment, his skills, his finesse, and his maneuvers, Chapman left a rich heritage. Within a span of 30 years he rose from a buccaneer and freebooter in 1818 to a highly respected man and an important leader in Los Angeles.

The Count of Monte Cristo fared no better.

62
Los Angeles—Born in 1781

The Los Angeles Harbor Area Hispanic group outlined in good perspective their Bicentennial goals.

FOR MONTHS the Hispanic Bicentennial group, a historically inclined and community conscious people from the Harbor Area have been meeting twice a month at Los Angeles City Hall, in large meeting rooms provided through the courtesy of Commissioners David Lozano of the Department of Public Works. Their Bicentennial is based primarily on the awareness of their Hispanic past, of the accomplishments of their present, and the possibilities of their future.

From a historic point, they have much of which to be proud. The Spanish-Mexican (Hispanic) heritage is uppermost in the Los Angeles Harbor complex. From Cabrillo to Pio Pico the Hispanic Californians have left landmark names that testify to their pioneering spirit. The first ship that landed in our harbor was built in Acapulco in 1542. Hispanic pioneers were the first to discover California, first to people it, first to cultivate it.

For their Bicentennial they want a centralized headquarters, such as the old Catalina Terminal at the foot of Avalon Boulevard in Wilmington, where they could display and interpret the story of the founding, growth, and evolution of the Los Angeles Harbor. Fiestas and siestas where senoritas performed with their Tipica Orchestras, and other festive events featuring song, and dance and poetry, will celebrate their rich, romantic California history.

Their Bicentennial has implanted a permanent monument to the glory of our state, and to our community. History-conscious Carlos Villabolos of Wilmington is chairman of the Harbor Hispano Bicentennial Committee.

Here is a partial list of the Hispanic landmark names: Alvarado, Bandini, Dominguez, Figueroa, Sepulveda, Del Amo, Carson, Pio Pico, Coto, Lugo, Del Valle, Cabrillo, Biscailuz, Olvera, and Feliz.

The mayor's office is already planning an all-out Bicentennial in 1981 to celebrate the founding of the Pueblo of Los Angeles.

The new settlers in 1781, all Hispanic-Americans, dug deep into the soil of California, and planted the seeds that made Los Angeles grow, and the Los Angeles Harbor bloom. There were 44 of them, men and women with their families recruited as colonists from Mexico, courageous people who could stand the hardships and knew how to work the fields.

They were the families of Basilio and Alejandro Rosas, Antonio Villavicenco, Jose Lara, Jose Venegas, Pablo Rodriguez, Antonio Navarro, Luis Quintero, Manuel Camero, Jose Moreno, Antonio Mesa, Francisco Lugo, Jacinto Costa, and their corporal, Jose Feliz.

What was California like in 1776? Seven missions had been established: San Diego, Carmel, San Gabriel, San Luis Obispo, San Francisco, and San Juan Capistrano. Mission Ventura was built in 1782; Santa Barbara, in 1786; and San Fernando, in 1797. These missions were the religious, social, and economic centers of California. They controlled all the land, all the adobes, haciendas, orchards, vineyards, workers, farming, and live stock.

From San Gabriel, the largest and most influential, a hundred dashing caballeros rode out the mesas from a thousand hills. In deference to the padres, their home life was quiet and peaceful.

The well-chaperoned senoritas wore colorful shawls and mantillas and were wont to dance at mission parties, weddings, and receptions with their castanets in perfect rhythm with the musicians.

It was a romantic era of fiestas and siestas, of barbeques, of general hospitality and camaraderie, and home-spun closeness. They were devoted to their church. No Anglo visitors had yet arrived in California. They were contented, healthy, and happy.

What was it like in Boston in 1776? Uprisings and tenseness, tea parties in reverse, and caballero Paul Revere riding 100 miles down the New England Pike urging his horse faster and faster, shouting warnings to the populace. The cold war with England suddenly became hot, and the skirmishes at Lexington, Concord, Ticonderoga, and Bunker Hill brought about the wrath of the people and the signing of the Declaration of Independence, July 4, 1776.

The Revolutionary War lingered on until the British surrendered at Yorktown in 1781. It was heroic, it was patriotic, and it was glorious for the Americans. But it was war.

In California the first land grant was not given until 1784, when Juan Dominguez received some 75,000 acres from which the following towns were platted: Redondo Beach, Torrance, Palos Verdes, San Pedro, Harbor City, Lomita, Gardena, Carson, Wilmington, and Dominguez Hills. This was the beginning of shipping from warehouses, in commerce, in hides and tallow, and free enterprise in bartering, and communication with the world via the ship's captain and crew.

According to Villabolos, their Hispanic Bicentennial is not unfriendly or opposed to any other Bicentennial group which plan alternate programs. "We were a continent apart from Boston in 1776, and under Spanish rule," Villabolos says. "We plan to celebrate the occasion and make the occasion a celebration of what California was like in 1776, not what Boston was like in 1776."

63
Cristobal Aguilar, Benevolent Mayor

A two-term mayor of Hispanic extraction planted seeds of progress and happiness in 1866. Harbor people are grateful.

THE CITY OF LOS ANGELES was incorporated by the California Legislature on April 4, 1850. The first mayor was Dr. Alpheus Hodges, a leading physician who was elected without opposition, although the city's population of about 1,700 was mostly of Hispanic heritage.

Before 1850, all the mayors (Alcaldes) back to the founding of Los Angeles in 1781, were of Spanish or Mexican Blood.

Antonio F. Coronel became the first mayor of Hispanic heritage for incorporated Los Angeles in 1853. He was a merchant, rancher, orange grower and school teacher who established the first department of public works.

A man of letters and arts, Coronel assisted Helen Hunt Jackson with research in creating her book, *Ramona,* which is the basis for the annual outdoor spectacular in Hemet each spring.

Coronel also was an avid collector of Spanish, Mexican, and Indian artifacts and items, many of which are on display today at the Los Angeles County Museum of History.

Cristobal Aguilar was the next Los Angeles mayor of Hispanic background.

He was elected in 1866, served a two-year term, then was elected to another two-year term in 1871.

Aguilar came face-to-face with many firsts. It was the period of national reconstruction as an aftermath of the Civil War, and although Los Angeles did not suffer from actual battle wounds, tension was prevalent in the community.

Aguilar was press and public relations conscious, and one of the first things on his agenda in 1866 was to call all local editors and writers to his office for a friendly conference.

He served his guests vintage brandy and asked them to be calm, honest, studious, and sober in their writings about the conditions in Los Angeles.

Eastern newspapers, he said, had reported news about Los Angeles which was distorted and inconsistent with the facts.

Aguilar told the editors and reporters that growing communities must inevitably face certain trials and tribulations, and he would like to see the press cover the community without resorting to sensationalism.

He pinpointed newspapers from New York, Boston, and Washington, D.C. which, he said, were guilty of gross misrepresentation and had maligned the city with half-truths.

The conference was apparently a great success as Aguilar made friends with the press and truthful reporting began to keep pace with the facts of progress.

There were a whole line of firsts during Aguilar's terms as mayor. He signed an ordinance creating a park site which became Pershing Square. He directed the publishing of the first Los Angeles directory. The first agricultural fair was promoted and held at Exposition Park. The first Los Angeles bank was opened with a boastful capital of $100,000. The first ice factory opened, with ice selling at 4 cents a pound. People now could spend a full day fishing in the Harbor Area and return with their catch without fear of spoilage.

Industry got a toe-hold with the opening of a long-needed woolen mill in 1871. The mill provided employment and export possibilities.

Also under Aguilar's administration the first steam fire engine was purchased and stationed in the plaza next to the Pico House on Olvera Street. The Spanish-language newspaper *La Cronica* made its debut, with Cristobal Aguilar the featured columnist. It is said he reported factual items in faultless Spanish. One lengthy article was an interview Aguilar had with himself about the progress he had made in palm tree planting, street paving, and irrigation.

Phineas Banning supplied Aguilar with eucalyptus seedlings from Wilmington, and several streets were lined with these trees.

Many birds began to flock to Los Angeles for the first time including the mockingbird, blue jay, wren, and chickadee. All these birds later found their way to the Harbor Area.

Aguilar was proud of his Los Angeles and of his Mexican heritage. The day he left office he strode up to the top of Temple Hill to observe the handiwork of his two administrations. He saw many of the firsts that had begun under his direction, including rows and rows of palm trees which had been planted under his careful direction and now swaying gently in the breeze almost as if in a farewell gesture to a loving friend.

64

Ex-Mayor Commits Suicide at City Hall

This was a period of much business and political activity. The Civil War started, Drum Barracks was built, and telegraph wires strung.

WHEN DAMIEN MARCHESSAULT became mayor of Los Angeles in 1859, the whole community was going through a definite metamorphosis. It was the beginning of the end of the flush gold mining boom of the 1850s, and of the old rancho days of town fiestas, fandango soirees, and siestas.

Damien was mayor from 1859 to 1860, and from 1861 to 1865. After his tenure in office, the pueblo would henceforth be recognized by its rightful designation as the City of Los Angeles.

Marchessault gained the reputation of being an aggressive mayor. He initiated several civic projects, many of them completed by mayors who followed. Marchessault was mayor during the Civil War period and aided Phineas Banning and Don Benito Wilson in establishing Drum Barracks in Wilmington.

Damien was the product of the early migration to California by a large and influential French colony. During the gold boom years, several thousand Frenchmen landed on our shores under the direction of Le Societe du I'Ingot d'Or.

It is said that the French were second to the Chinese in clannishness and picturesqueness. After the gold hiatus, some of their numbers became leading California merchants, importers, and bankers. Records show they have blended well with the social, political, and economic development of the state. Certainly, no people have left such an indelible and honorable imprint on the American scene as has the pioneering spirit of the French.

From friendly and gallant Lafayette to the unpredictable DeGaulle, American foreign policy has been closely linked with the French. They were the first fur trappers through the American wilderness. Even the Lewis and Clark expedition of 1804 did not meet an Indian tribe who had not first seen a Frenchman. The French have been elastic in mood and method throughout their history; their language is the favorite in diplomacy.

There was much work to be done in Los Angeles, and Marchessault, unlike any other mayor before his day, set the wheels in motion. He would not let the Angelenos resign themselves to the status quo in the ebb and flow of a fast-changing economy. Unprecedented activity began to chip away at the old *laissez faire* lethergy, and Marchessault's successor, another Frenchman, Jose Mascarel, was grateful.

A gas company was organized by the city in 1865, and for the first time gas-lit lamps were in the offing. Water pipes began to cross the community, and town pumps were established for the convenience of water users. Household plumbing, as we know it today, was still a long way off, but progress in sanitation was being noted, and the French importers of perfume did a thriving business.

The population was less than 7,000. Sam F.B. Morse had invented the telegraph in 1844, but the hook-up was slow in arriving in Los Angeles. Marchessault directed the wires be connected at Drum Barracks. This was accomplished in 1862, and the dots and dashes to the East Coast was a welcome miracle to Los Angeles and the Harbor Area.

It was Phineas Banning's horse-drawn coaches that carried the mail pouches from harbor ports to Los Angeles and the Pacific Southwest. Banning helped Mayor Damien prod the telegraph company to hurry and complete the line to our community.

In 1870, Banning entertained Morse at the Banning Mansion at a sumptuous dinner banquet at which Collis P. Huntington, Leland Stanford, Mark Hopkins, and Charles Crocker were present. Banning's railroad from Los Angeles to the harbor had just been completed, and they all toasted the genius of Morse, whose telegraph poles paralleled their railroad tracks.

Although Marchessault had been well disciplined in the chicanery of political demogoguery by his friend, Count Gaston de Raousset-Boulbon, a French nobleman who came to California to recruit hundreds of French for a filibustering campaign to Sonora, they both fell victims to other cohesive forces.

Raousset's denizens of the Mexican oases succeeded in capturing Guaymas and Hermisillo, but they themselves were later captured by Mexican Gen. Blianco in 1854. Marchessault fell victim to the bitter stings of malicious gossip over his construction of wooden water pipes which decayed in the acrid soil.

Three years after leaving as mayor of Los Angeles, the stress and strain was too much for Marchessault. He took his own life in 1868 in the city council room as a parting farewell against the system—this time against the finger-pointing and whispering campaigns of political scandal-mongers.

65
SAINT SCISSORS

In 1878 Lucky Baldwin bought 10,000-acre rancho, which became known as Baldwin Hills. There was a hanging aboard the S.S. Crickett.

THE OLD RANCHO FAMILIES left many landmarks on our horizon. One of the largest and most prominent was the Rancho San Pedro of some 75,000 acres, from which the towns of Redondo Beach, Torrance, Palos Verdes, Rolling Hills, Lomita, Gardena, Carson, San Pedro, Harbor City, Wilmington, and Dominguez were carved.

Perhaps the most poetic of all the rancho names was the "Rancho 'O Paso de la Tijera," which is Spanish for a pass resembling scissors. Most all the ranchos and the offshore islands were named for saints, but a name like "Saint Scissors" would hardly cut the mustard.

In 1843, Mexican Governor Manuel Micheltorena cut up a large parcel of the San Gabriel Mission lands, now known as Baldwin Hills, and gave it to Vicente Sanchez, a favorite of Mexico for his heroic services at the Texas Alamo. Sanchez did not live long after his landfall gift. It seemed to be too much for him; he was used to fighting for land, not getting it gratis.

Vicente's son, Tomas A. Sanchez, and two daughters, Dolores and Maria, were delighted to accept this inheritance which included about 10,000 acres and an adobe home in the pueblo near the Olvera Street Plaza. There, on special occasions, dozens of pretty senoritas would perform singing and dancing in colorful costumes, flaming dresses and castanets.

We can find no other mention of the Sanchez senoritas after they moved to the pueblo, but one good guess is that they became a part of the lively entourage of the many social functions given by the *alcalde* (mayor) to entertain the political and military leaders who often visited the pueblo on important missions. Old history files mention that there were many soiree's of music and dancing during this period of Mexican control.

Tomas Sanchez became sheriff of Los Angeles County and served from 1860 to 1867, often picking up army deserters and returning them to Drum Barracks in Wilmington.

These also were the hectic days of the vigilante, and Sanchez depended heavily on his friends to lead posses and track down the "bad guys" who were active in raids and murder against the rancho "good guys."

An interesting episode happened in 1863, when Ranchero John Rains was robbed and murdered in Azusa. His assassin, Joe Cerradel, was caught, tried, and found guilty. But the judge sentenced him to only 10 years in San Quentin.

The "good guys" thought this verdict a travesty of justice, and when Sanchez brought his prisoner to Wilmington to board ship for San Quentin in San Francisco Bay, the vigilantes forcibly took Cerradel, hanged him to the flagpole in Phineas Banning's SS Crickett, took the body down, weighted it with rocks, and dumped it into San Pedro Bay. Such was the vigilante law south and west of the pueblo.

In 1875, Sanchez sold most of the Rancho 'O Paso de la Tijera for about $75,000. A few years later, Lucky Baldwin became the sole owner and it became known as Baldwin Hills and was named for him.

Baldwin's real estate ventures were centered in his Los Angeles Investment Company. It made a national reputation advertising and subdividing this property as Angeles Mesa, which made many millions of dollars for Baldwin.

Lucky Baldwin died in 1909 during the period when Los Angeles annexed San Pedro and Wilmington.

Maybe Lucky Baldwin was not so lucky. He certainly had vision and knew what he was doing. His real estate investments included some harbor and Peninsula property, and it was rumored that he helped finance George Peck in some of his land deals, including the Harbor City-Lomita complex, and Manhattan Beach, where Peck owned one mile of beach property.

66
Bravo, the Queen!

At San Fernando five tons of wild honey was discovered from wayward bees from the Palos Verdes Hills. The bees won a stinging victory.

A TERRIBLE DROUGHT OCCURRED in the years of 1862 through 1864, when no flowers bloomed and nearly all vegetation disappeared. Honey bees died by the millions.

Honey bees were first imported to San Pedro in 1854 by John T. Gordon. He investigated the merits of buying the German black bee or the larger Italian honey bee. Gordon decided the well-groomed Italian bee would be superior for our kind of flowers and climate. He paid $65 for a queen bee, and his first order was for 600 hives (300 queen bees). Forty-eight of them went to the Palos Verdes Peninsula.

Even during mild droughts, these bees could draw upon instinctive knowledge inherited back to the dawn of history, but three full years of complete drought was too much; only a few escaped, and these buzzed their way to the more lush western slopes of San Fernando Valley.

There they found a protective rift which penetrated into rock formations 160 feet deep with an orifice 20 feet long and 15 feet wide, hiding secret passages. A one-foot opening was found where bees could come out in a nearly solid column.

From 1864 to 1868, the bees were unmolested in their comfortable retreat, where they worked and multiplied by the millions and lived contentedly.

They fared well and in time became lords over an underground superhive of some 5 tons of pure wild honey. At $1.25 per pound, this was a bonanza coveted by both man and beast.

Wild bees have five enemies—man, moths, lizards, bee-birds, and bears. Moths will spread their larvae, if possible, in the beeswax, lizards will gulp bees whole, bee-birds will outfly and outmaneuver for a billfull, and a bear will wallow in them with exalted gluttony.

But man was the biggest enemy for the bees of the San Fernando Valley. It was inevitable that man would find this honey El Dorado—and he did in June 1868.

The first men to brave the descent of this immense honey storehouse were driven back like firemen trying to quench a roaring fire with a squirt gun. Some were stung to death and others maimed and seriously injured.

The honey bees may have been squatters, but they were there first and they would not give up their home without a fight to the bitter end.

Finally, mining engineers were consulted. A 125-foot high scaffold was built with the idea of running a draft into the rock, but this proved a dismal failure.

The engineers had a conference. They could do nothing about getting the honey out, they agreed, unless they blasted the place with dynamite. And doing that, they figured correctly, would defeat their purpose.

Saloon keepers in Los Angeles were laying two-to-one odds in favor of the bees.

"Hack out to the bee rocks and see the fights," was a familiar call at livery stables.

Finally, the miners gave up.

The lovers of our fauna and our flora can admire with awe the intelligence and tenacity of the honey bee: his masterful techniques in warfare, his onslaughts and his field maneuvers against all comers, and his quick draw and the prompt reformation of his disturbed hive.

The queen reins supreme, proud and elegant in her domain. She appoints soldiers, nurses, guards, judges, spies, and other personnel to maintain her colony intact.

Their winged victory over man in the hills of San Fernando in 1868 was a stinging success. The bees proved their point on the field of battle, thus sustaining their squatter's entitlement with special privileges by right of conquest.

Since that time, more than 100 years ago, the bees have left that haven in the San Fernando Valley to find homes elsewhere. But that victory will live on.

Bravo, the queen! Long may she reign.

67
Old Landmark Delights

Problems in maintaining old landmark homes from the bulldozer can be answered eventually by members of the historical societies.

A RECENT ARTICLE by John Pastier, published in the *Los Angeles Times,* stated that Los Angeles is suffering from a retarded historical consciousness. Even San Diego, according to Pastier, is doing much better in preserving old buildings than L.A. on a per capita basis.

Recently, the author talked to Robertson Collins, an official of the National Trust for Historical Preservation, who said that Los Angeles, including the Harbor Area, may have the greatest quantity of high-pedigree historical architecture in any western city. Collins recommended a formal survey of all historical places to determine age, significance, architecture, and priorities. He stated that the alternative would be like being subject to a never-ending series of crises resulting in demolition and oblivion.

A case in point, Collins said, is the total bulldozing of the old Dodge House, the Richfield Building, and the Von Sternberg House, "due principally to our historic ignorance, indifference, and apathy."

At a recent meeting at the historic Hale House, one of the few that has escaped the bulldozer in Heritage Square, just off Avenue 43 exit on the Pasadena Freeway, a few historians met and planned for action to save our heritage. Architect Raymond Girvigian complained that the California Cultural Heritage Foundation should be more locally responsive to the $250 million state appropriation that has been going almost exclusively into parks and recreation use, and not into historical resources and preservation. (The 117-year-old Civil War Drum Barracks in Wilmington is a good example of this kind of neglect).

But this unfortunate circumstance, Girvigian thinks, is due principally because community groups are not lobbying and proposing preservation on the local level. He ended his comments by declaring that "historic preservation has been kicked in the teeth for a century or more."

These summations are only too true here in the Harbor Area, where even during the last five years we have seen the Gaffey Chapel on Bandini Street, preserved for a time by the new YMCA, completely bulldozed, as was the old Amar Home at Twelfth and Mesa Streets, and the old Carnegie Library on Beach Street across from the Post Office.

Fortunately, we still have a few old landmark homes in San Pedro and Wilmington; and Dick Wolfe and the author took a circle tour of them. Wolfe is an old-time local historian and an occasional contributor to the *News-Pilot.* The author contacted two other knowledgeable history buffs, Ed Hauck and Bill Olesen, both guiding his path in a landmark direction.

Some of the old houses we surveyed are masterpieces of architectural art, such as the one at 324 West 10th Street, a combination of Victorian and Green Renaissance. It has a carriage house in the rear. We believe this is the oldest house in San Pedro, and, if properly restored to its former elegance, it should become a real showplace in the harbor. Another unusual house is the old Cyrus Butterfield home at Thirty-sixth Street and Pacific Avenue with its quaint oriental roofing.

We were greatly impressed in meeting 96-year-old Wilbur Wood, and his 90-year-old wife, whose 73rd wedding anniversary was on June 25th, 1975. Wood built the Southern California Fish Cannery, which was the first on Terminal Island. They live in a modest, but gracious, old home at 4026 Bluff Place in San Pedro. (A chapter elsewhere in this book is devoted to Wilbur Wood).

The old house at 4074 Bluff Place, now owned by Mrs. Grace MacDonald, is another old ocean-view showplace built precariously near the edge of the cliff. The old Charles Perham home at 3541 Kerckhoff Street is another showplace abode nested on a panoramic cliff. Perham had the first jewelry store in San Pedro. The Jesse Bourgeois House at 511 Paseo Del Mar is, according to Ed Hauck, the oldest house in the whole length of the Paseo.

It was impossible to visit all the old homes on this trip, but the author was heartened to know that the old James Dodson residence at 13th and Parker Streets and the mansion of the late Lucy Banning at 1118 West Anaheim Street in Wilmington will be preserved by the present owners.

It is well to know that the San Pedro Bay Historical Society was founded in 1974 with local preservation of landmarks as the main objective. Carlin Soule, one of the founders of the Society, almost immediately and without help from anyone other than a letter from the Society, had the Los Angeles Department of Recreation and Parks save the Pt. Fermin Park Restaurant Building as a landmark. The club has appointed active committees that meet regularly to study and solve the problems of local landmark places.

Some of the leaders in this activity are Grace Hoxworth, Hilda Hager, Flora Baker, Adm. Frank Higbee, Pete Mandia, Clara Ostoich, Charles Ember, and of course, Bill Olesen and Pam Bleich.

The 40-year-old 30-Year Club, with its 1,000 members, is also active in local historical preservation, under the guidance of Olesen. (A chapter also deals with the 30-Year-Club).

68
First Protestant Churches

The religious faiths were devoid of biogotry during Protestant and Catholic church expansion.

VISITORS AT THE Phineas Banning Mansion in Wilmington often ask about the religious life of the Banning family. Phineas and his wife were Episcopalians, and they founded St. John's Episcopal Church in 1882. It is still the oldest church in continuous service in the Harbor Area.

In 1882, under the supervision of their pastor, the Rev. Carlos Linsley, the church was built by volunteers at a site on Canal Street, now called Avalon Boulevard. The major cost of all building materials was paid by the Bannings. In 1943, the church was moved to its present location at 1537 Neptune Avenue in Wilmington.

There are several antique stained glass windows in the church, one of them in memory of Gen. Banning. The bell in the cupola is from the S.S. Cricket, an early side-wheeler which Banning used both in local waters and for trips to Catalina Island.

The altar piece is a fine specimen of Catalina black marble, which the Bannings donated in 1925. St. John's is a modest, stave-type church of colonial architecture.

The church has been designated Historic Culture Monument No. 47 by the Cultural Heritage Board of Los Angeles. The present pastor, Fr. James Corbett, administers to more than 100 active members with Holy Communion every Sunday.

The old St. Peter's Episcopal Memorial Church, which was moved in 1956 to Harbor View Memorial Park at 2411 S. Grand Avenue, San Pedro, was built originally in 1884 at First and Beacon Street in San Pedro. It is under the sponsorship of St. John's in Wilmington. It also has been designated a cultural historic monument.

The Calvary Presbyterian Church in Wilmington was possibly the first Protestant church built in the harbor community.

The original site of this church property consisted of 3.5 acres donated by Don Benito Wilson, a partner with Banning in the purchase of 2,400 acres in 1857 for the town of Wilmington.

The church is now known as "Memory Chapel" and is located next to the current sanctuary at L Street and Marine Avenue. It is no longer in use, but due to Mrs. Fred Lorenzen this chapel has been designated a historical monument.

The first Protestant church in Los Angeles was built in 1864 under Catholic

Mayor Damien Marchessault. But Protestant building began in earnest during Mayor James R. Toberman's (of Toberman's Settlement House) administration in 1878 due to a greater influx of midwestern residents. They represented many Protestant denominations, principally the Presbyterian, Methodist, and Baptist faiths.

Toberman proved to be an excellent administrator. He served two terms from 1872 to 1882. He was a good friend of Phineas Banning and was a guest at the mansion on several occasions.

A significant number of firsts took place under his mayoral leadership. The Chamber of Commerce was organized, the Los Angeles branch of the University of California was established, the first issue of the *Los Angeles Herald* was published, and the first synagogue was built.

As mayor, Toberman accomplished drastic fiscal reforms, according to historian W.W. Robinson. He reduced the city's indebtedness by $30,000 while cutting taxes from $1,60 to $1 per $100. He left a surplus of $25,990 in the city treasury, a tidy sum in those days.

Main Street was paved, and Los Angeles turned on its new electric lights on New Year's Eve, 1881. San Pedro turned its lights on in 1882.

Toberman came to California in 1864 after being appointed revenue assessor by President Lincoln. He served for six years as a Wells Fargo agent before going into politics.

During the days of the dashing dons and the old rancho haciendas, church worship was confined solely to the Catholic Padres. However, there were no reports of religious bigotry during this vital transition of Protestant church expansion.

69
Tears From Wounded Knee

The Indians were the first Americans. In the early migration westward our pioneers fought them every mile from the Atlantic to the Pacific.

IN THESE TIMES there are many themes on how to portray the American scene in our celebrations, and it seems most appropriate to remember the American Indian and give him credit for his many contributions in the settlement of our Nation.

Actually, without the help of the Indian, all the first white settlers might have starved to death: The friendly Indians supplied them with food, as well as furs and skins for warmth. For the most part in California the Indians were peaceful. They got along with their neighbors and enjoyed well-established channels of trade. They lived off the land, hunting and gathering, making use of almost everything, destroying very little.

There should be a willingness to admire the ways these first Americans lived in harmony with their environment. California was then as now a land of beauty and variety, of magnificent forests, broad deserts, vast areas of grassland and wildflowers, from which great herds of elk, antelope, bears, and many other animal species grazed contentedly on nature's bountiful offering.

The Gabrielino Indians carried on a brisk canoe trade between San Pedro and the off-shore islands, where they exchanged cow hides, tallow, hand-woven baskets, acorns, pigment and reeds, for soapstone and slate, agate, and mineral rock for carvings.

Juan Rodriguez Cabrillo came in 1542 and Sebastian Vizcaino came in 1602. In each instance the Indians brought fresh fish, vegetables, and meat to both Cabrillo and Vizcaino, whose ship crews were sick and dying of scurvy and hunger. The Indian tribes had all the land to themselves. They hunted and fished and set up villages where cities now stand. The white man found many appetizing foods among the Indians not known to Europe, such as corn, pumpkin, squash, tomatoes, potatoes, peanuts, maple sugar, avocado, artichokes, snapbeans, limas, blackeyed peas, and about fifty other kinds of foods. Most of these foods found their way back to Europe for planting and cultivating to enrich their own meager larder. The turkey is also native to America and was not known in Europe before Columbus.

Indian chiefs Massasoit, Squanto, and Samoset, made the Mayflower settlers acquainted with corn and taught them how to cultivate it, grind it into meal, and bake it as bread. Tobacco, first found in America, cultivated by the Indians, became the colonist's first cash crop for export. The Indians also introduced new medicines: quinine, ephedrine, ipecac, witchhazel, and medical herbs.

The life of the American Indian has been deeply imprinted in the history of a Bicentennial of 200 years, since which time the passing of the many moons, the rains of many winters, and the suns of many summers cannot erase. Every state west of the Mississippi has an Indian name except for Washington and California. States east of the Mississippi also have Indian names, save for New York, New Jersey, New Hampshire, Rhode Island, Pennsylvania, North and South Carolina, Virginia and West Virginia, Georgia, Louisiana and Maryland.

Even our mighty rivers, Mississippi, Ohio and Missouri, are Indian, not to mention the Tennessee, Kentucky, Colorado, Arkansas, Delaware, and Connecticut Rivers. The Indians were the pathfinders for the Lewis and Clark Expedition of 1804 which saved for the U.S. the Oregon Country in the "54-40 or fight" threat.

Princess Pocahontas saved the life of Virginia leader Capt. John Smith, and married the tobacco planter and economic leader John Rolfe, and saved a state from poverty and ruin. Hiawatha is known as the heroine in the beautiful poem by Longfellow, and Chief Sequoya helped his people adjust peacefully to new ways. The tribes of the Cherokee had an alphabet and their language gave us names like hominy, succotash, chipmunk, woodchuck, and skunk.

Today there are about 600,000 Indians living in the United States, about 60,000 in California. It is often difficult to decide just who is an Indian. In the U.S. a person's ancestry determines his race, but anyone with one-quarter Indian blood is considered an Indian.

The Indian taught the white man how to survive in the rugged New World of America, but ironically in the course of his destiny the Indian himself could not survive. When the white man came armed with gun and ax, plow, crowbar and Bible, he transformed a peaceful wilderness of 3 million square miles into a mighty new nation, evicting the Indians along the way.

In celebrating our Bicentennial, let us stop and pause, reflect, ponder, and think about our First Americans, the Indian, and of our cruel treatment of him with broken promises, forced marches when thousands perished, the willful slaughter of his food supply of buffalo, and the shame and sorrow in the hearts of a hundred thousand "WOUNDED KNEES."

70

A Chamber of Commerce is Born

San Francisco leaders got a charter for a Chamber of Commerce, on February 24, 1906, paving the way for progressive development of one of the world's most honored ports. The chamber has been steadfast in holding high the torch for improvement.

RENEE McNETT, MANAGER of the San Pedro Chamber of Community Development and Commerce, recently asked this writer if he had any information about chamber activities before the San Pedro chamber was incorporated in 1906.

Eileen Pulliam, manager of the Wilmington Chamber of Commerce, is also interested. Here goes.

The profile of Los Angeles changed in 1888 with the coming of the Santa Fe railroad, San Pedro's incorporation as a political entity and the knowledge that larger and more passenger and cargo ships would arrive in the future and berth in San Pedro and Wilmington.

A few leading Los Angeles businessmen met for the purpose of founding a chamber of commerce with the welfare of the harbor uppermost–a chamber, though founded in Los Angeles, that would be highly acceptable in the Harbor Area and treated by them with proper deference.

They were an imaginative group, creative and innovative.

The spark plug was Harrision Gray Otis, publisher and editor of the *Los Angeles Times.* Another stalwart was Joseph J. Scott, father of Msgr. George Scott, and William D. Stephens, an attorney who became governor of California in 1914.

Another was Willis H. Booth, whose grandson, Arch, is currently president of the United States Chamber of Commerce.

Their secretary, Charles D. Willard, arranged many meetings in the Harbor Area with the objective to train local men to exercise leadership and eventually form their own chamber.

From 1888 to 1899 their big fight was against Collis P. Huntington and the Southern Pacific railroad who insisted that the Congress transfer the port and build a breakwater in Santa Monica Bay and eliminate the ports of San Pedro and Wilmington.

The fight grew furious. The L.A. *Times* and the L.A. Chamber carried the ball for San Pedro against the railroad influence in Congress under the leadership of Sen. William P. Frye of Maine, chairman of the powerful Senate Commerce Committee.

In the meantime, the L.A. Chamber sponsored the election of Stephen M. White as senator for California and urged him to take leadership defying the vast power of Huntington in national politics. White won.

Sen. White's successful debates against his colleagues, Sen. Frye and the outsider, Collis P. Huntington, so endeared his constituents that they erected a bronze statue of him on the grounds of the Los Angeles County Courthouse and named a street for him in San Pedro.

During the contest, L.A. County population allowed only one representative in the lower house of Congress. He was James McLachland, a Pasadena attorney who worked hard for San Pedro. The fight was bitter and lingered for nine years.

The Free Harbor Jubilee on April 27, 1899, sponsored by the Chamber, was a spectacular event.

It had been planned to have President William McKinley press a buttom in the White House that would dump the first barge load of rock to start the breakwater construction, but the large crowd at Point Fermin watched in vain. Something went wrong with the button and the load had to be emptied by hand.

Through many local community working committees, the Free Harbor League led to a charter granted by the State on February 24, 1906, creating the San Pedro Chamber of Commerce.

The charter members were C.C. Abbott, Lewis Hansen, E.H. Bautzer, P.P. Ferl, S.M. Storer, Frank Burns, W.H. Wyatt, W.H. Savage, Joseph Atchison (father of Al and Floyd Atchison), W.O. Drishaus, C.A. Pearson, F.D. Foot, Morris A. Rosenfield, F.H. Percival and W.H. Wickersham.

Frank Burns was elected president, W.H. Wyatt, secretary, and S.M. Storer, treasurer. The secretary received $20 per month. Rent at the Masonic Hall was $5 per month.

On April 5, 1906, a resolution was adopted which stated: "The people of San Pedro are opposed to the mooted proposition to consolidate with the city of Los Angeles."

The consolidation, however, took place in 1909, since which time the entire Harbor Area, including San Pedro and Wilmington, has been a part of the city of Los Angeles.

On April 12, 1907, a resolution was passed expressing the chamber's appreciation to Mrs. Rudecinda F.S. de Dodson for a gift of 25 acres of valuable land to the city of San Pedro. This is the land now known as Park Plaza.

Fifteen years ago, this writer was membership chairman of the San Pedro chamber when its office was in the old Carnegie Library Building across the street from the post office.

Evie Bullock, office secretary, saw some strange things while looking through the south window—a station wagon with two men in a large vacant area with measuring equipment.

Evie suggested I see them. When I arrived, the head man introduced himself as David Tallichet, the other man was Jerry Sutton.

This was the beginning of the Ports O'Call Village project, and I brought back a newly signed membership. Sutton was the first manager of Ports O'Call and is former owner of the Princess Louise Restaurant. Tallichet is the owner of Ports O'Call. In the Los Angeles Harbor, fact is often more strange than fiction.

71
Olvera Street is Alive

This area was the birthplace of Los Angeles in 1781, known as the pueblo. It is getting a new face-lift in historic restoration.

IN 1965 THE CITY of Los Angeles and the state of California combined to restore and refurbish Old Olvera Street. This was the place where Phineas Banning's wagon trains were outfitted with fresh horses and mules for the long pull hauling equipment and provisions for the U.S. Army at Fort Tejon, Fort Mojave, and Fort Yuma.

This is a project that all history lovers should get behind and support. In the recent budget, the Governor blue-penciled a big slash in an appropriation sorely needed by Mayor Bradley's commissioners who were appointed to remake Olvera Street into an exciting and authentic replica of the Old Pueblo. When completed, it is calculated to draw millions of visitors and have the effect of a perpetual fair.

What did old Olvera Street look like? It had narrow streets, pastel-colored houses with the frilled windows of Spanish Colonial times. There were pleasantly shaded "portals" where one could go to drink rum, or gulp a cactus stingeree and watch dashing dons on gaited horses gallop by. The ornate bandstand in the plaza acted as a magnet in attracting young and old to sit under its "yum yum" trees and hear the marimba band with clown-like guitarists parading up and down the square. For overnight visitors, the Bella Union Hotel or the Pico House offered cool spaciousness and gracious dignity.

During fiestas the streets were ablaze with beautiful senoritas, castanets and tambourines in hand, dancing the light fantastic. It was said to be a colorful picture to observe them in their gaily decorated shawls and mantillas. Many Indian types would stroll lazily in the street and in the market place.

Some of them were proud little figures newly arrived from Sonora or Mazatlan and other fabled places from Old Mexico. Many were Zapotec and Mixtec, blended exotically with our Indian tribes. A few of them brought precious gold filigree and silver artifacts to peddle for a song. Our Gabrielinos offered bright-colored textiles and other handcrafts.

"Even today one will find Olvera Street relaxing like a trip to the past in modern comfort. When fully restored, it should be a world of color, of grace, and of fascination," observes the curator in charge, Jean Bruce Poole, who is doing an excellent job of restoration.

72
Harbor City Has No Harbor

It is older than Lomita. Harbor City is still a part of Los Angeles. Lomita is not. Harbor City almost became the port for Los Angeles.

PEOPLE HAVE often questioned why Harbor City is called Harbor City. After all, it is an inland community with no harbor facilities.

Well, when it was annexed by the city of Los Angeles on November 12, 1906, Harbor City was part of the grand scheme of the city to have its own harbor. And, in fact, an old map in Councilman John S. Gibson's office confirms the fact that the original annexed Harbor City did, indeed, include a large stretch of land that touched the San Pedro Bay just east of the west basin Channel.

After the annexation of Harbor City, Los Angeles city officials had the land promoters plan for a canal that would permit ocean-going ships to dock on Harbor City property. It was an escape in case the voters in Wilmington and San Pedro turned down the annexation proposals, which were approved in 1909. After that, the plans for a harbor in Harbor City were dropped, and the land that was a part of the original Harbor City stretching to the bay became parts of Wilmington and San Pedro.

Most of the land area of Harbor City was once a part of the Palos Verdes Rancho. It was purchased by George H. Peck in 1899 and cut up into small farms selling from $80 to $100 an acre.

Ed Anaker, a prominent local history buff formerly in charge of the Harbor Lake complex of water and tules for the city department of Recreation and Parks, has followed the history of the area for years.

"The pioneers who first bought land in Harbor City," says Anaker, now a leader in the San Pedro Toastmasters Club, "were J.J. Lembke, Herman Dempke, Andrew Large, and Oliver McCoy. They all purchased 100 acres or more, and all of them farmed their land in grain."

In 1911, the W.I. Hollingsworth Co. of Los Angeles bought out Lembke, Dempke, Large, and McCoy as well as all the land Peck had left of his personal holdings. Hollingsworth bought the land for about $200 an acre and began subdividing Harbor City in 1912.

By 1920, Harbor City had three thriving business enterprises. The Harbor City Canning Co. made tomato paste and shipped it all over the nation. The Harbor City Sash, Door, and Mill Co. sold its products to the building contractors of San Pedro, Wilmington, and Long Beach. That company also did a substantial business among the builders in the new Harbor City community.

Harbor City Sash, Door, and Mill Co. also operated the third largest industry in town with its three brick yards which did a thriving business. The right consistency of clay was found nearby, and Harbor City, like San Pedro, was on its way to becoming a progressive and prosperous integrated city.

G.E. Preston became the tract agent for the Hollingsworth Co. in 1916. He constructed a two-story brick building at the northwest corner of Belle Porte Avenue and 253rd Street. He leased the building for use as a store and the Harbor City post office.

G.G. Todd was appointed the first Harbor City postmaster. He was succeeded by A.H. Funk, Al Pifer, Ed S. Smith, G.G. Preston, and Charles Hofstetter. Jack Snider is the present postmaster in Harbor City.

Another former postmaster in Harbor City is Wilbur Hammond, the new postmaster in San Pedro.

Hammond was also postmaster in Lomita where he was one of the driving forces behind incorporation of that city. He is also a local historian of both Lomita and Harbor City. Alan W. Larsen is now postmaster of San Pedro.

Although Harbor City no longer touches San Pedro Bay and has no direct link to the harbor, it is still a thriving community of industry, commerce, and homes. Included among its residents is Rep. Glenn M. Anderson.

Harbor city is an integral part of the Harbor community.

73

Gen. George S. Patton and His San Pedro Connection

The Patton family were pioneers and prominent leaders in the early development of Los Angeles and the San Pedro Harbor Area. Through marriage the Pattons were merged with the Bannings.

THE EARLY LIFE of General George S. "Blood and Guts" Patton is closely linked to San Pedro, Wilmington, and Catalina Island. His father, George S. Patton II, was a prominent attorney and served as district attorney of Los Angeles County. Patton Avenue in San Pedro was named for him.

The elder Patton became a partner in the law firm of Smith & Patton, whose clientele included several affluent landowners and developers in the Harbor Area. When certain local land disputes and building codes dictated, the general's father would bring his young son to San Pedro with him and let him fish and play at the beach until his business was completed. Then they would return to their 1,800-acre ranch home near San Marino, property which was once owned by Don Benito Wilson, young George's grandfather.

In 1844 Wilson bought the Jurupa Rancho near Riverside from Juan Bandini of San Pedro. Wilson then married Ramona Yorba, whose father owned the large Rancho Santa Ana, most of which is now Orange County. After Wilson's wife Ramona died in the 1860's he married Margaret S. Hereford, widow of Dr. Thomas Hereford of Los Angeles. The couple had two daughters, Annie and Ruth.

George S. Patton II married Ruth, and their son, George S. Patton III, who became the general, was born at San Gabriel on Nov. 11, 1885.

Patton's family roots are deeply entrenched in America, especially in Virginia, where nearly all male Pattons were graduates of the Virginia Military Institute (VMI). During the Civil War all of them fought on the side of Robert E. Lee.

The first George S. Patton, who became a brigadier general at age 26, was killed in the Civil War. He was Gen. George S. Patton III's grandfather and namesake, his inspiration and his idol, whom he strove to emulate.

The first Patton's young widow was left with two sons and a daughter. Shortly after her husband died, she married Col. George Hugh Smith, a cousin and a wealthy, noted attorney. After the Civil War he came to Los Angeles to practice law, later becoming a California Supreme Court Justice. Smith was extremely fond of his stepson, George Patton II, and doted on George III, "a frisky, tow-headed lad who could ride a fast horse virtually before he could walk."

Young George's two loves were the classics and soldiering. It is said that at 7 years of age he could recite passages from the Iliad and knew the Bible by heart. He would startle his sister, Anne, two years his junior, by suggesting they play what he called Hector of Troy. "I'll be the horse and you'll be Hector," he proposed, then dragged her all around the yard.

Anne later married Phineas Banning's son, Hancock, and founded the Assistance League, whose members are pledged to devote many monthly hours to community projects. They have a chapter at Weymouth Corners in San Pedro.

In 1902 it was arranged that George would go to VMI to prepare for West Point, but at this time an attractive young girl came into his life, Beatrice Ayer, daughter of a Boston textile magnate, whose uncle, Joseph Banning, and his wife had a summer cottage on Catalina Island not far from the Ayers summer home.

At first Beatrice merely watched the Patton boy from a distance, not daring to hope to become friends with the hard-playing, rambunctious youth. But soon the family gave a reception, and George and Bea met face to face. It was love at first sight.

Beatrice was a tiny girl, small for her 15 years, and still playing with dolls. George was a six-footer and still growing, but Patton was never to court another girl, and Bea never had another beau. On Catalina they went sailing and horseback riding together. Before the summer ended, these teenagers, deeply in love, had forged an understanding that lasted all their lives.

After George graduated from West Point, he wanted to marry Beatrice, but first he had to get her father's permission. Frederick Ayer was one of the richest, most successful and aristocratic industrialists in America. He was a Brahmin to the core.

Ayer asked George why he chose the military for a career. "I feel it inside of me," he said, "and it is as natural for me to be a soldier as it is to breathe."

George and Bea were married in grand style on May 26, 1910, at Beverly Farms Episcopal Church on Cape Cod.

Nearly everyone is familiar with Patton's fabled Third Army, which he rode roughshod over Hitler's legions in 1944, thus becoming possibly the most famous fighting general in American history.

In May, 1951, this author had the honor as a representative of Sen. John Sherman Cooper to visit Hamm Cemetery in Luxembourg and to cover Patton's grave with fresh flowers passed to me by Minister Perle Mesta. On the plain headstone of the grave were 4 stars above his name: GEORGE S. PATTON JR., GENERAL 02605 3d ARMY.

Minister Mesta wrote the following letter to Mayor Robinson of San Pedro:

Dear Mr. Robinson:

One of your fellow citizens, Oliver Vickery, recently came to see me in Luxembourg.

He is indeed charming and I greatly enjoyed meeting him.

We visited Hamm Military Cemetery when he was here and laid a wreathe of flowers on the grave of General George Patton, who is buried there. The cemetery is situated in a perfectly beautiful spot, very quiet and serene. They are now replacing wooden headstones with large crosses of white marble.

It was a great pleasure to see Mr. Vickery and we had a wonderful talk about San Francisco. It is one of my favorite cities and I was very happy last spring to address the Commonwealth Club there.

With kindest regards, I am

Sincerely yours,

Perle Mesta

American Minister

July 31st, 1951

74
San Pedro and Wilmington Over a Barrel in 1909

A lively election campaign is described in this interesting narrative on how Los Angeles politicians protected themselves in event the harbor area did not vote for consolidation.

SINCE THE independent cities of San Pedro and Wilmington consolidated with Los Angeles, August 19, 1909, waterfront property, because of its strategic location, has had a growing demand with an ever-diminishing supply. And because of this fact the entire harbor has been the subject of major controversy ever since the merger.

The author has in his files the complete reports, numbering 25 typed pages on large legal size paper, all of them approved by the L. A. City Council. These working committees consisted of the L. A. Consolidation group which was chaired by Stoddard Jess, whose vice chairman was Joseph Scott, father of Msgr. George Scott. William D. Stephens, who became governor of California in 1917,

Harris Newmark, leading merchant, F.J. Hart, land developer, Leslie Hewitt, and Frank Simpson, legal advisors.

Other working committees represented the L. A. Chamber of Commerce, the Municipal League, Associated Jobbers of Los Angeles, the City Council and County Supervisors, the L. A. Merchants and Manufacturing Association, the Consolidation Committee of San Pedro, including John T. Gaffey, James H. Dodson, O. C. Abbott, A. P. Ferl, Benjamin F. Gross and James Swinford.

The Wilmington Consolidation Committee consisted of E. Opp, Charles Menvig, F. S. Cary, W. S. Moore and F. F. Breen. In addition all the recommendations of the various committees were ratified, confirmed, and approved by the following newspapers: *San Pedro Pilot, Wilmington Journal, Los Angeles Times, Los Angeles Examiner, Los Angeles Herald, Los Angeles Express, Los Angeles Record, Los Angeles News, Los Angeles Financier, Los Angeles Graphic,* and the *Pacific Outlook.*

During the campaign for votes, the City of Los Angeles distributed pamphlets and letters to strategic associations stating that the future development of San Pedro and Wilmington harbors would require large sums of money, and to accomplish this it would be vital that the City of Los Angeles have control, since it has sufficient financial strength to formulate and carry to successful completion the plan to construct and operate public docks, wharves, piers, and warehouses, and in connection therewith such means of municipally owned and controlled access and transportation thereto and therefrom as the needs of commerce should demand. [Also, it was noted that a municipally owned and controlled ferry be at once established at San Pedro, connecting said portion with Terminal Island, such charges to be made as necessary to pay the cost of operation, but in no event to exceed a two-cent fare, either leaving or returning to San Pedro.]

The consolidation also promised that a fire station be provided at San Pedro, the same to be fully equipped with modern equipment, and, as soon as practical after merger, that a municipally owned and controlled, adequate supply of fresh water be provided, for both private and public use.

The same "Whereas" was also inserted for an efficient police station, a public library, a fish market and a fisherman's wharf, as well as a system of kindergarten, primary and grammar schools and high schools.

"As now organized in the present city of San Pedro it will be immediately placed upon the same footing as to the course of study, manual training, equipment and accommodation and as to salaries of teachers and other attachees and employees of such school department as is now established in the present City of Los Angeles." This same "Whereas" was also provided for the City of Wilmington.

These recommendations were submitted to the Los Angeles City Council and

: 1. Harbor panorama in 1905, showing Dead Man's Island and dredge deepening the nel.

: 2. The SS Warrior and the SS Falcon, ships of Banning's Wilmington Transportation ıpany that transported passengers and freight from Wilmington to Avalon harbor on lina island in the 1880s through the 1900s.

Plate 3. Dead Man's Island viewed from Timms' Landing, foot of Tenth Street, San Pe
1870s. The island was removed in 1929 because it was a shipping hazard. (Photo courtes
Southwest Instrument Co.)

te 4. Schooner General Banning, 1883, sailed between San Francisco and Wilmington h freight and passengers. (Photo courtesy George Hugh Banning)

BUILDING A HARBOR

Plate 6. The Great U.S. White Fleet in San Pedro Harbor in 1908, three years before the breakwater was completed.

Plate 8. A barge containing rock from Catalina, circa 1899. (Photo courtesy Southwest Instrument Co.)

Plate 10. Phineas Banning's Wilmington Wharf, 1870, showing terminus of Banning's Los Angeles & San Pedro Railroad. (Photo courtesy Southwest Instrument Co.)

Plate 11. The Ferryboat Islander gave 10-minute service across the channel from the Pedro Ferry Building to Terminal Island. It provided service from 1940 to 1963, when Vincent Thomas Bridge was completed. (Photo courtesy Southwest Instrument Co.)

Plate 12. The SS Columbian, the first ship through the Panama Canal, at dock in Wilming Harbor, 1914. (Photo courtesy of Southwest Instrument Co.)

Plate 13. San Pedro Harbor in 1903, showing sailing ships unloading lumber from Eureka, Calif. (Photo courtesy Title and Trust Co.)

SAN PEDRO.
LOS ANGELES CO.,
CALIFORNIA.
1 CEMETERY
2 ELECTRIC LIGHT WORKS
3 MARINE HOSPITAL
4 "TIMS POINT"
5 S.P.R.R. WAREHOUSE, WHARF ETC.
6 PALACE BATH HOUSE
7 CITY PARK
8 HARBOR VIEW HOTEL
9 M.E. CHURCH
10 CATHOLIC CHURCH
11 CITY WATER TANK
12 PRESBYTERIAN CHURCH
SAN PEDRO HARBOR
PACIFIC OCEAN
EAST SAN PEDRO
PUBLIC SCHOOL BUILDING
BANK OF SAN PEDRO
RESIDENCE OF GEO. H. PECK
EISEN'S GENERAL MERCHANDISE STORE
CLAY BUILDING
EPISCOPAL CHURCH
BATH HOUSE
BOATS
CATHOLIC CHURCH
PRESBYTERIAN CHURCH
"TIMS POINT"
M.E. CHURCH

Plate 15. Artist's conception of the Rancho San Pedro home of Manuel Dominguez, showing Phineas Banning's Los Angeles & San Pedro Railroad Station, 1869. (Illustration courtesy George Hugh Banning)

Plate 16. Typical Phineas Banning stage coach in 1859. (Photo courtesy Southwest Instrument Co.)

Plate 17. These three Indian women returned to the Mission San Luis Rey for its rededication ceremony on May 12, 1893. They worked as young children in 1811, carrying adobe bricks for the mission's construction.

Plate 18. Avalon Boulevard in Wilmington, circa 1915

Plate 19. San Pedro's first railroad station, foot of Sixth Street, showing the first and only windmill in the harbor area, in 1889.

Plate 20. Headstone at the burial site of Jose Rodriguez Cabrillo, discoverer of California 1542, buried on San Miguel Island, 1543. (Photo courtesy Ernie Ehrke)

Plate 21. During the campaign by Los Angeles to take over San Pedro in 1909, a sign appeared over Beacon Street in San Pedro, shown here in reverse but reading "Take all but our harbor." The clock tower identifies the Bank of San Pedro, Beacon and Sixth Street. (Photo courtesy Southwest Instrument Co.)

Plate 22. Point Fermin Lighthouse built by [illegible] in 1874. (Ph[illegible]

Plate 23. Front Street in San Pedro in the 1880s. Upper left residence is the Rudecinda Sepulveda Dodson home on Seventh Street. The First Presbyterian church is shown upper right. (Photo courtesy Southwest Instrument Co.)

BIG BONANZA
FURNISHED ROOMS
GERMANIA
BEER HALL
6th St
Front St

Plate 25. Lumber cart and employees of the San Pedro Lumber Co., circa 1880.

Plate 26. San Pedro Public Library in 1906, located on Beacon Street across from pres
location of San Pedro Post Office. (Photo courtesy Southwest Instrument Co.)

Plate 27. Brighton Beach Resort on Terminal Island in 1890—a "Coney Island of the Wes
where many Los Angeles residents weekended. (Photo courtesy Southwest Instrument Co.)

Plate 28. Canal Boulevard in Wilmington, circa 1910. Stores and homes were on stilts. Mud from dredging was used to elevate the land level. This boulevard is now Avalon Boulevard. (Photo courtesy Security First National Bank)

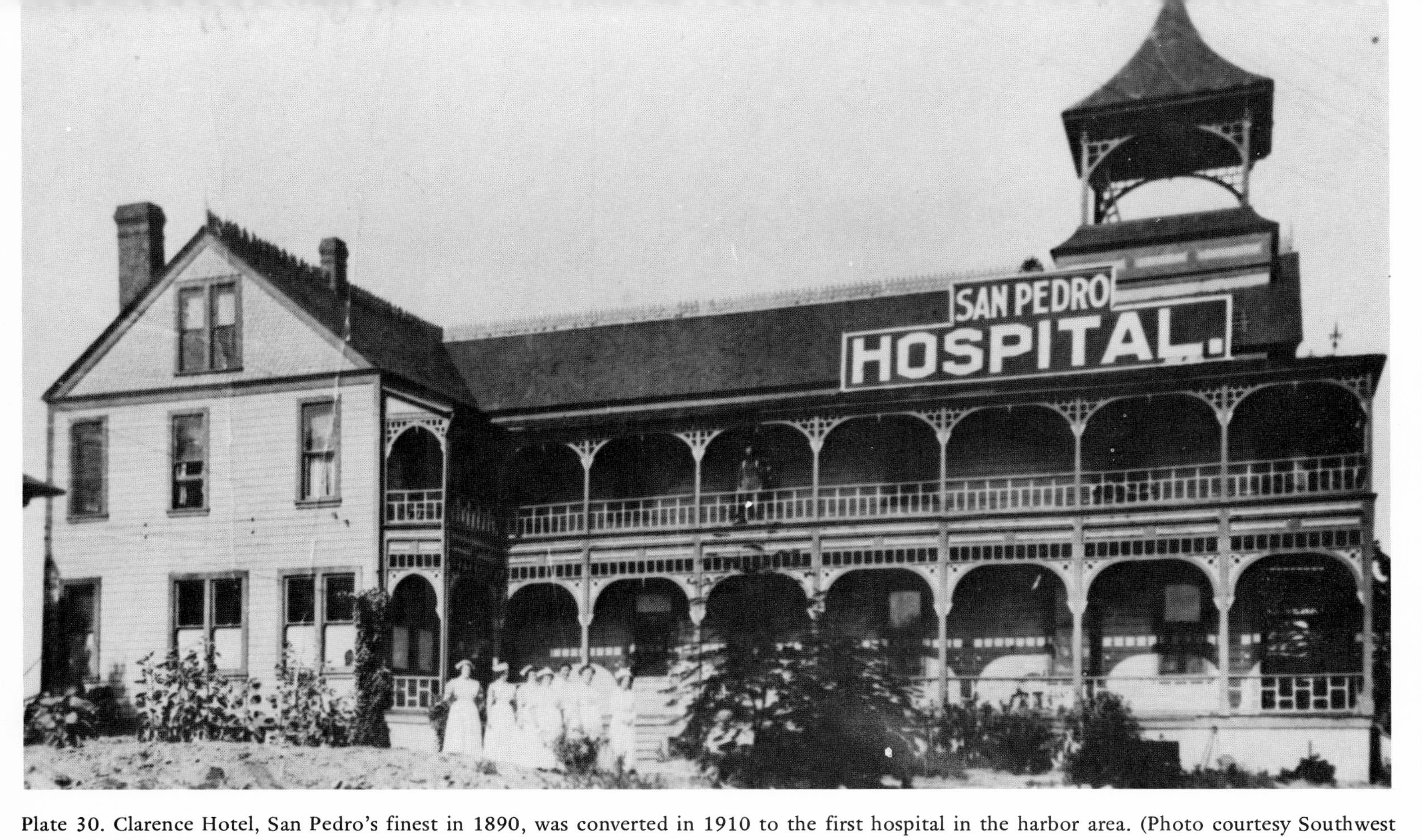

Plate 30. Clarence Hotel, San Pedro's finest in 1890, was converted in 1910 to the first hospital in the harbor area. (Photo courtesy Southwest Instrument Co.)

Plate 31. San Pedro was served by the Big Red Cars of the Pacific Electric Co., which on
served 100 million passengers yearly through 56 Los Angeles area communities but w
dismantled in favor of gas-driven vehicles.

Plate 32. Beach attire was somewhat more modest than today's, as these ladies demonstrat
during a sedate stroll down the Esplanade at Newport Beach in 1905. (Photo courtesy Ti
Insurance and Trust Co. and California Historical Society)

ıte 33. Phineas Banning at age 22. He arrived in San Pedro in 1851 and quickly proceeded
develop the Port of San Pedro and foster the growth of communities and the local
onomy. He was the founder of Wilmington, Calif. in 1858. (Photo courtesy of George Hugh
nning, grandson of Phineas Banning)

te 35. Banning's stagecoach in 1864.

te 36. A horse-drawn streetcar serving Los Angeles passengers in 1885.

Plate 37. Artist's conception of trading in hides in San Pedro Bay area, circa 1850.

Plate 38. Depot and cars of the Los Angeles and San Pedro Railroad in Los Angeles, 1869. The railroad was one of many projects Phineas Banning pursued to develop the Wilmington-San Pedro area.

Plate 39. Don Juan Bandini and daughter. The latter helped with the first American flag ever made in Californi
The Bandini name is still prominent in Southern California affairs.

Plate 40. General Andres Pico at time he surrendered to General John C. Fremont at the close of the Mexican War in California. Pico subsequently became an outstanding American citizen.

Plate 41. General John C. Fremont was California'
governor and first U.S. Senator as well as the Repub
party's first candidate for President. When he was
tary governor of California, Los Angeles was the s
capital.

42. Phineas Banning in 1884, one year
'e his death.

Plate 43. General Phineas Banning, standing, with Mathew Keller, left, vineyardist, and Colonel John H. Hollister, noted cattle and sheep raiser.

.te 44. From an early photographic panel, four of the prominent financial and industrial
.nes in California history, left to right, Leland Stanford, Mark Hopkins, Charles Crocker,
d Collis P. Huntington.

Plate 45 Stagecoach of Captain William Banning in front of Banning House, Wilmington, about 1924

e 46. Mayor Tom Bradley of Los Angeles with Author Oliver Vickery, wearing General
ıeas Banning's Civil War uniform, at a ceremony in 1978.

: 47. Oliver Vickery with his wife, Grace, in front of the Banning Mansion and Museum.
author was curator of the Banning complex from 1965 to 1975. (Photo courtesy Port of
Angeles Public Relations Department)

Plate 48. The Danish Castle, an old San Pedro Landmark, built in the 1880s, with J
Mandia, Grace Hoxworth, and William Oleson, the executive committee of the San Pedro
Historical Society, on the balcony, 1978. (Photo courtesy Port of Los Angeles Pu
Relations Department)

Plate 49. At the Banning Mansion Wisteria Festival of 1972, from left, Oliver Vickery, Mrs. Fred Lorenzen, Robert Rocker, Marga Jean Lucas, Don Lucas, Fred Lorenzen, Patricia Clark, and Daniel Clark, were actors in a playlet of Phineas Banning's household in 1882.

Plate 50. Presentation of bronze plaque to Civil War Drum Barracks by the Daughters of the American Revolu
January 15, 1978, left to right, Mrs. Fred Lorenzen, President, Society for the Preservation of Civil War Drum Barra
Oliver Vickery; Congressman Glenn M. Anderson of Harbor City; Mrs. Everett E. Jones, Vice-President Genera
California, National DAR; Mrs. John M. Reed, Director, District 9, DAR; and Marga Jean Lucas, "Miss D
Barracks."

Plate 51. Civil War Gatling gun found in the Dominguez dump by two youths pictured, left to right, Herbert Cox, who with Joe Kerrico found the gun; Mrs. Fred Lorenzen, President, Society for the Preservation of Civil War Drum Barracks; Kerrico; and Oliver Vickery. The gun had disappeared for 15 years.

passed. After the election, they were signed into law, August 19, 1909, allowing a $10 million harbor bond issue, guaranteed by Los Angeles, to give the harbor a good financial start under the new consolidation.

People often ask what really prompted our leading citizens to turn over our harbor, over which they had control, to Los Angeles and lose control. The vote was not too impressive. San Pedro cast 726 votes for merger, and 227 against the merger. Los Angeles City voted 11,478 for consolidation, 109 against.

Let's give our local leaders credit for squeezing the best possible concessions they could get out of Los Angeles. It was inevitable that the control would fall into Los Angeles' hands regardless of the vote. Surely they knew that when Los Angeles annexed Harbor City on November 12, 1906, that it was the grand scheme of the city to have its own harbor since Harbor City included a large stretch of land that touched San Pedro Bay just east of the west basin channel. Plans called for deepening a canal, permitting ocean-going ships to dock on Harbor City property. [It was an escape valve in case the voters of San Pedro and Wilmington turned down the annexation proposals. That part of Harbor City stretching to the bay became parts of Wilmington and San Pedro. Actually the "independent" cities of San Pedro and Wilmington were over the proverbial barrel—this time a water barrel!]

75

Streets Are Named for Meyler and Fries

These engineers helped enormously in building the San Pedro bay breakwater, and streets named for them have become landmarks.

THE TWO MEN who engineered the building of the San Pedro Bay breakwater, started in 1899 and completed in 1911, are landmark names of men honored by having streets named after them. Capt. James J. Meyler, (Meyler Street in San Pedro) and Capt. Amos A. Fries, (Fries Avenue in Wilmington). Both men worked for the Army Corps of Engineers.

It was these two men who struggled through masses of government red tape and financial pressures to produce the world's largest man-made port.

Through the advantageous contracts they negotiated, the work was done cheaply enough to allow for lengthening the breakwater by 750 feet at the outer end to a total of about 12,000 feet.

The breakwater up to low water is a rubble-stone mound. The granite rocks below low water weigh from 100 pounds to 15 to 20 tons each, two-thirds averaging more than 1,000 pounds each.

As originally designed, the width of the sub-structure at low water was 38 feet, but this has been increased to 48 feet by a berm (a narrow ledge) on the harbor side.

The superstructure begins at low water and ends 14 feet above the two walls being laid in courses with rectangular blocks of granite rock. On the ocean side there are four courses, each 3½ feet thick with no stone weighing less than 16,000 pounds.

The harbor side is built up of seven courses, each two feet thick, with no stone weighing less than 6,000 pounds, while the interior is filled solidly with all sizes of rocks. The width between the outer edges, ocean and harbor, at the bottom is 38 feet; at the top, 20 feet.

It was necessary to build a double standard railway trestle to haul the huge rock boulders which came from quarries, first near Chatsworth and later from a granite mountain near Riverside.

The very first barge load came from Santa Catalina Island.

Two traveling cranes converted from steam shovels were used to unload the heaviest boulders for both the superstructure and the substructure.

Even before the breakwater, in 1871, the year Dead Man's Island was connected by a jetty to Terminal Island, the annual commerce of the harbor was 50,000 tons. In 1888 it rose to 450,000 tons, and today it approaches 30 million tons.

Before 1900 most of the ships that came to San Pedro bay were sailing vessels with huge lumber cargoes. This tonnage meant the arrival and departure of several hundred ships each year. There being no anchorage completely protected from storms, a ship was occasionally wrecked by being driven against Dead Man's Island, or ashore on the mudflats. It was these wrecks which caused a strong demand to form a harbor of refuge with a breakwater.

About the time of the Civil War, the best landing place was shifted from San Pedro to Wilmington, and Mormon Island came into prominence as the center of barge and lighter construction. The island is now connected with Wilmington proper at the end of Fries Avenue, and is controlled by the U.S. Borax Corporation. Mormon Island is the only tideland property not subject to harbor department rentals.

The port's comprehensive master plan presents a view of the Port of Los Angeles as it will look and function by the end of the century. This study defines the effects of dredging various areas with the harbor, 65 feet for the outer harbor for a deep-water channel and turning basin which should accommodate the 165,000 DWT ships. Dredging would be required to a depth of 82 feet.

Waterfront property is in growing demand as availability diminishes and is the subject of major controversy. Assemblyman Vincent Thomas, D-San Pedro, until recently carried the ball for many years on behalf of the harbor department in relations to tideland monies, insisting that these dollars belong to the harbor department and not to the City of Los Angeles.

76

Faults Are Thick Where Love is Thin

In pre-war days, the local Japanese made White Point in San Pedro a popular hotel resort center that attracted visitors from far and wide.

THERE IS AN old saying that "faults are thick where love is thin." This axiom became obvious within our own local ethnic social structure when the Japanese government attacked Pearl Harbor, Dec. 7, 1941.

The U.S. government set up a civilian defense system to protect the Los Angeles Harbor, and all Japanese were classified as enemy aliens, even those nisei who were born in America and were actually American citizens.

At the time there were several hundred Japanese in and around San Pedro. Many owned homes and property on Terminal Island, where they had erected a Shinto temple. Most Japanese were farmers and gardeners on the Palos Verdes Peninsula; some of them were expert albacore fishermen.

Shortly after Pearl Harbor our local Japanese were given only enough time to grab a handful of personal belongings and dispose of their farms and homes at a fraction of their worth. They were immediately sent to relocation centers far removed from the coast, to Arkansas, Utah, Colorado, and other states.

For many years the Japanese ran a successful and fashionable health spa at White Point, with five natural hot sulphur pools supplied from a flowing spring nearby. They also operated a two-story hotel and restaurant under the management of the Agami brothers, headed by Tamiji who kept the hotel and baths fully occupied most of the time. While the abalone fishing was in its prime in the 1900s an amusement center know as "Japanese Village" was built. A bus line ran between White Point to the red car line depot in San Pedro. There was a steady flow of visitors from "Little Tokyo" in Los Angeles to White Point.

However, when war broke out the Japanese had already left White Point. Many became farmers on the large Sepulveda mesa lands above the cliffs. The old hotel and bath area was used by the U.S. Navy for gunnery practice. All that is left there today is a cement skeleton of a fountain and several large concrete slabs.

Art Almeida, 47, born in San Pedro, graduate of S.P.H.S. and Harbor College has become the recognized authority on White Point and the Japanese families of the harbor community. He has researched many archives, prowled old cemeteries, interviewed most of the Japanese who came back to the harbor after their forced removal during the war, and has written several articles on the subject that have appeared in the *Los Angeles Times, Long Beach Independent-Press Telegram,* and the *Rafu Shimpo,* a Japanese daily newspaper.

Mr. Almeida is of the opinion that the Japanese-American, although unsung, unknown, and unheralded, has contributed greatly to the economic and social development of San Pedro and the Palos Verdes Peninsula. Mr. Almeida also found that in the 1890s the Japanese were diving for abalone off White Point, and pin points where the Japanese pioneers erected abalone racks, jetties, and storage sheds. His great delight is showing old Japanese albums and interviewing close relatives of the first pioneers.

"The Japanese," Mr. Almeida observes, "are sensitive people, and their love for their ancestors and their close-knit families motivated them to save most of their picture albums when they were forced to leave most everything else to the war defense authorities."

A San Pedro community advisory group made up of close relatives of the Japanese pioneers is assisting Mr. Almeida in his search for more information about the early San Pedro and Palos Verdes Japanese. They are Masaichi Ishibashi, Yikio Tatsumi, Sumi Seo Seki, Sumako Inouye Nishiaka, Peachy Imanaka Shimizu, Midori Yasuda, and Kanichi Kawasaki.

It is well known that before the war Japan had been buying considerable scrap iron, steel, rubber, cotton, aircraft equipment, oil, and gasoline through the Port of Los Angeles. In 1940 we stopped all exports to Japan, and also froze all Japanese government assets in the United States. Most historians believe this inflamed Premier Hideki Tojo and made the Second World War inevitable. However, subsequent investigation and intelligence have proved the Japanese Americans in California knew nothing of the shenanigans between Japan and the U.S. State Department. But when Hawaii was bombed all of them became suspect.

Recently the author met knowledgeable Louis Sepulveda, 85, whose father Ramon Sepulveda, owned all of White Point and leased it to the Japanese. Louis said this geographic location was named White Point over 100 years ago because of its white cliffs, visible for many miles. Moreover, Louis mentioned the late Wilbur Woods and his first fish canning factory that became a new force in the harbor economy. Louis also complimented Art Almeida for his scholarly interest in the Japanese, whom his father found to be honest, hard working, loyal, and highly respectable.

This reminded the author of the time in 1951 when Cliff Duffy, warden of San Quentin, invited him to inspect the prison on behalf of the *Oslo Aftenposten* to ascertain that there were no Norwegians among the 5,000 inmates. Come to think of it, neither were there any Japanese prisoners—not one.

77

Pioneers in Leaded Glass windows

On display at the San Pedro Elks Club are four beautiful leaded stained glass windows depicting leaders who gave San Pedro greatness.

SAN PEDRO has been fortunate in producing many unselfish leaders who have given more than cursory attention to our historic past, and who glory in our rich harbor heritage. Among them are Al Atchison, the late Leon Dwight, and Thomas Benton Roberts.

In Shakespeare's *Tempest,* he wrote, "What's past is prologue"; and in 1911, when the late James H. Dodson, Sr., and his wife, Rudicenda Sepulveda Dodson, contributed four leaded mosaic stained-glass windows to the San Pedro Elks Club, they gave four historic sermons in prologue in the likenesses of Juan Rodriguez Cabrillo, Sebastian Vizcaino, Gaspar de Portola, and Stephen M. White. They were originally installed as windows in the old Elks Club at Seventh and Palos Verdes Streets, where for a time they lay in attic dust—unsung, unheralded and almost forgotten.

When the Elks moved to their palatial new home in the San Pedro Hills, four blocks above Western Avenue, these precious windows were carefully cleaned, packed, transported and installed as lighted displays in the Main Bar overlooking the ocean waters these four men once knew.

However, it was the dedicated efforts of Roberts who preserved and made it possible for posterity to see and to enjoy the genesis of our harbor history in these masterpieces as they are now displayed. They are indeed a work of art and worthy of careful scrutiny.

CABRILLO. In 1542, just 50 years after Columbus, Cabrillo sailed from New Spain (Mexico) and landed on California soil, thus providing the undisputed factor in Spain's successful claim to California, which it controlled until Mexico took over in 1822. An imposing statue of Cabrillo towers above the bay at Cabrillo Beach. Recently this writer was a guest of the U.S. Coast Guard aboard its Cutter, Walnut, to visit Cabrillo's grave on San Miguel Island, where he was buried in January 1543. Cabrillo named our area Bahia de Fumos, Bay of Smokes.

VIZCAINO. This great adventurer was in the old Spanish galleon trade with the Philippines. In 1602, he made a California voyage to check on Cabrillo. When he came to the area Cabrillo named The Bay of Smokes, Vizcaino promptly renamed it in honor of Saint Peter–San Pedro in Spanish. Vizcaino was the Marco Polo of the sea, observing coast contours, drawing outlines, taking soundings, and classifying the fauna and the flora. Moreover, it was Vizcaino who named all but one of the offshore islands for saints–Santa Catalina, San Clemente, Santa Barbara, San Miguel, Santa Cruz, Santa Rosa, and St. Nicholas. Vizcaino said Anacapa Island, made up of rugged crags and mountain tops, was unworthy of a saint.

PORTOLA. His coming with Father Serra in 1769 made the world conscious of California, prompted, no doubt, by fears of Russian and English encroachment. Portola would build praesidios, embarcaderos, and pueblos. Serra would build missions and convert the Indians. It was this expedition that discovered, by accident, San Francisco Bay. Portola was searching for the famed Monterey Bay, highly recommended by Vizcaino, but Portola missed it by 100 miles. Many historians believe that had Sir Francis Drake discovered San Francisco Bay during his pirating voyage in 1579, world history would have been different.

WHITE. United States Senator from California, Stephen M. White, became famous in Congress and the Los Angeles Harbor community in 1899 with his brilliant oratory and debating skill as the one man who saved the Port of San Pedro and Wilmington from being removed to Santa Monica. Collis P. Huntington and the Southern Pacific Railroad had built a mile-long pier and spent fortunes in their abortive attempt to transfer the port of entry to their monopolistic shipping empire to Santa Monica. In Los Angeles, there is a life-size bronze statue of White at Hill and First Streets. In the Los Angeles Harbor area, he is also honored with a Stephen M. White Boulevard, and a Stephen M. White Junior High School.

78

Chambers of Commerce Beams

The San Pedro and Wilmington Chambers are a necessary adjunct in disseminating community information to the public without charge, and are the basis of good citizenship and an aid to business.

SINCE A CHAMBER OF commerce is an association which promotes the interests of its members and the community in general, it is well to know something about its functions and history, especially in San Pedro and Wilmington.

Both chambers have been successful in bringing new industries and home buyers to the Harbor Area, furnishing free information and pamphlets about the advantages of locating here.

Pertinent facts are offered about transportation, climate, housing, schools, churches, and utility rates. The chambers also provide information about steamship berths, religious sites, such as Wayfarers Chapel, and such scenic and entertainment highlights as Marineland, Cabrillo Marine Museum, and Ports O'Call Village.

More and more people are asking the chambers about the 117-year-old Civil War Drum Barracks and 115-year-old Banning Manor in Wilmington, as well as the 105-year-old Point Fermin Lighthouse in San Pedro, still standing majestically, proud in its old age retirement where one may reminisce about the old clipper ships which her beaming lights guided safely to our port.

San Pedro also has been the gateway to Catalina Island for many years, reached by the Big White Steamer, the SS Catalina, or by yacht or seaplane.

The first idea of an association of business people originated in the old Roman empire. The first group, however, to have the name of "chamber of commerce" was organized in Marseille, France, in 1899. It has since caught on throughout the world since.

The San Pedro and Wilmington Chambers of Commerce have been, and still are, active in building a community of which all can be proud.

When the San Pedro chamber was organized in 1906, there were 21 charter members. Within a short time, however, several other prominent local landmark names were added to the membership, including Ramon Sepulveda, James M. Dodson, Philip M. Gaffey, and C. H. Cleveland.

Others were George Peck, Edward Mahar, R. C. DePuy, B. B. Lippman (97 and still going strong), Eloi Amar, Ray Mitchell (founder of Marine Hardware Co.), and Jess Knight, father of Goodwin Knight, who became governor of California in 1953.

During its formative years, the chamber faced many problems, as it still does, but it seems to have resolved practically all of them.

At this April 19, 1906 meeting, members oversubscribed their request for funds to help the San Francisco earthquake and fire victims; and on April 19, 1907, on motion of A. P. Ferl, the surplus of $766.09 was turned over to local charity causes.

On June 9, 1906, the chamber authorized a representative with expense money to accompany the first yacht race to Honolulu.

On June 30, 1906, the chamber worked with our harbor commissioners for the location of the fish canning industries.

A mass meeting was held October 13, 1906, to protest articles published in the *Los Angeles Herald* derogatory to the reputation of San Pedro (a tactic calculated to soften us up as unworthy so Los Angeles could take us over).

O. C. Abbot, Ray Mitchell, W. H. Wyatt and Joseph Atchison were appointed to "journey to Los Angeles and complain bitterly about such trash editorials."

On March 21, 1907, plans were laid for holding an annual "water carnival" for the Fourth of July each year. Also at this meeting, a committee was appointed for a cleanup campaign in San Pedro just as when Henry Soto was appointed for the same job in 1970. Tons of debris were collected by volunteers, mostly by junior chamber members. (Page Soto, San Pedro could stand another cleanup.)

In January 1908, the chamber appealed directly to President Theodore Roosevelt to have the Great White Fleet stop in San Pedro during its around-the-world tour. The chamber was successful.

On March 27, 1908, the chamber elected a new board of directors, including John T. Gaffey, E. H. Bautzer, W. F. Bickenback, Charles Adair, A. K. Maloy, Frank Burns, A. L. Selig, S. M. Storer and E. L. Blanchard. They were instructed to protest to Washington, D.C., against the sale of Fort MacArthur reservation. Three of the committee members went to the capital to protest personally on behalf of San Pedro. History often repeats itself.

Under the date of October 16, 1908, it was resolved that "the chamber urgently recommends the adoption of an up-to-date fire alarm system for San Pedro as soon as possible."

On September 1, 1910, Mr. Mahar was thanked for the use of the Banning's S. S. Hermosa for moonlight excursions to raise funds for the chamber and the San Pedro Publishing Co. was thanked for its donation of display cards and advertising space in the *San Pedro News* about the moonlight trips.

On April 17, 1915, J.T. Gaffey suggested the establishment of a U.S. naval station in San Pedro. During this month, measures were also started for the acquisition of Cabrillo Beach.

As a result of chamber of commerce activities, San Pedro did get a naval base here in August, 1919. The fleet was commanded by Adm. Hugh Rodman, who was given a rousing welcome by some 100,000 people.

This was the base for 12 dreadnaughts and the personnel of the unit at once became a part of the San Pedro community, buying homes and sending their children to the new schools built for this purpose.

Long Beach finally got our fleet base away from San Pedro for Terminal Island. However, the chamber prevented it from going to other ports such as San Francisco. They tell us even while we sleep the chamber is always working for the best interest of San Pedro, Wilmington and the harbor.

The late President Harry S. Truman, a former Kansas City haberdasher, said in one of his speeches, "If we didn't have a chamber of commerce, we would have to invent one."

79
ORIGIN OF THE SUFFIX MARU

More ships come to San Pedro Harbor with the suffix Maru than any other type. Japan is our biggest customer.

WHILE THE AUTHOR was a guest speaker recently at San Pedro High School in Marian Grinnell's popular class on harbor history, an alert student asked a question on the origin of the word Maru, which he said he often sees on ships in the harbor.

It was a good question. It prompted some extra research that has brought out some unusual and interesting historical items missed in college history. There have been diverse opinions by different authorities on the derivative of the word Maru, but the word originated in China and was borrowed by Japan. Emperor Kublai Khan of China bestowed the suffix Maru to Marco Polo, an Italian traveler, during his exploits in Cathay in 1292.

In the December 19, 1928, issue of *Moji Shimpo,* a Japanese magazine, there is an extensive article on the subject of Maru, by Enosuke Nakamura. He wrote, "According to legend in ancient China, during the reign of Emperor Kotei, there was a man by the name of Tae-tes-shi to whom a messenger from heaven, called Hakudo-Maru, appeared and taught him the heavenly art of shipbuilding. Since then Japanese ships have been named with the suffix Maru in deference to the heavenly instructor, Hakudo-Maru."

To call a ship Maru is, according to the heavenly system, to give ships due reverence to this deity. According to Nakamura, in olden times, Japanese leading families had the name Maru appended, which added greatly to their stature and social level. It also was given to the names of male children of noble birth or pages serving in Buddhist Temples.

"To express a man, or to express oneself, Maru Maro, was often used in the old times," Nakamura wrote. "Thus, there were the names of Fukiwara-Maro, Hito-Maro, Marco Polo-Maro (Maru)."

The article also mentions that in ancient times domestic animals, such as horses and dogs, were called Maru, such as Setzu Maro for a horse, and Okina Maro for a dog. Names of swords used to guard oneself often were suffixed with Maru. Even favorite castles and towers in Japan are called in the endearing term of Maru.

Nakamura states his own views of Maru as follows:

"It is true that from old times male children were named with suffix Maru and the reasons for so naming are, first, it sounds euphonious; secondly, Maru stands for roundness and for shapes more symmetrical than a triangle or a square and therefore beautiful; thirdly, Maru signifies harmony and possesses the meaning of encouragement for the future, braving all the difficulties of life and the reaching the shore of success with the same intention applied to the names of ships.

"It also felicitates the future of ships so they shall ride over dangerous seas without mishap, thus, Maru applied to a ship personifies it and felicitates its future. Contrary to the Western usage, treating a ship as a 'she' of the feminine gender, the Japanese and the Chinese consider ships as a 'he' of the opposite sex."

Pete Mandia, harbor department economist, gave the author a few statistics of the economic impact of the Japanese and other Asiatic ships that come to our port.

"For many years Japan has been our best customer," he said. "In 1977, 329 Maru ships came to the port, Great Britain was second with 262, Norway was third with 242 ships."

The 1978 Annual Harbor Report shows that, tonnage-wise, Japan imported more goods through the San Pedro port than all other nations combined with 1.5 million tons. Next highest was the Netherlands with 365,000 tons. Korea was next with a quarter million tons.

"Let's be realistic and face the facts," Mandia said, "All port cargo business is highly competitive with Long Beach and other California ports, and historic records show that the Los Angeles port business increases when personal contracts are made by sending, periodically, harbor commissioners and other department experts to Japan, Hong Kong, Taiwan, Korea, and other foreign ports. It is not an expense to the taxpayers, but a prudent investment that pays big dividends for the continued development of the harbor."

80

Understanding Through Travel—Out Mexico Way

While in Mexico the author researched the National Archives for California land grant titles, and for other historical knowledge for this book. His impressions herein are published at the request of local Mexican groups.

THERE IS MUCH more to Mexico than can be seen by automobile or by plane trips. Much more than meets the eye at Tijuana, Mexicali, or Juarez. To bring this truth into its proper perspective one should take a train trip as we did recently.

It was a tour of 43 people, boarding the Pullman train at Mexicali and, after a few side trips, riding all the way to Mexico City. It was a grand, awesome, and thrilling travel experience. When you glue your eyes and ears attentively on the tour guide, you will understand how the archaeologists, geologists, and ethnologists have dug deep into the ancient ruins of pre-Columbian history and brought forth a new concept in American research.

You will learn that it was in Mexico that early Western man first observed that seeds falling on the earth produced a new growth of corn. Because of this simple knowledge, man in Mexico changed from a hunter about 1,500 B.C., to a farmer, and from a destroyer to a creator. Thus the seeds of civilization on our continent took root.

At San Blas, about 300 miles south of Mexicali, the group made a never-to-be-forgotten side tour east to the mighty Sierra Madre mountains. The trip is over a new railroad that has opened for viewers one of the most remote and isolated sections in the world. You cross the Continental Divide three times, traverse 73 tunnels and ride over 60 bridges to get to a "believe it or not" spot called Barranca del Cobra. This is a recently discovered and mostly unexplored mountain range where the untamed Tarahumara Indian Tribe live in a gorge larger than our own Grand Canyon. The train stops long enough for an unobstructed view at a place where Indians meet the train and sell their wares. The government guides will tell you that most of the valleys and mountains you see have never heard the footsteps of modern man.

You travel through mountains and tropical forests, over rivers and canyons of indescribable beauty. It is said that it cost Mexico more money to build this railroad than it cost the United States to build the Panama Canal. However, the guide proudly informs you that during the 10-year construction period, surveyors and engineers found enormous mineral wealth for Mexico including gold, silver, platinum, copper, lead, zinc, iron and even precious gems.

The trip from San Blas to the barrancas and back took a full day. The Pullman cars which had been side-tracked at San Blas were waiting for the trip to Guadalajara and Mexico City. From the train windows and observation car could be seen evidence that in many sections the good earth of Mexico had been shamelessly mistreated. Like the spindly legged burro, the soil had been over-worked, neglected, and barely cultivated. Perhaps this contributed in large part to Mexico's early poverty and social decline, but no more. Today a water canal system traverses the heart of Old Mexico, transforming it into an agricultural paradise.

For hundreds of miles on either side of the train one may see luscious growth comparable to California's Imperial Valley. Sugar beets and cane fields, a great variety of fruit orchards, vegetables, grapes, alfalfa, pineapple, corn, wheat, rice and other grains ripen under an abundance of sun-kissed cloudless skies. This was particularly noticed from Hermosillo to Mazatlan, then southeast all the way to

Acapulco. There are a few shanties and hovels left, but one should go by train to see and appreciate the great step forward Mexico is now making for its people. From the train, and by bus from Mexico City to Acapulco and Taxco, one can view the high central plateau. It is an awe-inspiring series of mountain ranges that surround and separate one valley from another. Some highways snake through high mountain passes, but only by train can one behold the real majesty of Mexico and feel the new national consciousness of its people.

In Mexico City one sees where Agustin de Iturbide paraded his army through decorated streets on September 27, 1821, when bands blared, bells rang and cannons roared at which time Mexico took control of California from Spain. It was Mexico's most jubilant hour. At the Historical Museum were seen records of some of Governor Pio Pico's communications in 1845, with old California families such as the Pioneer Sepulveda, Dominguez, Bandini, De Valle, Carrillo, William Workman, Manuel Garfias, Hugo Reid and others.

Mexico City itself is one of the most cosmopolitan centers in the world. It has a population of nearly 6 million. Even Paris does not excel her in educational and cultural attractions. Her museums are rich in history and folklore. Her art galleries are conversation pieces, Mexico's world-famed Folklorico ballet ranks with Moscow's Bolshoi, and, like the Bolshoi, reservations must be made weeks in advance to secure a seat, otherwise stand.

Mexico's ancient Pyramids, built by advanced civilizations of antiquity, are about the same distance from Mexico City as are the Egyptian Pyramids from Cairo. Guide Bruce Thomas demonstrated that a high voiced yodeler can bridge the distance. It is that close. The Mexican pyramids are just as mysterious, inspiring and thought provoking as any ever found.

The Paseo de la Reforma reminds one of Paris' Champs Elysee, but the Reforma is wider, longer, more interesting and makes one less foot-sore in walking its intriguing length. The old Castle in 2500-acre Chapultepec Park is a miniature Versailles. Here one can relive the love, hope and despair of Emperor Maximilian and his Queen Carlotta. The Palace has recently been refurbished in gilt elegance precisely as when political fate overtook these royal pawns by the intrigues of Louis Napoleon in 1867.

Mexico's intelligentsia are changing Mexico from an essentially agrarian and cattle economy to an industrial one. Large steel mills, chemical and fertilizer plants, appliance, generator, and cement factories have sprung up. American names are prominently displayed on factory buildings such as Ford, General Motors, Chrysler, Dow Chemical, International Harvester, Aluminum Corp., General Foods, Campbell Soups, Pepsi-Cola, National Distillers, Kodak, and many others, altogether employing thousands of Mexican workers with good wages. Mexico still has many basic problems in building a prosperous nation. Presently she has no major fiscal worries. Her economy and political stability is on a sound basis, and the American dollar is interchangeable by mutual agreement. If you have pesos left after your trip any Mexican bank will give you the equivalent in dollars—no questions asked, and no fees taken.

The population and tourist explosion have created a new era in the hustle and bustle of her people, who take it in stride and ask for more. Modern hotels are being built steadily; during the past five years a new one has been opened almost every month. The National Lottery is their Social Security. It is big business, centered in an imposing building on de la Reforma Street, where it is said a lucky ticket holder can win unheard-of wealth for a few pesos.

The Mexican peasant and his family are smiling again as their children play and eat under the benevolent school administration of cultural opportunity for everyone. These are projects financed solely by their social security. Gone are the old haciendas once staffed with indentured peons. In their place are schools offering instruction in the new technology of how to become stalwart citizens in the know-how of modern civilization.

Throughout the centuries no people have suffered more or complained less than the Mexican. He has been damned, admired, satirized, envied, and serenaded, and with it all no one enjoys a siesta or fiesta with its frills and thrills and fandango more fully or more romantically or with more abandon than our friends south of the border.

Adios, Amigos!

81
Banning High School in Wilmington

The old Phineas Banning High School in Wilmington, and the Richard Henry Dana, Jr., High School in San Pedro, were condemned in 1972.

AN IMPORTANT Harbor landmark was occupied in the fall of 1975 with the completion of the new Phineas Banning High School in Wilmington. It was a great relief for Principal James Hanley and 3000 plus students.

For the previous years, classes had been cramped in rows of bungalows while the new school was completed. Most of the bungalows were moved the following summer to Dana Junior High School in San Pedro and made ready for classes during the erection of a new Dana Junior High.

At the Dana Advisory Council board meeting February 1, Principal J. W. Pluim of Dana outlined the plans with a chart depicting the set-up of how the Banning High bungalows and other changes were to be made for his classes in the fall. The Council then voted unanimously to accept the plans as presented.

Principal Dave Carter of San Pedro High School was there and promised full cooperation from his school.

Hanley is enthusiastic about his new school structure at Banning. He pointed out on a chart the five new master buildings including the Main Classroom Building housing 87 classrooms; the Fine Arts Building with a 520-seat auditorium; the cafeteria with a multi-purpose room holding 450 people; the Physical Education Building with two latest-style gyms; Second Arts Building with six classrooms; a new half-Olympic size swimming pool approved, but subject to financing from a local assessment district. "It may take two years before the pool is ready," Hanley said.

He calculated the total cost of the new school and the pool at less than $13.5 million, "and this will probably be the last of the new, big comprehensive high schools in the Los Angeles School System."

Hanley emphasized the pool will be a community center with proper lighting, a facility sorely needed in the Harbor Area. We were happy to know that Hanley will personally supervise the placing of the metal plaque on the main building which honors Phineas Banning. It reads: "The Class of 1929 Dedicates This High School To The Wonderful Spirit and Vision of General Phineas Banning." This steel plaque was taken from the old Banning High Main Building.

There are many notable graduates from Banning High School. Among them are: Mildred Naslund, superintendent of the large Area "A" Los Angeles School District of which Wilmington and San Pedro are a part; Robert Shepherd, president, Allstate Insurance Co.; Walter H. Putnam, president, California Fish and Game Commission; Dr. Albert Anderson, founder, San Diego Chargers; Jack Gifford, specialist in space techniques; and Dr. James Morse, prominent orthopedic surgeon.

Education is big business, the largest industry in the country. It consumes a large percentage of our national and local budgets. Practically all of our population is directly involved with it, in one capacity or another. In every city, no exception, education claims the lion's share of the local budget. And rightfully so.

No one appreciates this more than Dr. William Johnston, superintendent of the Los Angeles School System, and Mildred Naslund. They are both doing their best to provide the finest in educational facilities in accordance with their limited budgets.

This writer is not unfamiliar with their problems. Years ago when Bill Johnston was principal of adult education at Gardena High School, he and the author went house to house ringing doorbells asking for votes to pass bonds for education. It is still the finest investment in all the world.

The present Banning High School and the Dana Junior High School have been condemned as unsafe. Both schools have maintained high scholarship standards throughout their existence, thus preparing its graduates for life and livelihood and making the Harbor Area a finer place in which to work, play, and live.

A school system is much more than teachers and students. It is construction, maintenance, and utilization of facilities. It is purchasing, warehousing, and distribution. It is administration, accounting, and personnel. It is transportation and food service. We in the harbor district have an important role to play in all these developments, as parents, as citizens, and as businessmen. Education in the arts and sciences is the backbone of our future, the only hope we have for our moral, economic, and social prosperity.

The spirit of Phineas Banning and Richard Henry Dana, Jr., should become more indelibly imprinted in the hearts of our citizens in the construction of these two progressive educational institutions. Both should be edifices that will continue to hold even higher the torch of scholarship standards, and become great schools of which every student, every parent, and every citizen should be proud.

82
Wilmington's First Bank

The Banning family sold most of Wilmington in lots. The first houses did not have "inside plumbing," only out-houses with two and four holers.

RECENTLY Los Angeles Harbor Commissioner Nate DiBiasi, who is an ardent history buff, met the author at the old First National Bank Building at the southeast corner of Avalon Boulevard and "C" Street in Wilmington.

This old building, constructed in the 1890s, has undergone considerable repair and is now occupied by Olney, Levy, Kaplan, and Tenner, a large law firm that offers special advice to the port commission pertaining to maritime law.

In one of the rooms is the remnant of a bank vault, and on the shelves were some old cancelled checks bearing the signatures of several well-known local citizens of the 1900s such as the bank's founder Paul Eubank, J. H. Dodson, W. T. Gaffey, E. W. Sandison, Don Fohl, J. P. Widney, F. D. Foote, T. F. Keavenly (once owner of the property where Drum Barracks is located), W. I. Travis (first high school principal in Wilmington), William Lambie (once owner of the largest ship propeller firm in the harbor), A.J. Lembke (the town baker) and Albert Boschke (for 50 years the caretaker of the Banning Plot, known as the Wilmington Cemetery).

The Bank of America let the author see a copy of a deed to a lot at 203 W. Opp St., Wilmington, that was sold for $10 to a Mr. and Mrs. Bert M. Forbes of Los Angeles. The deed was signed by Joseph B. Banning in 1910.

The deed reads: "No house costing less than $1,500 plus a necessary "out-house" can be erected on this lot; nor shall any building erected elsewhere be removed or placed upon said premises."

The deed is quite comprehensive and stated emphatically "that no part of said premises shall ever be used directly or indirectly for the purpose of rending malt or vinous spirits or any intoxicating liquors therein . . . and in the event of a breach of any of said conditions, the title to said premises hereby conveyed, shall immediately revert to and rest in the grantor, his heirs, or assigns, who shall thereupon be entitled to the immediate possession thereof."

Today there is a very modern apartment house on this lot that is probably worth about $500,000.

In 1909 after Wilmington, along with San Pedro, was annexed to the City of Los Angeles, Joseph B. Banning, son of Phineas Banning, was put in charge of selling some of the extensive Wilmington property from his father's estate. Joseph did very well. There is no record that any property he sold was ever repossessed. In 1909 Wilmington's population was about 1,200; today it is 50,000.

The Banning heirs insisted that every applicant for lots be carefully screened so they could pick the people who would most likely contribute to the economic, social, and cultural progress of Wilmington and the community.

The Bert M. Forbes family and their succeeding generations have contributed generously to the historical atmosphere of the Banning Mansion and Museum. While the author was the curator there for more than 10 years, he saw an historical marker imprinted with the name of Mrs. A. S. C. Forbes attached to a large display of antique canes and walking sticks, used mostly by the Banning family and their guests.

The Forbes family moved to Wilmington from Los Angeles to a house they built in 1912 that cost less than $1,500, including the inevitable out-house. Even the 30-room Banning Mansion, completed in 1864, had no plumbing to begin with. For years well-trained gardeners kept the four-holers in two out-houses clean and in good order.

83

SOAP, SOUP, AND SALVATION

One of the world's finest non-profit organizations contributed much to area welfare with its gracious ministration to the spiritual and economic welfare of millions of grateful people.

THE SAN PEDRO Salvation Army opened its doors in 1890, and ever since has helped nearly every hardship case referred to it. Sometimes it was not an easy task, but the Army seems always to provide the help where it is most urgently needed.

The local church, known as a corps, at 439 S. Grand Ave., serves a congregation that includes Wilmington, Carson, Harbor City, Lomita and San Pedro.

In 1977, grocery orders were issued during Christmas for 216 families, many with several children. In addition the church has cooperated fully each year with the San Pedro Chamber of Community Development and Commerce in its Christmas programs for needy families.

Lt. Jerry Ames, local commander of the Corps, said the needs will be even greater this year due largely to increasing inflation and unemployment. More families are applying for aid this year than ever before.

"My staff is straining every effort to meet the need of the indigent families," Lt. Ames said. "Especially their children who are already asking about Santa Claus and toys—worried about being ignored."

Alice Hall, who has been a soldier of the Salvation Army for over 40 years, is possibly the most historically knowledgeable person in the local corps.

She says there are more than 16,000 churches in 82 countries using 109 different languages.

"There is absolutely nothing in San Pedro or elsewhere that can take the place of the Salvation Army," she said.

Delving further into the statistics found in the Army's recent yearbook, the author was amazed at the enormous size and influence of the world-wide Salvation Army. It maintains 250 large food distribution centers and serves more than 20 million meals a year, provides more than 10 million beds, and manages 70 maternity homes for unwed mothers and 13 institutions for the blind.

Moreover, it maintains 10 homes for the crippled and serves 721 leprosy patients in Hawaii, Asia, and Africa.

Worldwide, the Army has more than 26,000 officers, all of them ordained ministers. It also owns or leases 131 fresh-air youth campsites. The San Pedro

Corps controls one in the Santa Monica Mountains, open yearly from June to August.

The Salvation Army was founded in 1865 by William Booth, an English Methodist minister whose aim was to preach the gospel and to help the poverty stricken. Booth organized his followers along military lines, and his congregation appointed him a general. He gave full equality to women, and many of them were ordained to preach. Up to this time public speaking by women was unheard of.

Booth was the first to organize musicians with trumpets, clarinets, tambourines, and drums and preach outdoors from street corners. Saloon keepers yelled competition, often hailing the soldiers into court.

But Booth and his corps maintained their courage, and in the slums their motto was, "Soap, Soup, and Salvation; clean them, feed them, and convert them."

It is recorded that Booth in 1867 was determined that his brood should have a fine Christmas and a happy, old-fashioned celebration. But when he returned from preaching at Whitechapel Christmas morning he was sad and grim.

Suddenly he burst out, "I never want to see a Christmas like this again." Then stalking the room like a lion, he told of the sights he had seen:

"The poor have nothing but the public almshouse—the terrible spectacle of children crying for bread on the streets is too awesome and heartbreaking. Many children are not born into this world, they are damned into it!"

The next year Booth was in the slums again, this time distributing plum puddings, many of them having been made in the Booth kitchen. It is said this was a foreshadowing of the millions of Christmas dinners the church was later to distribute in the Whitechapels of the world.

In 1880 Commissioner George Railton and seven women came to the United States as the first official delegation of the Salvation Army. They set up a corps in New York and Philadelphia and soon were working in the slums of America. Ten years later they arrived in San Pedro.

The San Pedro Kiwanis Club has made a yearly project of having members service Salvation Army Christmas kettles and ring the bells on street corners.

84
Suang-Na Indian Rancheria

San Pedro had the largest Indian Rancheria of about fifty that were scattered in what is now Los Angeles County. Suang-Na Rancheria has been honored.

THE LOS ANGELES City Recreation and Parks Department recently accepted title of some surplus land offered by the federal General Services Administration, consisting of 49.5 acres of Palos Verdes Drive North, between Western Avenue and Gaffey Street in San Pedro. This land is adjacent to the U.S. Navy Depot and is to be used in perpetuity only for park and recreation purposes.

At the recommendation of Councilman John S. Gibson, the Recreation and Parks Commissioners voted to name the site "Suang-na" in honor of the Indian village which Juan Rodriguez Cabrillo saw when he landed in San Pedro Harbor in October 1542. Cabrillo named the whole area "Bahia de Fumos" after observing smoke emerging from the hills.

This name was recorded by Cabrillo and sent to the king of Spain. It was not changed until the arrival of Sebastian Vizcaino in 1602, when Vizcaino renamed the area in honor of Saint Peter. However, the Indians still called it Suanga na. It was the largest Indian Village among about 50 others in what is now known as Los Angeles County.

The Indian Rancheria in Los Angeles was known as Yang-na; in San Gabriel, their village was called Sibag-na; in Palos Verdes, Chowig-na; and in Catalina Island, Pineug-na. Gibson suggested to the park board that the name be spelled as pronounced, adding a hyphen and two letters to the word. It was originally spelled Suanga na.

There were about 1,500 huts in the Indian village, composed largely of bullrushes and tules, and the Indian family would live in the hut until it was unservicable and then build another. The Indians usually burned these huts, and some historians now believe it was the smoke from these smouldering fires which Cabrillo saw, and not smoke from rabbit holes, as Cabrillo reported. The area provided abundant game of all kinds. Rabbits were plentiful and easy to catch.

This site, which will now be made into a public park and recreation center, formerly housed a series of quonset huts built during World War II for the Navy. There is a 2.5-acre tract compound on the property which contains six homes. All of them have recently been heavily vandalized.

Gibson has been working to have the compound buildings cleaned up and leased at $1 a year to the American Youth Hostel Association and the Boy Scouts. Gibson's office reported the Federal Bureau of Outdoor Recreation in San Francisco is currently discussing the possibility of leasing the property, as requested by Councilman Gibson. The Recreation and Parks officials have already approved a bikepath development from Western Avenue to Five Points adjacent to the 49.5-acre property.

Hugo Reid, a native of Scotland, came to Los Angeles in 1834. After a few years, he retired to San Gabriel, where he married the daughter of the Gabrielino chief, an Indian tribe named for the San Gabriel Mission. Reid devoted himself to the study of Indians. He died in 1852, leaving perhaps the most complete authentic Indian history and folklore records of any extent. Reid's essays, customs, languages, and legends of the California Indians are still valuable texts in many schools of the Los Angeles Unified School System.

According to Robert Glass Clelland's book *From Wilderness to Empire,* Alfred A. Knopf, publishers, there were about 250,000 Indians in California. When Cabrillo and Vizcaino arrived, the Indians were not nomadic; each group lived within a limited territory. It was one great family under distinct chiefs. Clelland said the Gabrielinos and the Chumash of Santa Barbara, together with the San Pedro Shoshones, were the wealthiest Indians in California. Reid said these tribes spoke nearly the same language, with the exception of a few words, and each tribe could be distinguished by its local intonations in speaking.

Reid also pointed out that the San Pedro Indians were not aggressive fighters as were the Indians of the eastern states. They depended more on language, food sources, and topography than upon political or social organization.

The San Pedro Suang-na Indians had close trade relations, selling their wares to other Indian groups including the Indians of Los Angeles, San Diego and Santa Barbara. Even today Indian trade relics are often found in the San Pedro hills by amateur archeologists.

85

Art Linkletter Lived Here

Linkletter is not a stranger to San Pedro. He has extensive roots in its life and lore.

A RECENT NEWS-PILOT article by Joseph Bensuoa about the poet and storyteller, Richard Armour, a former San Pedran, reminds one of another famous storyteller, Art Linkletter. He also lived with his parents in San Pedro as a youngster and attended kindergarten here. It was where he first learned that "kids say the darndest things."

The author first met Linkletter in San Francisco in 1939 when he was there representing the import-export firm of Owesen & Company of San Pedro. Linkletter was a roving radio reporter for the Roma Wine Company.

When Art put a mike in front of the author in the lobby of the St. Francis Hotel and asked where he was from, Art seemed to feel a closeness with him when told the author was from San Pedro. His face lit up when he said he spent his early life in San Pedro.

After he interviewed others in the hotel lobby for his 30-minute live program, which was broadcast over station KPO, the author made it a point to get better acquainted with him. The author was invited to be his guest at some of the shows at the fair (his favorite was the Folies Bergere).

Just before the fair ended in October he wanted to give a farewell champagne party for the Folies before they returned to Paris and asked if he could use the author's penthouse apartment for an all-night shindig.

It just so happened that an affluent importer friend had asked the author to live in his full-floor penthouse home while he and his wife took six months to see the world. The author was delighted to let Art entertain his friends there. It turned out to be a grand affair with a professional violinist, pianist, and a xylophone player.

Right after the Fair closed, Linkletter joined up with early television and became a leader in the entertainment world. He is the author of several books and is a sought-after dinner speaker.

The author thought his contact with him was ended but took a chance and invited him to be his guest when he was being honored with a testimonial dinner in 1976. But Linkletter has a good memory and a good heart and surprised the author when he wrote an amusing letter to Jerry Bresnahan, the emcee, to be read at the dinner. It is dated March 27, 1976, and reads:

"I was alarmed recently to hear that a number of folks in the L.A. Harbor community are giving Oliver Vickery a testimonial dinner.

"Things must really be at the bottom of the well to dedicate an entire evening for this kind of event when you could all just as well be home figuring out how to cheat the IRS. I would be there myself but I have a much more important event. . . I have been asked to emcee the annual Miss Live Bait Barge in Tijuana. However, I do know something of Oliver and his past. . .

"He was so dumb that he lit a fire in a simulated fireplace in his apartment where he was entertaining the Folies Bergere with an all-night party of some 50 guests. It was during the 1939 World's Fair at San Francisco, of which I happened to be the official emcee. Had it not been for a couple of chorus girls of the Folies putting out the fire with their shawls, the house could have burned down. Oliver takes chances like this . . . he likes to see girls putting out fires!

"This was during a time I had a radio show and interviewed people from the street. I met Oliver, asked him a few questions, and he talked so loud and fast that it blew out a fuse! I might add that the Roma Wine Company, my sponsor, provided all the champagne for Oliver's penthouse party. Oliver is like that, you provide the free champagne and he'll give a party, give him a testimonial dinner and he'll eat it up.

"Seriously, San Pedro and the Harbor brings back pleasant memories for me because my folks settled at Point Fermin when they came from Canada and I had my first job in the Point at the age of 6, licking ice cream cones as a shill for the vendor.

"Every good wish to all of you, and I know this party will be a wonderful evening of camaraderie and insults." Art Linkletter.

Of course, the soiree in 1939 was all arranged by Linkletter. Notable celebrities have a clever way to take the conceit out of anyone having a testimonial and to cut them down to size. The author is still in touch with Art, who has promised to make a long overdue trip to San Pedro and tell something of his early life here.

When Linkletter does come to visit the harbor, the author intends to turn him over to a bevy of attractive local women, who, although not especially of the Folies Bergere type, would, nevertheless make him feel at ease. They are, Renee McNett, manager, San Pedro Chamber; Volney Scott, president, Woman's Division of the Chamber; Mary Jo Olk, supervisor, Pac Tel and Tel; Grace Hoxworth, president, San Pedro Bay Historical Society. Plus a few beauties among the local Angelenas tribe, starting with Marga Jean Lucas, Betty Bloom, Lillie Trudnich, Jackie Pike, Emelyn Parslow, Joan Lorenzen, Katie Papadakis, Angie Papadakis, Wilma Deets, Beryl Olds, Barbara Sonneborn, Thora Pratt, Barbara Hopkins, Isabel Willingham, Eileen Pulliam, and Sarah Hampton.

This group of darlings is bound to impress Art Linkletter no end. In fact, the author bets his last paragraph that Art will find them much more attractive and knowledgeable than the Folies Bergere from Paris. Besides, they speak our language and can keep step to any tune. Come on down, Art.

86
Elks Come to Graze

The BPOE Elks from its beginning in 1905 has contributed millions of dollars to worthy causes in San Pedro. Good Americanism is their forte.

THE OLD three-story building at the southwest corner of Seventh and Palos Verdes Street in San Pedro, was built by the Elk's Club in 1909. It is fireproof and has met the test of time with its reinforced steel beams, large timbers, girders, and columns which support the structure.

The interior of the building is soundproof. The third floor had rooms for eight bachelor quarters, the second floor was the Lodge room and the secretary's office. The first floor was reserved for clubrooms consisting of pool and card tables, and a recreation room with steam bath, dining space, bar, and kitchen. On the Palos Verdes Street, ground floor side, there were rental stores. In 1958 these rental spaces were closed and used for more office space and for storage rooms. The total cost of the building when completed in 1910 was $65,343.15.

The lodge edifice was built to last, but, due to a large increase in membership necessitating larger quarters with additional athletic facilities, the members moved on March 18, 1968, to a 11.4-acre tract into their present home in the San Pedro Hills, four blocks above Western Avenue, off Morse Drive.

It is reported that on June 5, 1905, when Elkdom first started in San Pedro other Elks traveled from near and far via horse and buggy, automobile, special train and ship, congregating on San Pedro from all points of the compass, during which time the community was bedecked in red, white, and blue bunting. Beer flowed freely and good cheer and camaraderie reigned throughout the harbor area.

The BPOE Elks Club was founded in New York City on February 16, 1868, by Charles A. S. Vivian, and it has grown nationwide with approximately 2,200 lodges with almost two million members. Its principal ingredient is loyal Americanism and all that it implies in freedom and charity.

In the 1920s the San Pedro Lodge became famous for its traveling band that went throughout California for performances, winning the acclaim of other lodges that gave generously of their cups and other honors. For a short time San Pedro Leader B. B. Lippman was a member of this fifty member group. Msgr. George M. Scott became Chaplain in 1956, and Grand Chaplain in 1965. Scott is always urging members to become active and participate in community affairs for worthy causes.

It has recently come to light that Rudecinda Sepulveda de Dodson donated one of her homes in 1910 for a raffle to raise funds for the interior furnishing and decoration of the club at Seventh and Palos Verdes. Tickets sold for one dollar each, and about $10,000 was raised for antiques and art work. Bill Russell, a long-time Elk and history buff, is a good source of information about Elkdom in San Pedro.

In addition, Rudecinda donated four leaded mosaic stained glass windows in the likeness of Juan Rodriguez Cabrillo, Sabastian Vizcaino, Gaspar de Portola and Stephen M. White. They were originally installed as windows in the old building. For a time they lay in attic dust, untended and almost forgotten. However, when the Elks moved to their new Lodge, member Tommie Benton Roberts took charge of these precious pieces, carefully cleaned and repaired them, and personally transported and installed them as lighted displays in the main bar room overlooking the ocean waters these four men once knew. These masterpieces actually represent the genesis of our harbor history. For permission to view them get in touch with any San Pedro Elk who may vouch for you.

Records at the Lodge show Roberts as an engineer, electrician, artist, and musician. He supervised the construction of the new building. Moreover, *Popular Mechanics* in its March 1946 and March 1949 issues features Roberts in glowing terms as the "Admiral" of Hollywood's Navy, having propped and skippered over 100 boats for movie thrillers, including, "Two Years Before the Mast," "Mrs. Miniver," "Captains Courageous," "Fast Life," "Frenchmen's Creek," and "Mutiny on the Bounty." He is given credit for building models of rum-runners, speedboats, kyaks, dugouts, sampans, skiffs and clippers, and using Harbor Lake for MGM, 20th Century Fox, Warner Brothers, and other studios that came to film some of their sea thrillers.

A few years ago Roberts invited me to his home in Wilmington, and I found it a symphonic lesson in lights and shadows; of art and artifacts, of fiddles, flutes, drums, trombones, piano-halves, horns and organ interiors, all wired to music with the slip of a switch. On the mantle was a framed letter from Tommy and Jimmy Dorsey thanking Roberts for resigning in 1919 from a professional band to give them a chance to make good.

With delicate tools and harp-like wires Roberts creates wonders out of rosewood, pine, spruce, cedar and hemlock, and with pride and persistence he usually gets it done in harp-like harmony.

87
AYRE'S CASTLE

Vern Ayres was an imaginative aviation stuntman and a creative builder of a San Pedro landmark.

THE SIX-UNIT apartment building at 3437 Peck Ave., San Pedro, known as The Castle, was built and owned by the late Vern Ayres, who enjoyed a colorful and spectacular career, often adventurous and dangerous.

Ayres was a World War I veteran. He flew biplanes in the war; was one of the early stunt aviators and one of the first Alaskan bush pilots; taught aviation and stunt flying; and owned the Ayres Aviation Service in Seattle and Portland.

His life and experience paralleled the history of aviation.

In June 1922, Ayres wrote a thrilling aviation episode for the Portland Oregon Rose Festival. In a full page advertisement in the *Portland Oregonian* of June 18, 1922, he featured his main attraction, "Miss Elfleda," in glowing terms:

The text began:

"The world's most famous and fearless little lady wing walker, Miss Elfleda, a mere slip of a rosy-cheeked girl who knows no fear and has no nerves . . . the same girl who created a coast sensation last year at the beach when she fell to a CERTAIN DEATH but EMERGED ALIVE with a smile of triumph for having again scientifically demonstrated the EXTREME SAFETY IN AVIATION with that old army aviator whom you all know so well—Vern Ayres. . ."

Ayres married Miss Elfleda. They moved to San Pedro in 1925 and started construction of The Castle, inspired by a classic Scottish castle. They chose the highest peak on Peck Avenue for an unobstructed view of the ocean and the breakwater panorama.

Elfleda told the author that the foundation and the building itself are reinforced with steel rods, so the building should have a comfortable life-span into the next century.

The Castle's new owners, Mr. and Mrs. Gordon Millman, are doing considerable repairing, refurbishing, and painting. They showed this writer crates of old papers and memorabilia left by Ayres.

One of the items is a document in Imperial script, signed by the Emperor of Japan, which appears to be the official declaration of war on the United States and Great Britain.

The document, which is accompanied by an English translation, carried a notation written by Ayres:

"Tokyo, Japan, Oct. 1945, translation made for Vern Ayres by Miss Jessica Kawasgee, who is one-half Japanese and one-half Persian, speaks English, Russian, Japanese, Chinese, French, Persian and German."

Ayres added a postcript:

"P.S. I 'borrowed' this from the Emperor's Gold Room at the Diet Building, Tokyo."

The author believes this record has important historical significance and, with the consent of the Millmans and the Ayres' heirs, he is donating it to Pete Mandia, president of the San Pedro Bay Historical Society for its archives, directed by Flora Baker.

Several years ago, Ayres spoke of his experiences before the San Pedro Kiwanis Club at the old Hacienda Hotel.

The minutes of that meeting reveal that Ayres said he started flying before World War I in Chicago. He signed up as an instructor of pursuit combat aerial gunnery with the Canadian Royal Flying Corps when he had only 12 hours of solo flying experience in the Jenny (JN4D), the "flying coffin" that had a Curtis engine of "90 doubtful horses," he said.

Ayres also told the audience that he flew Pacific Marine Airways' HS2L flying boats. These were passenger planes serving Catalina Island. The aircraft utilized pusher motors from Pacific's headquarters at the foot of 22nd Street in San Pedro.

He said Cecil B. DeMille and William Wrigley were frequent passengers.

Ayres also told about another episode involving the bravery of his wife. It seems she broke several fingers once, while dangling above Portland from a rope 20 feet from the wingtip of Ayres' biplane.

She was unable to pull herself up the rope to the wing, as she was supposed to do in the act, so she hung on for dear life while Ayres flew in close to the ocean so she could be dropped in safety.

In the *San Pedro News-Pilot* of Jan. 21, 1961, the late Bynner Martin wrote:

"Vern Ayres wired President Kennedy yesterday asking him as his first official act as President to give relief to a disaster area by getting a skunk out of his castle."

Martin said Ayres told him that the skunk somehow got in his home during the night and took refuge under his bed.

After he divorced Elfleda, and in the sunset years of his life, Ayres became a lonely man in his castle.

His son, Vern Jr., a retired San Pedro fireman, says of Ayres:

"In his retirement he dreamed of putting a moat around The Castle and erecting a drawbridge to keep out invaders like the Feudal lords of old."

88

George Peck's Mansion

This mansion is still an attractive landmark in San Pedro. It is reconstructed and fully occupied.

THE OLD George Peck Victorian mansion built in 1887 at the foot of 14th Street, near Timm's Landing, is still standing in simple modesty and fully rented at 380 W. 15th Street in San Pedro. The house was moved there in 1914.

The home was originally erected on a wooded hill, fringed by a large pepper and two eucalyptus trees on a bluff overlooking the ocean immediately above the port facility known as Timms' Landing. Nearby was another old palatial home owned by Aurelia Sepulveda, who was a brother of Ramon Sepulveda, and Rudecineda Sepulveda de Dodson. Ramon had a home at 438 Fifth Street, where his son Louis Sepulveda now 83 was born, and Rudecinda lived with her husband James H. Dodson, Sr., in their mansion on 7th and Beacon Street, which has been moved to Parker and 13th Street.

In 1961 this writer went into partnership with George Ash, local landowner and manager of several San Pedro properties, to purchase this old home, which was owned by Mr. E. Cammerenesi. His three daughters, Mrs. Mary Caprio, Mrs. Julia Mardesich, and Mrs. J. Bergstrom, handled the sale for their father. Mrs. Bergstrom was the principal negotiator for her father and took care of his interests for many years prior to his death.

Mrs. Bergstrom told us that her father's purpose in purchasing the Peck Mansion was to move it to its present site on his lot and converting it into an apartment building over a 66 x 34 foot cement foundation where he had built space for two stores on the street level. When the Peck home was made secure over the foundation, the Cammerenesi family moved into the second floor. In 1939 this floor was converted into two separate apartments. The third floor was rented to others, and during the housing shortage during the World War II the third floor space was occupied by two families, both sharing the same bath and kitchen. Mrs. Bergstrom and her husband occupied the third floor apartment for a time. But in later years her father kept the third floor apartment for his personal use, renting out the two apartments on the second floor, and the two store spaces on the ground floor.

From 1957 to 1961 this writer also was manager of Andreassen & Co., successors to Owesen & Co., a marine electric ship supply and export firm that supplied electric winches and parts for foreign ships. The firm rented the entire ground floor and combined the two stores. In the rear of one of the stores was an old bakery oven which seems to have been the first pizza and bread oven of Pietro Di Carlo. When the author left the premises in 1961, the oven was still there.

George Peck's attractive daughter, the late Rena Peck Anderson, spent many delightful and happy years in the early days of this imposing Victorian home, with picture windows, breezy verandas, extra wide front staircase, and the many gables, fancy shingles, rosettes, and cupolas affected in the architectural style of the period. Rena practiced her music lessons on a solid ebony upright piano, since generously donated to the Drum Barracks Museum by her proud son, Herbert Peck Culler.

The bathroom was adequate for the period, containing large zinc tubs encased in wooden frames. At first water was heated on a wood stove and carried in, as at the Banning Mansion in Wilmington. The Peck residence was elegantly furnished with soft Victorian settees and chairs which sat on flowered and plush carpets. Like the Banning home, the Peck mansion had a marble fireplace and carved wooden mantles which held art objects typical of the time.

According to the reports, quilting bees took place in the parlor rooms, and tea and receptions were served in another room. There was a six-by-ten foot mirror, framed in red velvet, and heavy sliding doors which could separate the living room from the rest of the house. After 1900, Peck purchased some leaded plate glass windows which were used to enclose part of the veranda overlooking San Pedro Bay. They are still there.

Property values have risen enormously in San Pedro in the intervening few years. A good example is the old Peck Home. When the property was bought in 1961, the price was $15,000. Recently, George Ash, sole owner in 1977, turned down an offer of $100,000 for it.

And values didn't start going up until right after the author sold his interest!

89
John Gibson's Lookout Point

Rare judgement was used by the City Council in buying San Pedro land at bargain prices and using it for strategic benefit to the public.

SAN PEDRO'S popular Lookout Point, at the top of Gaffey Street between 34th and 36th streets, was saved by a narrow margin in 1958, when the plot of 1.42 acres was put up for grabs by the federal General Services Administration.

The area was part of the Fort MacArthur land deed and was declared surplus by the GSA, which sent out applications for bids.

Ernie Ehrke, San Pedro supervisor for the Los Angeles Department of Recreation and Parks, heard about the sale offer and alerted his boss, George Hjelke, general manager. Ehrke felt the city should turn in a bid for the site; otherwise, the land might go to a building promoter who would construct an apartment complex.

Sure enough, a building contractor, Joseph C. Ash, of Los Angeles, offered the high bid of $35,000 to be consummated at an auction on May, 28, 1958. The auction was attended by nearly 100 residents. Ash told them he would erect a large apartment building on the site if the city did not exercise its priority privilege.

Immediately, numerous San Pedro civic and service organizations protested the sale for private use. Telegrams were sent to U.S. Rep. Cecil King, Los Angeles Mayor Norris Paulson, Assemblyman Vincent Thomas, and to Councilman John S. Gibson, who had just started his second term.

Gibson got busy, called a special meeting of the city council and, when they approved his proposal, contacted Hjelke to go ahead and use the city's priority. The priority gave the city the right to buy the site for one-half of the highest bid, or $17,500, when the land was to be used for recreational purposes.

At the same time Gibson also had the council approve the purchase of another scenic spot consisting of 6.46 acres as government surplus by the GSA. This land is adjacent to Point Fermin Park, between Paseo del Mar and the ocean, extending from Roxbury Street, 1,700 feet to the east to the park proper.

The land is actually a rocky slope extending from the edge of the street to the ocean.

The property was bought by the city for $151. "The greatest bargain since Phineas Banning, in 1857, bought 2,400 acres from the Rancho San Pedro for $1.10 an acre for the town site of Wilmington," Gibson said. "I am extremely happy to hear that Lookout Point has been preserved for the residents of San Pedro and for thousands of other visitors who will be attracted to this historic site."

Both checks were drawn on the funds set up by the 1957 Recreation and Parks bond issue passed by the voters. The author was told there hasn't been another bond issue passed by the voters for recreation purposes since that date, although many efforts have been made.

On May 28, 1958, Hjelke wrote a letter to Udell C. Hoft, acting chief of the disposal branch of GSA: "It is understood that these two payment checks will be held by you as a deposit until such time as the proper deed or deeds can be granted to the City of Los Angeles." Both deeds were now under the control of the Los Angeles Department of Recreation and Parks.

The ocean front site is now the Nature Trail project, created by local poet Dick Wolfe, in close cooperation with Gibson and approved by the city council. The acreage has become an active site with well-kept trails where thousands of school kids and others come in busloads during the year to hike, study, and learn something about the region's wild life.

The Nature Trail Society meets regularly, keeps minutes, discusses educational and recreational projects, and often has tours in conjunction with John Olguin, Bill Olesen, and the Cabrillo Marine Museum.

Possibly, the most pressing need right now in San Pedro is getting a suitable location for a new library. Ann Rumery, local librarian, has said, "With Gibson's demonstrated expertise in obtaining surplus sites, as he did recently for the Korean Bell location, the Friends of the San Pedro Library Association are looking forward to this accomplishment in the very near future."

90

Nick Zorotovich and Benjamin Franklin

The accomplishments of Benjamin Franklin should live forever in the hearts of the American people.

NICK ZOROTOVICH, chairman of the San Pedro Bicentennial Committee, asked if the author could write about someone other than Phineas Banning, who would be of unusual interest to the people of the Harbor Area in the spirit of our Bicentennial anniversary.

The author thought of several, some of whom signed the Declaration of Independence, but the greatest of all, he decided is Benjamin Franklin. His contributions have affected all in the harbor community. He was a statesman and a diplomat, a scientist and an inventor, a philosopher and a humorist, a printer and a journalist.

Franklin touched greatness in many ways. He was the only man to sign four of the essential documents that made American democracy function: the Declaration of Independence, the Constitution, the Treaty of Alliance with France, and the Treaty of Paris that ended the Revolution. The alliance with France, signed February 6, 1778, allowed Franklin to enlist the services of Lafayette and the French navy that enabled Washington to win at Yorktown in 1781. The author saw evidence of this during his recent trip to Yorktown.

Franklin led all the men of his time in his concern for the happiness, well-being, and dignity of mankind. George Washington expressed it succinctly in a letter to Franklin in 1789:

> "If to be venerated for benevolence, if to be admired for benevolence, if to be admired for talents, if to be esteemed for patriotism, if to be beloved for philanthropy, can satisfy the human mind, you must have the blessing to know that you have not lived in vain."

Franklin's face has appeared on postage stamps, and on the silver and paper money of the United States. Two of our Presidents bore his name. Franklin Pierce and Franklin D. Roosevelt. He became Postmaster General in 1775 and organized the first postal system. He gave his salary to the relief of wounded soldiers.

During the signing of the Declaration of Independence ceremonies, John Hancock warned the other signers: "We must be unanimous, there must be no pulling different ways; we must all hang together."

"Yes," Franklin replied, "we must indeed all hang together or assuredly we shall all hang separately."

Franklin's discoveries showed Americans how to improve acid soil by using lime. In the tense period when California ranchers changed from cattle to agriculture this knowledge was a great benefit. This piece of wisdom came from copies of *Poor Richard's Almanac,* a publication that made Franklin famous and rich even before he entered politics. Franklin was the first to advocate daylight savings time and the first to organize a city hospital. He invented bifocal eyeglasses and a stove that gave more heat than other stoves and with much less fuel. His lightning rod demonstrated his saying that, "An ounce of prevention is worth a pound of cure."

Moreover, Franklin discovered the Gulf Stream in the Atlantic Ocean and charted its course, temperature, and depth. And he showed sailors how to calm a rough sea by pouring oil on it. He was the first to organize a fire department and the first to establish a subscription library, where members contributed money to buy books, and then used them free of charge.

He established an academy that grew into the prestigious University of Pennsylvania. In 1788 he became the first president of the first antislavery society in America.

Franklin knocked himself unconscious when attempting to kill a turkey with an electric shock. When he regained consciousness, he said, "I meant to kill a turkey and, instead, I nearly killed a goose!"

Franklin tells how he started his almanac: "In 1732 I first published my almanac under the name of Richard Saunders; it was continued by me about 25 years and was commonly called *Poor Richard's Almanac,* I endeavored to make it both entertaining and useful and, accordingly, it came to be in such demand that I reap'd considerable profit from it, vending near 10,000 . . . it was generally read, scarce any neighborhood being without it."

Some of *Poor Richard's* sayings were:

"The worst wheel of the cart makes the most noise."

"If you know how to spend less than you get, you have the philosopher's stone that turns into gold."

"Keep your eyes wide open before marriage, half shut afterward."

"When you play, play with all your might, when you work do not play at all."

"A man's years should not be counted until he has nothing elese to count."

"The person who throws the most mud loses the most ground."

"Early to bed and early to rise makes a man healthy, wealthy and wise."

Franklin died April 17, 1790, at the age of 84. He was buried in the cemetery of Christ Church in Philadelphia. When his will was read, it began with these simple words: "I, Benjamin Franklin, printer. . ."

Franklin left $5,000 each to the cities of Boston and Philadelphia to be used for public works. At compound interest this money has accumulated into a sizable fortune. Part of this fund has already been used to establish the Franklin Technical Institute in Boston and the Franklin Museum in Philadelphia.

Nick Zorotovich, may you enjoy these recollections of a great American and a prolific, creative spirit whose works and words still have meaning and inspiration for all. The author and countless readers are indebted to you for your part in stimulating this article.

91
Bicentennial Visit to Jamestown

The beginning of American history, and some unknown items about Collis P. Huntington of Southern Pacific Railroad fame, are dealt with.

JAMESTOWN, VA., together with Yorktown and Williamsburg, loomed higher in portraying the American scene in the Bicentennial than possibly any other section of our nation. Jamestown was the first permanent English settlement in America, founded in 1607 and named in honor of King James I of England.

King James I succeeded his cousin, Queen Elizabeth I, to the throne upon her death in 1603. It was James who translated the Bible which became known as the King James Version and the early settlers built the first church in America here which was based on that version of the Bible. The ruins of the old church tower are the only remnants of the settlement still standing.

Anchored nearby are full-sized replicas of the three ships that brought the settlers, the Susan Constant, the Godspeed and the Discovery. All of them look like glorified lighters with sails. Capt. Christopher Newport, for whom Newport News is named, commanded this fleet. The original colony consisted of 100 men and four boys (women didn't arrive until 1619).

The settlers were looking for treasure such as Cortez found in Mexico, along with Indians to do the work. The colony was harassed by the Indians from the start, and more than half of them died of starvation during the winter of 1609. Were it not for the leadership of Capt. John Smith, whose imposing large bronze statue stands high facing the water, all of the settlers would have died.

Smith wrote in one of his books, *True Relations of Virginia,* in which he mentions that the Indian Chief Powhattan's beautiful daughter Pocahontas saved his life by placing her head upon his and begging her father to spare him. But Pocahontas married settler John Rolfe in 1614, while Smith went exploring and gallavanting in a section of the country which he named New England. His glowing reports impressed the English Pilgrims, who chose that place to flee from England and landed on Plymouth Rock in 1620.

Rolfe discovered how to cure tobacco for English smokers and how to cure and smoke pork and hams; these, along with Indian corn, peanuts, and hogs became the basis of Virginia's economy. They still are.

Rolfe took Pocahontas to London where they were royally entertained. She died there in 1618 of smallpox. Rolfe returned to Jamestown and was killed during an Indian uprising in 1622.

Under what circumstances did the author get to Jamestown? He left San Pedro by plane on October 16, 1975, for Knoxville, Tenn., and was met there by Dr. Mack Roberts, a cousin and a prominent physican from the author's native Kentucky. With his wife and daughter Marilyn the party drove for two weeks to learn more about historic America. Through the Great Smokies to Cherokee, N.C., they saw more Indian artifacts than ever seen in the West.

North Carolina grows more tobacco, manufactures more cloth, and makes more furniture than any other state. Sir Walter Raleigh tried to establish a permanent colony in 1585, but failed. In 1590 his colony of 100 settlers on Roanoke Island disappeared, and no trace of it has ever been found. Virginia Dare, the first white child born in America, was one of the missing.

The first airplane flight took place at Kitty Hawk in North Carolina in 1903.

The party drove through the center of South Carolina to Georgia. In Savannah they saw that Gen. Sherman in his destructive march from Atlanta to the sea in 1864 did not destroy this historic town, settled in 1733 by James Oglethrope. Most of the old mansions are intact.

Many historic firsts occurred in Savannah. The first steamship to cross an ocean arrived at Liverpool from Savannah in 1819. The first nuclear ship is named Savannah. Savannah was the first planned city in the United States. Eli Whitney invented the cotton gin there in 1793 and created a new dimension in world economic prosperity. The Girl Scout movement was founded in Savannah in 1912.

Savannah is a busy port and one of the chief naval storage centers in the world. The Savannah canneries processing crab meat, shrimp, oysters and tuna remind one of San Pedro.

Driving to Jamestown from Savannah the party stopped at Charleston, S.C., founded in 1670 and named for King Charles of England. The city is famous for its heritage preservation. John Galsworthy called its magnolia gardens the most beautiful in the world. Charleston holds an important place in American history as it was there where railroad building was pioneered in the 1800s and where the first steam locomotive was built in 1830.

At Ft. Sumpter, in Charleston Harbor, the Civil War began when the Confederate troops bombarded the fort on April 12, 1861. In the fort the travelers saw the footprints of Capt. Abner Doubleday, who invented baseball while a schoolboy in Cooperstown, N.Y. The Baseball Hall of Fame is located in Doubleday's hometown. Doubleday, who became a major general, is buried at Arlington National Cemetery.

During the trip through the Carolinas, the party saw two alligators, lush crops of soy bean and rice and a continuous forest of pines, cedar, oak, hickory and sycamore on either side of the highway. In the land of hominy grits, the party ate a side dish of them almost every day from breakfast to dinner.

After returning to San Pedro in November, the author made his report to Commissioner David Lozano, Chairman of the Hispanic Bicentennial in Los Angeles.

A footnote in the report recorded finding, while in Norfolk, Va., some items of unknown history about Collis P. Huntington, who founded the profitable Newport News Shipbuilding Company in the 1880s and built several U.S. battleships there for the government.

Huntington also became president of the Chesapeake & Ohio Railroad, centered at Newport News. Even in those days Huntington attempted to have Norfolk's port of entry moved to Newport News. But he failed just as he did in his abortive attempt in 1899 to have the port of San Pedro and Wilmington transferred to his long wharf at Santa Monica.

Huntington resigned as president of the C & O Railroad in 1889. Soon thereafter he became president of the Southern Pacific Railroad after forcing Leland Stanford to resign the post.

Huntington said that what he could not control he did not want.

92

Union Oil Names Sansinena

When all is said and done, we can be grateful for the fine achievements Union Oil has made in the economic progress of our community.

THE UNION OIL Company Refinery in Wilmington was opened in 1917. It has over 300 tanks ranging in size from 138 barrels to giants of 133,000 barrels. It occupies 450 acres, operates day and night, and employs an average of 1,000 people, including subcontractors, many of them living in San Pedro.

Pipelines from producing fields throughout Southern California and from overseas tankers run directly into the facility. It is one of the largest and most modern refineries on the Pacific Coast, capable of processing approximately 110,000 barrels of crude oil into gasoline and other products every day. Their other refinery in San Francisco is about the same size as the one in Wilmington.

The Wilmington refinery achieved an important scientific breakthrough in 1964 resulting in obtaining 120 barrels of high-octane gasoline for every 100 barrels of semi-refined oil fed into the unicracker. This method is now used by most other refiners, all paying royalties to Union Oil Co.

Actually, during the past 20 years, the Wilmington refinery has been quite proficient by cooperation with their Research Center in Berea, California, and developing successful and profitable petroleum refining techniques. Many of these improvements are licensed to other oil companies and are in use in more than 400 refineries throughout the world.

The Company's research scientists have now dedicated some of their team to the development of new and more economically attractive processes to meet the needs of the Federal Energy Administration in Washington, D.C.

Some of these processes are used for making chemicals, in particular, chemicals such as styrene, methacrylic acid, vinyl acetate, aldehydes, glycols, films, synthetic fibers, and resins, an official explains.

President Jimmy Carter mentioned in a TV message to the nation that there are several alternative energy sources besides crude oil or natural gas. They are coal, shale, geothermal, solar, and nuclear.

Union Oil has been a pioneer in researching all these potential energy forms. They own 20,000 acres of shale deposits in Utah, Colorado and Wyoming, which they claim can supply at least 150,000 barrels of shale oil per day for 25 years.

A Union Oil official told the author that it is easier to make liquid fuels from shale than from coal and that enormous additional oil reserves are in oil shale deposits. "It must be heated to a temperature of 700° to 900°F, then the solid organic material in the shale breaks up to yield petroleum-like oil. Such a treatment of oil shale is known as a retorting process, and we have ways to refine the oil to make products indistinguishable from those made from petroleum crudes," he said.

The opinion among most oil executives is that in future years as the domestic supplies of petroleum and gas decline, nuclear power plants will use uranium for fuel. Union's subsidiary, Minerals Exploration Company, is pursuing the development of uranium production by conventional underground mining. It involves in-place chemical extraction of uranium from low-grade buried ores that cannot be mined economically by normal mining methods.

Union Oil also operates The Geysers geothermal field in Northern California and sells the steam to the Pacific Gas & Electric Co. Union is now testing the potential of thermal heat in the Imperial Valley, Nevada, and Utah.

The Union Oil Company of California was formed in 1890 by Lyman Stewart and various partners in Newhall. Their first petroleum laboratory was in Santa Paula, where they developed a large field.

In 1855, Gen. Andreas Pico, brother of Pio Pico, the last Mexican governor in California, set up a crude still at San Fernando that extracted axle grease, lamp oil, and medicine oil from outcroppings he found near Newhall.

This was the feeble beginning of California's oil companies. It was unnoticed at the time because more ventursome fortune seekers were still digging for gold and silver. In fact, it was a prodigious producer drilled in Pico Canyon, named for Andreas Pico, that saved the early Union Oil Company group from bankruptcy.

In 1945 Union Oil opened the 3400-acre Sansinena tract in La Habra. The first well, Sansinena No. 1, was abandoned due to a series of accidents. But the field later proved to be profitable. They named a tanker Sansinena in honor of this oil field.

Union Oil has achieved an amazing number of firsts, first modern tanker, first offshore oil well, first locomotive converted from coal to oil burners, first two-mile-deep wells, the world's greatest gusher, first using asphalt for road building, first in discovering oil in Australia, and the low sulphur oil fields in Indonesia. Union Oil also is the largest petroleum company originating in California. Their growth and achievements have been phenomenal.

93

History of Harbor College

Records recently found reveal that the Wilmington Chamber of Commerce members created and dedicated Harbor College.

LOS ANGELES Harbor Junior College, now known as Los Angeles Harbor College, was dedicated on October 28, 1949, on a 37-acre campus, with an enrollment of about 400 and a staff of 41.

Today there is an enrollment of more than 12,000 and a full-time faculty of 180 on 85 acres.

Establishment of the college began in the offices of the Wilmington Chamber of Commerce in the 1940s, when George H. Moore, secretary-manager, wrote more than 100 letters proposing it. He urged all the leading business firms to lend their support, including the Union Oil Company, General Petroleum Corp., the California Shipbuilding Corp., and many others. There were many years of follow-up meetings after the letters.

A typical letter, dated January 25, 1940, to the superintendent of the Los Angeles city school system, said, "The Wilmington Chamber of Commerce has been interested, as you know, in the establishment of a workable and flexible vocational training program. The first fruits of its efforts are the extension classes at Phineas Banning High School, started about a year ago, and the results with the employers and the students have been excellent.

"We have been emphasizing the fact that within a radius of eight miles from the chamber office are the communities of Redondo Beach, Torrance, Gardena, Compton, Long Beach, and San Pedro. No other location in the south area holds such strategic geographical position in relation to vocational training. We are adjacent to most all the shipbuilding, oil refineries and aircraft centers, and more and more they will need trained specialists."

The Los Angeles school system provided the first vocational equipment, electrical welding facilities and a machine shop. But when World War II started, the demand for trained vocational workers and administrators became too large for a high school, and a junior college was indicated.

The Wilmington chamber helped in getting a $2 million appropriation from the federal government for the college project. In the interval there were many meetings in the chamber office with committees, including the San Pedro chamber.

The site was finally picked at 1111 Figueroa Place in Wilmington. It is the fourth largest of the nine junior colleges in the Los Angeles Community College District, which happens to be the largest junior college district in the United States.

Eugene Pimentel, president of the college, together with Pamela Bleich and Lawrence Frank, history professors, took the author on a recent tour to some of the new campus buildings: the astronomical observatory, the life science, physics and chemical building, two technology centers, a gym that seats more than 1,000 people, and the new learning resources center embracing the library of more than 85,000 volumes and 700 periodicals, plus many current local and national newspapers.

Pimentel remarked that this library, where students can hear recordings of technical lectures, see films and slides covering almost every phase of academic learning, is the finest and most modern among California colleges.

A part of the library is set aside for the perusal and study of local historic memorabilia and pictures which the late librarian, Camille Baxter, was instrumental in collecting and preserving. It is, according to Bleich, "the largest of its kind in Southern California, and the collection is being added to almost every month."

"And requests come from far and wide," Pimentel said. "From throughout the west, including historical societies, asking for answers to certain harbor area questions of historic significance. Miss Baxter's reputation and dedication to historic facts are well known."

Of the first faculty group, only two of them are still active: Francis Clines, coordinator of vocational education, and Regina Myers McClain, professor of business subjects.

Nicolas Zorotovich, local historian and one of the original faculty, has served as president of Harbor College Alumni Association.

Professor Cline said that in the beginning there were classes in petroleum technology, and transportation techniques, as well as a class on horology, and a watch and clock repair group. "Our placement record for jobs has been excellent from our first graduation," he said.

"We also had courses in hotel and restaurant management. The students were the cooks and they went all out in cooking and serving sample dishes for the faculty, during which time nostalgic odors of succulent cooking things permeated the corridors. Something we haven't had since. I'm not sure, but I believe the whole class graduated with honors!"

The dedication program lists Raymond J. Casey as director in charge of the college. Later the title was changed to president, which was, in turn, conferred to his successor, Dr. Wendell Black, and to Black's successor, Pimentel.

Also on the program was the name of George H. Moore, the man who initiated the Harbor College idea, as the principal speaker. At the time Moore was the 15th District Councilman of Los Angeles, as well as serving as general manager of the Wilmington Chamber of Commerce.

94
30-Year Club is 40 Years Old

This active club provides landmark signs, keeps records of historical events, and charges only one dollar a year for membership. Best bargain since Noah.

IF A MUSEUM is an expression of the educational and cultural part of a community, then so is the San Pedro 30-Year Club, an organization that has, for the past 40 years, contributed greatly to our local heritage.

The club was founded November 27, 1937, by Clyde "Lucky" Foot (his family started the Foot Transportation Co. that later merged with the Mayflower Worldwide Movers) and other community leaders, including the late Harry Fairall, James H. Dodson, Sr., (a former president of the San Pedro Chamber of Commerce), Christina Gaffey (a member of the pioneer Gaffey clan), Elio Amar, Robert Baley (one-time cashier of the old Bank of San Pedro), B. B. Lippman (who recently celebrated his 97th birthday), Arthur Quamma, Agnes Oswald Mead, Margaret Tansler, Martin Yturralde, William Crocker, and C. Henry Olsen.

The fundamental objective of the club is to get early residents together for camaraderie and to be an active forum for the discussion of local history. The club is specifically interested in preserving historic landmark homes and buildings.

The society has been successful from the start; today it numbers about 1,000 members. The membership fee has never been increased from a dollar a year, and anyone who has lived in San Pedro, Wilmington, Harbor City, Lomita, or the Palos Verdes area for 30 years is eligible. But the applicants are screened, and nobody gets a free ride. The author is presently serving as membership chairman, having been on the board for 20 years, and anyone interested in joining may write him in care of the *San Pedro News-Pilot.*

It was the 30-Year Club that secured adoption of Angel's Gate for the harbor entrance, provided anchors for the approach to Cabrillo Marine Museum, and began the campaign that saved the old St. Peter's Episcopal Church. The church was moved from Second and Beacon Streets to its present site in Harbor View Cemetery at the south end of Grand Avenue.

Moreover, the 30-Year Club relocated the drinking fountain provided originally by the newsboys of San Pedro in memory of their friend and benefactor, Luke Kelly. The society also initiated the restoration of Point Fermin Lighthouse under the careful guidance of Bill Olesen. Together with John Olguin, Bill put together a 100th birthday party for the lighthouse which was attended by some 10,000 on November 2, 1974.

The 30-Year Club also supports in spirit the restoration of the 115-year old Banning Mansion and the 117-year-old Civil War Drum Barracks, both in Wilmington. The club recently contributed to the Point Fermin Nature Trail, which is headed by another notable historian, Dick Wolfe, and helped in the preservation of the old Point Fermin Park cafe building, sorely needed for a community center.

The club does not limit its interests to history. It also bought a piano for the San Pedro Retarded Children's Foundation and also sponsors a scout troop.

The 30-Year Club holds a general membership meeting every two months. The 25-member board of directors meets the second Friday of each month at 7 p.m. at Ulabrand Hall.

The community leaders who have served as president of the club are Clyde Foot, A.M. Rosenfeld, C. Henry Olsen, Clinton Rechtwig, Harry Fairall, Art Harkness, Alice Parker, Herbert Cleveland, Sr., Margaret Kreider, Frank Perkins, James Byrnes, Ernest Pia, Al Eachus, Frank Camillo, Ambrose Rossero, Howard

Taylor, Manuel Mello, Anker Peterson, John Korthe, Knud Jorgensen, Earl Uhlin, Everett Weldon, Raleigh Newton, R. W. "Duke" Decker, Oscar Nelson, Everett Hager, Jesse Kopp, Mildred Hards King, Dennis Stake, Geraldine Lind and Bill Olesen. Some of them have served for more than the customary one-year term, including Bill Olesen.

Grace Harkness Linane is the current president.

95
Civil War Comes to Life at Banning Park

Realistic Civil War skirmishes have occurred at Banning Park in Wilmington. A rare Gatling gun was returned to Drum Barracks.

GREEK HISTORIAN Herodotus wrote around 450 B.C. something about the mails, which has been turned into the theme of postal workers throughout the world. "Neither snow, nor rain, nor heat, nor gloom of night stays these couriers from the swift completion of their appointed rounds."

These words were apropos on Sunday April 6, 1975, at Banning Park in Wilmington, when more than 100 uniformed soldiers evenly divided between the blue and the gray, with their arms and five field pieces of large cannon, enacted three Civil War skirmishes during rain downpours. The rain failed to stay their appointed rounds.

The event was viewed by about 2,500 people.

Confederate Lt. General G. L. Helms, field commander and head of the Civil War Association, expressed delight that the program came off so well and with such a large viewing audience in spite of the rain.

This writer was dressed in Brig. General Phineas Banning's Civil War uniform, but was outranked by Helms, who, upon inspecting Banning's uniform, invited him to be his guest at the Blue-Gray Ball aboard the Queen Mary the following Sunday. He was requested to explain the part Banning played in the Civil War at Drum Barracks. The Civil War activity was part of the Wisteria Festival of which the author happened to be the general chairman from 1968 to 1976.

Many community leaders were present, including John S. Gibson, Jr., president of the Los Angeles City Council; William Frederickson, general manager of the city Department of Recreation and Parks; Adm. and Mrs. Frank Higbee (U.S.C.G., ret.); Col. and Mrs. Harper Cowles, former commander of Fort MacArthur; James Hanley, principal of Banning High School; Capt. and Mrs. Roger Mairs, commander of the Los Angeles Police Harbor Division; Mr. and Mrs. Paul Shonafelt, a prominent educator; and Mr. and Mrs. John Sonneborn, district manager of Pacific Telephone Company. Marga Jean Lucas paraded in her Miss Drum Barracks uniform and held the umbrella for the Channel 2 television crew during its 1975 taping of the proceedings. Ken Williams, president of the Wilmington Chamber of Commerce, presided.

The scheduled 1:30 p.m. program was held at the Banning Ballroom, where several showcases were filled with Civil War memorabilia. The item causing the most curiosity was the old 10-barrel Gatling gun which was borrowed from Drum Barracks for the occasion.

The 350-pound bronze gun was stolen from the barracks in 1962. It is not often that a Gatling gun is stolen, buried and lost for seven years, then dug up and returned intact, save for a few brass fittings.

After the recovery, the gun was taken to the Drum Barracks headquarters where Col. Vincent Manchester, caretaker and part-time gunsmith, put the pieces together in good working order. When the barracks is restored in 1979, it will be mounted and put on display.

The gun is essentially a Civil War relic. We wonder philosophically if Jordan Gatling (1818-1903), the inventor, may himself have revolved a few times in his grave for putting that revolutionary touch on a mechanical instrument that has through the years possibly killed and maimed more people than all other manual weapons combined.

In his later years, Gatling did research in agriculture and, like his contemporary Alfred Nobel, inventor of dynamite and TNT, contributed to foundations in peace studies and other research for the betterment of mankind.

We give thanks to the Harbor Division police for Sgt. Harry Stine's unravelling of the records that proved the theft of the Gatling gun was reported in 1962.

Stine took copies to the Long Beach Police Department, where the gun had been turned in and where other claimants had filed for the find. With the evidence provided by Stine, the Gatling gun was released in care of the author. Joan Lorenzen, president of the Society for the Preservation of Drum Barracks, also was there as a witness.

This is a good example of why people should report stolen property to the police immediately. Otherwise, according to police Lt. Mike Markulis, long delays and expensive litigation may occur when the property is recovered.

Herbert Cox and Joe Kerrico, the youths who found the Gatling buried in a trash heap in the Dominguez Dump in 1969, deserve the sincere and lasting thanks of the community for returning the historic weapon to its rightful place.

96
EVOLUTION OF PORT COURTS

Phineas Banning was appointed a temporary judge in 1869. His are compared with the court techniques of modern jurisprudence in the local courts of Judge Walter Binns and Judge Michael Yelovich.

MUCH IS BEING written about crime, mugging, purse snatching, break-ins, and car thefts. The author has often wondered what crime was like during the time of Phineas Banning in the harbor area, from 1851 to 1885.

Research discloses that during Banning's era, cattle rustling and horse stealing were rampant; stage coach holdups were numerous; and recurrent clashes with posses and the sheriffs were recorded. Even during this era juveniles would steal horse-drawn buggies and coaches for joy rides, pretty much as they do today in stealing automobiles. Likewise, fishing skiffs and small lighters moored at the dock would be stolen, together with all the gear and tackle.

Culprits were often caught, but long overdue cases were awaiting trial, and local courts were swamped. Also phony gold mine stock swindlers were active. Something had to be done about it.

In 1869 Phineas Banning was appointed to a temporary judgeship to preside over some of the local cases that were piling up. At the time, Banning was head of a large and growing transportation business but was willing to do the governor a favor and dispose as best he could some of these irritating cases that were awaiting trial.

Phineas Banning had studied law in his brother's Philadelphia law office before coming to San Pedro in 1851, and he was sharp on Blackstone's Commentaries. In those days such knowledge was sufficient qualification for one to sit on the bench of a lower court.

Fortunately, Banning had a keen ability to assess human problems, but he knew they were subject to change by the vagaries of the day. However, he did his best to interpret the law, and analyze, weigh, and evaluate evidence. Banning was harsh but just. He never let his court become a marketplace of justice, where flagrant thieves and bold brigands could hope for leniency, nor would Banning countenance any political pharisee to interfere with justice.

Recently this writer observed the local courtroom trials of both Judge Walter Binns and Judge Michael Yelovich, and pondered in retrospect what Judge Banning may have done under the same circumstances, conditions, environments, and evidence.

After the court recess he interviewed Judge Binns in his private office. When asked why petty crime is increasing, Judge Binns clenched his fist, rose from his chair, and with a waving arm pleaded the historic difference.

Binns said, "In Banning's day there were no such things as psychedelic drugs, brain washing, hippies, or extra-sensory perception, and no bail bonds or Parent Teachers Association. In Banning's era a psychiatric examination of a guilty person, insane or not, to determine if he were responsible for his crime, would have been superficial and just plain wrong. But today the law demands it."

"Let us be realistic and face the facts," said Judge Binns. "We need a new rehabilitation method, a renaissance, if you will, in the code of morals of what is right and what is wrong, in the homes, in the schools, in business, and in the professions and on the streets, a conscious awareness of decency, courtesy, and responsibility.

"The court room should not be a garage," Binns continued, "to apply the first brakes on crime. The wheels of justice should turn only as a last resort after parents and schools and others have failed in teaching proper discipline in moral responsibility, and this lesson is far more urgent today than ever before—even in Banning's time."

Judge Yelovich entered the rebuttal, and stated tersely; "Poverty and suffering respect neither age, nor sex, nor color, nor creed, and to decide on the bench what is wrong requires considerable conscious effort, alertness, determination, and firmness of purpose and, above all, devotion to principle."

"In jurisprudence," Judge Yelovich continued, "the span of a century has seen tremendous change in trial techniques due mainly to backlogs of newly enacted laws and established precedents. Sometime, possibly in the days beyond tomorrow, the citizens may get to know and appreciate the procedures of the modern courts. But one thing is sure: Each case must be tried on its own merits, and justice should be tempered with compassion. We are dealing with human beings!"

After leaving the San Pedro Court House, the author felt that here were two judges that Phineas Banning would have greatly admired. And, like Judge Banning of old, he felt that Judge Binns and Judge Yelovich had kindred spirits with Banning in making for a worthwhile career in jurisprudence by attesting to a faith to live by, a self fit to live with, and a purpose fit to live for.

97
HOC IS A JOB PROVIDER

Over 8,000 have received good paying jobs after taking courses at the prestigious Harbor Occupational Center in San Pedro.

IN THE CENTER of our harbor complex is an important history-making educational facility known as the Harbor Occupational Center (HOC), 740 N. Pacific Ave., San Pedro.

This institution embraces seven buildings on 7½ acres of land, represents a capital outlay of $7 million, and has a 150-member faculty.

It was not easy to establish this facility. It required considerable initiative, courage, and stamina to renounce a popular and generally accepted theory that it "couldn't be done."

But Arthur McIntyre did it.

His faith in this project was so profound that he sold his ideas, almost single-handedly and after many attempts, to the Los Angeles City School Board.

It became a regional Los Angeles Unified School District project under McIntyre's management.

The school provides trainees with skills that are in demand in shipyards, business, and industry. Records indicate the school is on its way to becoming one of the finest facilities of its type in the nation.

McIntyre conceived his plan for HOC in the late 1960s.

As principal of Phineas Banning Community Adult School from 1964 to 1970, he saw the need for an occupational center of this kind; a place where potential workers could receive the finest training possible for about $10 per semester; a place which would emphasize skills that are in demand in our harbor community.

Since 1970, when the school opened in Wilmington, more than 8,000 HOC alumni have found employment after finishing their specialized training. About 2,000 students are enrolled at the present time.

The largest employer of former HOC students is the Naval Shipyard in Long Beach. Others are Todd Shipbuilding, California Shipyard, Bethlehem, Al Larson, and related enterprises.

The school curricula are varied and well balanced. Courses include electrical, marine, and diesel engineering; boatbuilding; machine shop; sheet metal; pipefitting; automotive body repairing and painting; refrigeration and air conditioning; drafting and blueprint reading; and arc welding.

Also taught are accounting, typing, secretarial, clerical, and nursing courses, as well as courses in commercial and deep-sea fishing and school bus driving.

Retired Capt. Edmund Miller, a commanding officer of the naval shipyard, paid McIntyre and the occupational center a high tribute when he said:

"The Harbor Occupational Center and the Long Beach Shipyard have a very close common interest. The skilled journey persons, technicians and mechanics produced by the center are essential to the success of the shipyard.

"I would like to praise the work the instructors are doing. They are, without question, filling a real need by providing training and practical job skills to persons in our community.

"I should also like to applaud the Los Angeles Unified School System and Supt. William Johnston for providing the funds which allow this facility to exist, to function, and to grow. The benefit of the education and training at HOC are proving the worth of this Center each day, as former students effectively fulfill their jobs and advance in responsibility through the ranks."

McIntyre is well qualified to carry out his mission. He has the master's degree from USC in vocational education and administration and in transportation law and regulation.

The demonstrated influence of his school in turning out thousands of technicians, who returned the investment in their education many times, is an inspiring example of how tax money is well spent.

McIntyre and HOC lend credence to our own oft spoken remarks that "the Harbor area is more richly endowed perhaps than any other section of California."

In 1977 McIntyre retired to become coordinator of training at the U.S. Naval Shipyard on Terminal Island. He was succeeded as principal of the Harbor Occupational Center by Dr. Robert F. Schenz. Jose Garcia is assistant principal, and Dan Stark is in charge of coordinating the training program. Steve Podesta is chairman of the advisory council, consisting of about 25 area business and professional leaders.

98

Riding Out the British Seas in World War I

This story relates why England enacted a law that lime juice be served three times a day aboard British ships.

WHILE THUMBING through stacks of old books and pamphlets at a museum recently, the author found the original manifest (interpreted into English) of the supplies aboard the Spanish galleon San Carlos that landed in San Pedro harbor on July 24, 1774.

It was carrying urgent supplies for the San Gabriel Mission, including several tons of food and other commodities.

When shown the list of food supplies, Ship Chandler Charles Crouthamel, owner of San Pedro Harbor Ship Supply, the state's largest ship supply house, was greatly impressed. But he quickly noticed there were no fruits or fresh vegetables included in the manifest.

"Fruits and fruit juices are absolutely necessary to prevent scurvy," Crouthamel said. "Because of this neglect all the ships' crews of those days got seriously sick, over half of them dying before getting to San Pedro.

"And another thing, the British passed a rigid maritime law in the 19th Century that every ship, under sail or steam, must issue each sailor, under strict penalty, two cups of limejuice daily to ward off the possibility of their coming down with scurvy. Even to this day our company sells many British and other ships large quantities of limejuice and other citrus fruits and juices."

The citrus juices are effective in battling scurvy because the disease is caused by a deficiency of Vitamin C in the body. It's characterized by weakness, anemia, spongy gums, and bleeding from the mucous membranes.

Crouthamel's comments about limejuice brought into sharp focus an exciting experience of the author's teenage days. In 1915, he foolishly ran away from home in Kentucky to see the world. He found himself in Philadelphia looking for a job.

At the foot of Chestnut Street, he was observing a British ship that carried the name Leonatus. The gangplank was down, the ship's bosu'n saw him and offered to take him aboard.

After he found out that the author was a long way from home and alone he offered him a job as an O.S. (ordinary seaman) and put him to work chipping the rusty iron deck (and without the usual protective eye goggles).

The ship sailed the next day down the Delaware River into the Atlantic Ocean to Hampton Roads for bunkers and a cargo of coal. The vessel was a coal-burning workhorse of the sea of about 2,500 tons.

After unloading the coal in Havana, the Leonatus sailed to Matanzas, a sugar port in Cuba, where it loaded large bags of raw sugar. It sailed in a convoy of about 25 other ships for England. The Leonatus went to Liverpool.

Those were tense days. England and Germany had been at war for a year and German submarines were sinking British ships right and left. The author was aboard the Leonatus when the Lusitania was sunk on May 7, 1915. Britain and her allies were clamoring for America to declare war against Germany as we did two years later.

President Woodrow Wilson's reply to Britain in 1915, however, became a famous phrase in history. He proclaimed that "Americans are too proud to fight."

After that quote, the author became a focal point aboard the British ship Leonatus. There were many unkind words, and he was even threatened with losing his precious ration of limejuice. The cook stated more than once that he was "not a limejuicer, anyway, but a damned Yank too proud to fight."

After unloading our sugar in Liverpool, most of the British sailors were transfered to men-o-war. Their substitutes were mostly blacks from the West Indies.

The Leonatus left for Boston in another large convoy. After arriving, the author left the ship hungry, skinny, and broke, save for the 12 British pound pay—at that time about $60.

He lost no time in buying a ticket for Kentucky and the protection of his worried parents. While on the train he noticed a headline in the newspaper reporting that the Great Lakes steamer Eastland had sunk in the calm waters of the Chicago River, and more than 1,000 drowned.

His convoy had lost five ships—three on the way over and two on the way back. But, as he looked back, he was sure he would rather have been surrounded by submarines on the Leonatus with his two daily cups of limejuice than be aboard the galleon San Carlos fighting scurvy from which few ever escaped.

99
California Historical Society Gets Rare Photographs

The largest historical society of all in the 50 states promises more and gives more. Membership is open to the public.

THE 107-YEAR-OLD California Historical Society exhibited rare photographs and artifacts at a special showing for the press recently at the society's new Southern California headquarters in Los Angeles.

Representatives from most all the area newspapers were present. The author represented the *News-Pilot* for this historical event, and brought back two old, seldom-seen photographs. One of them was Ducommun's oldfashioned hardware store of the 1880s. The other was an old saloon scene of the 1890s, which could be on Beacon Street in San Pedro. No one knew exactly, but it had the earmarks of that era on Beacon Street.

In 1871, the California Historical Society began to collect, preserve, and publish the records—in text and photographs—that reveal the history of California. The object of this special meeting was to display some of the 30,000 photographs recently donated to the society by the Title Insurance and Trust Co.

Dr. J.S. Holliday, director emeritus of the society, said, "In accepting the great resource of the Title Insurance collection we have an opportunity to present to our members and the public a pictorial treasure, which has had wide identity in Southern California. And from our new location the collection and its usage will be expended to scholars, researchers and the general public."

The society plans to place on microfiche the most important portions of the collection. It is calculated that this system will enhance the usefulness of the materials and preserve the original images. Until now the facilities and operations of the society have been focused in the San Francisco and San Gabriel areas.

The heart of the historical photograph collection is the Pierce collection, illustrating rare and curious photos of Los Angeles, the Harbor Area, Santa Catalina Island, and Southern California.

Pierce arrived in Los Angeles during the boom of the 1880s and established his studio in 1886. Within a few years Pierce amassed an impressive collection of thousands of views, which he sold in 1941 to the Title Insurance Co. The company used them for promotional purposes and over the years made the collection available to historians and pictorial researchers.

Like many pioneer photographers of that era, Pierce added to his holdings by trading with others or by copying the works of those who preceded him. Because of his interest in collecting and preserving picture records of Los Angeles and Southern California, Pierce was credited with creating the finest single pictorial collection devoted to Los Angeles. He died in 1946.

It was pointed out at the meeting that Los Angeles was not favored with a natural harbor or an adequate water supply. The city grew from human dreams and desires, through acts that brought a famous harbor, water supplies, railroads, tourists, citrus, oil, movies, aerospace, and other resources and industries. It has become one of the great cities of the world.

The exhibit chronicles the coming of the Southern Pacific in 1876, and the Santa Fe in 1886, heralding the beginning of Los Angeles as we know it today. The population jumped from 11,000 to 50,000 during the year following the Santa Fe's arrival.

The history of how the Hollywood movie industry was started came into sharp focus. It began in 1907, when the Selig Company arrived to film the second half of "The Count of Monte Cristo" using a different group of actors because the company could not afford train tickets for the regular cast in Chicago.

People seem to be more interested in history than ever before. During the past 10 years several historical societies have been organized and are doing well, including those in the communities of Long Beach, Torrance and Inglewood.

Recently Lomita-Harbor City and Palos Verdes established historical societies. The San Pedro Bay Historical Society was founded in 1974 and, according to Irene Almeida, treasurer, it has a membership of more than 200 and is growing rapidly.

Frank Fenton, in his book, *A Place In The Sun,* wrote: "This was a lovely, makeshift city (Los Angeles). Even the trees and plants did not belong here. They came, like the people, from far places, some familiar, some exotic, all wanderers of one sort or another seeking a piece of fortune or the last frontier, or a thousand dreams of escape."

100
GUNG HAY FAT CHOY FOR 1977

Chinese birthdays and New Year's are celebrated with a gusto unknown to the Western world. It is a time of paying debts and giving gifts.

"GUNG HAY FAT CHOY!" yelled David Chin, last year's honorary mayor in San Pedro, in a New Year's greeting.

He was in a local Chinese parade at South Shores Trading Center, wearing an impressive lion's head under which another participant carried the hind-quarters and the tail of the cloth-emblazoned monster. Firecrackers popped along the way.

This was the Chinese Year of the Dragon, which followed the Year of the Hare. The day before Chinese New Year, Feb. 1, Adm. Frank Higbee called to suggest this would be a good occasion to write the history of China's relationship to the Los Angeles Harbor.

No nation is older than China and no country has celebrated more New Years than the Chinese; none take it more seriously.

It is their New Year, Christmas, Thanksgiving and Fourth of July rolled into one. Also, it is a time of giving and receiving gifts, from toys for children to diamond bracelets and expensive automobiles for adults. Moreover, it is a time of gaiety and camaraderie.

The Chinese calendar has 12 animal creatures in its zodiac, such as the ox, pig, cat, dog, tiger, rooster, and the tortoise. The next dragon year will be 1988, when China is expected to have one billion population.

China covers more than a fifth of Asia. Only Russia and Canada are larger in area than China. The people of China take pride in their nation, its long history, and its influence on other countries, including the United States.

The whole world has borrowed much from Chinese technology, art, literature, science, religious philosophy, and language. The Chinese were the first to develop gunpowder, paper, procelain, printing, and silk culture.

Chinese art began before written history, and their painting has been an art form for more than 3,000 years. Chinese sculptors have produced many beautiful statues and temple decorations, carved jade vases and figurines. Many have been imported through the Port of Los Angeles. And are proudly displayed in local homes. Benny Low, owner of the Far Eastern Restaurant, is the possessor of many Chinese artifacts.

Chinese architects developed methods of building that have been adopted by modern American architects. For instance, Chinese pagodas were among the first home buildings with low, sloping roofs that extended well beyond the walls and blend artistically with their surroundings.

Chinese music has a sing-song sound to most listeners but, according to Dorothy Searcy, local critic and music teacher, the Chinese have a different scale of five or seven notes while our music uses an eight-note scale with five half-tones.

"In Chinese music," she said, "instruments and voices follow the same notes instead of blending in harmony."

The shores of three seas of the Pacific Ocean form China's coast. In the north, the Yellow Sea and the Gulf of Chihli cut between the mainland and the Korean Peninsula. Along some of these shallow coastal waters oil formations have recently been discovered. It has also been reported that oil has been discovered in the East China Sea Strait, from the Yangtze Delta to the Formosa Strait.

China's economy today cannot meet the basic needs of the huge, growing population for food, clothing, housing, and education. Factories of all types are urgently needed. There are vast mineral resources and most of them are undeveloped. Roads, railroads, and communication are still only partially developed. Many regions lack electricity and sanitation.

There certainly is a great potential for trade between our port and their ports. Authorities in Washington, D.C., are developing the possibility of future trade with China.

Ed Hauck, who works out of the office of Councilman John S. Gibson, Jr., let the author see a letter from Shanghai, written to his father and dated Jan. 1, 1925. The letter was from a Rev. H.G.C. Hallock, in which he describes the celebration of the New Year in Shanghai 52 years ago:

"This is Chinese New Year with its clanging cymbals, beating drums, flaming banners, and banging firecrackers. The many-hued cloth dragons about the streets are carried by men concealed within. They writhe and twist along and even climb poles to second story verandas to devour foods and money gifts handed them.

"While they go through these gyrations, thousands and thousands of firecrackers are exploded and drums add to the deafening din, while the dragon keeps twisting to the weird music.

"Every store is closed. No business is done, and most people are out in their best 'bib and tucker.' Most of them were up all night cleaning house, washing themselves, buying cakes, candy, food, paying debts, and storing food to last for several days when nothing can be purchased in China."

101
Big Bang and Black Holes

This chapter on astronomical science relates to Harbor Heritage *through the Los Angeles Unified School System, which presents the subject in a brochure sent to all schools, as well as the author's writing on local history. "On The Periphery of Eternity," the chapter which follows, also treats upon this subject.*

THIS STORY HAS NO bearing on the "Black Hole" of Calcutta, or of peoples and places on this earth. It is a story of a new theory in the formation, evolution, and dynamics of astronomical science, dealing with awesome laws of probability of mass distribution in the universe.

Whether 17 or 70, there is in every human being's heart the love of wonder, the amazement at the stars and starlike things; the undaunted challenge of places and events; the "what next" curiosity; all for the joy of the game of living.

Last year the author tried Bora Bora, Paradise of the Pacific. This year he would be a delegate—the observing kind—to the Astronomical Society of the Pacific Convention, USC campus, 1976, from June 10 to 13 inclusive, to try to fathom the immensity of time and space.

Bora Bora had this to a limited extent. But this year would be different. He would sit for three days while 53 top star gazers read carefully prepared papers, explain graphs and charts, all of them attempting to prove that there are billions of galaxies in the universe—each galaxy herding a billion and more stars. Maybe they proved it. The author didn't know. He is not an astronomer.

But an illustration of our own galaxy called the Milky Way with its billions of stars shepherding our sun and the solar system intrigued him very much.

"If the sun shines in your heart, the light should shine on your face," he thought.

When Dr. Phillip J. Peebles, a colleague of astronomer John A. Wheeler, of "Black Hole" fame, Princeton University, read his paper: "Development of Structure in the Early Universe," mentioning light ray spectrum from a galaxy of quasars on the edge of the universe, the author got shaky and a little confused.

Then, Dr. George O. Abell, chairman, UCLA Astronomy Department, reassured us. He reasoned that in the hierarchy of the universe, the Milky Way and our sun are on the bottom rung of existence; therefore, we will not have so far to fall!

"But matter in the universe is becoming more and more unevenly distributed as time passes," Abell said, getting down to the genesis of the subject.

At a special symposium, the "Black Hole" was discussed. We were told about the new 100-pound instrument, called SIT (sillicon intensified target), when attached to the Hale 200-in. telescope, can measure the brightness of objects almost at the edge of the universe 20 times more precisely than ever before.

It was predicted that with this highly sophisticated tool the future of the universe may be revealed within a few months to two years (it will not be long), when they hope to roll back the time machine of all galaxies.

In measuring light clusters from the edge of the universe, astronomers are literally looking at a probing from its formative stage. "This is the greatest breakthrough in modern astronomy," said Abell.

It is estimated 95 per cent of all astronomers adhere to the "big bang" theory of evolution, when all matter was released from an enormous homogenous whole scattering in all directions throughout the universe gaseous matter that in time created the galaxies and all the suns.

The "Black Hole" hypothesis is the "big bang" in reverse, when all mass will fall back upon itself creating a gravity so strong that no light or anything else can escape and the universe will again be devoid of light.

Dr. Alan Skandage, Hale Observatories, pointed out by proxy that a decrease of only 5 percent in the brightness of galaxies for each billion years of their lifetime would alter the calculations of expansion and fall into a "Black Hole."

Dr. Wheeler told the National Academy of Sciences last week that the collapse of the universe into a single, great "Black Hole" with the annihilation of all matter seemed inevitable.

Dr. Peebles concurs, stating: "The prospects of such a collapse confronts the physicists of our day with the greatest crisis in all the history of science."

And with it all, the author has never met an astronomer, during his 33 years in ASP, who is an avowed atheist.

The astronomers are apparently too close to time and space; they may feel that beyond and above all materiality there is something greater.

This was the most reassuring indication of all.

102
ON THE PERIPHERY OF ETERNITY

This writer had the privilege of meeting with and taking a special course from the world-famous physicist, Dr. Nils Bohr, at Copenhagen in 1951.

THE LAND AROUND San Onofre, center of a nuclear power consortium, was at one time a part of a 200-square mile rancho that embraced 18 miles of Pacific beach-front, including President Nixon's la Casa Grande at San Clemente. At the beginning of the century it consisted of 260,000 acres known as Rancho Santa Margarita. This is the same land that knew the footsteps of Fr. Junipero Serra. For a century many dashing dons, some from San Pedro, galloped over its great expanse. Today most of the old rancho is part of the Marine Base at Camp Pendelton.

In 1967 this writer had the dubious privilege of being present at the official dedication of this first unit destined to be the center of the most powerful atomic power complex in the world. This visit brought into sharp focus reminiscence of one of the most amazing experiences that a mortal could possibly witness on this earth. It happened in Copenhagen in 1951 at the Nils Bohr Institute of Nuclear Physics, where 100 scientists were in convention—six of them Nobel Prize winners. The author arrived just in time to witness a celebration in honor of a nuclear breakthrough over the great barriers and hurtles of neutrons and mesons. He was an unofficial but eager observer.

A humorous show was arranged and acted out by the scientists themselves, and it is believed it was unlike anything ever given before—a hilarious satire on dreams and fantasies, of theoretical formulations and physical manifestations realistically humorous but with mighty implications.

It was a sort of scientific escarpment bordering the valley of death, life and hope—a hilarious blueprint of scientific horseplay. There were lantern slides depicting fake atomic cloud chambers with fission and fusion mixed in delightful confusion; errors in research attributed to individuals whose names were mentioned with serious profiles in grotesque caricature of the six Nobel Prize winners present. During a flash of micro-instabilities, the group entered the realm of astrophysical phenomena. The show went on for two hours, during which time an "Authoritative Voice" acting as the "Master Atom" spoke from behind a cosmic cloud.

This experience was as though one had seen the beginning of time and was feeling deeply the impulse of creation and the totality of eternity. Before it was over, one had the consciousness that the universe and life itself were not a product of accident or chance—that the Great Maker definitely did not shoot craps with the cosmos; on the contrary, that every atom and molecule is numbered and accounted for in time and space. The perspective was clear that the universe is a preconceived pattern of infinite harmony and geometrical perfection.

In 1967 from the top of a green meadow glade the author gave a parting farewell to San Onofre and its atomic reactor. This was once prime cattle, hide, and tallow country with dons riding out on the mesas. One almost heard the galloping hooves of their spirited steeds as of old and voices crying out in violent disapproval of the inevitable transformation of this historic pasturage given over to tests by geiger counters to determine radiation and other measures to prevent future annihilation. For a while, in retrospect, the author was again transfixed on the periphery of eternity!

103

South of the Marquesas and West of the Easters

A romantic tale of a trip to the South Seas, where the author was sent to investigate the possibility of having a "Sister City" connection between Papeete and Wilmington.

IN THE SOCIETY ISLANDS, of which Papeete is the principal city, it is easy to be entranced by exotic sights, smells, and strange sounds, all enriched with the flavor and the flare of the Blue Pacific in the South Seas.

The island chain consists of Tahiti, Moorea, Raitea, Bora Bora, and ten smaller islands, all of them surrounded by coral reefs. On Tahiti, the largest island, there are several waterfalls and mountain streams amid the jungles.

On most of the islands there is a profusion of cocoanuts, rice, breadfruit, bananas and oranges. No one goes hungry. Fishing is particularly good. There are extensive pearl cultures operations in the many lagoons. In Papeete, there is a vanilla processing plant. Spices are abundant. Now we know where the Ports O'Call gets its saucy sauces.

The author went to Papeete on behalf of the Wilmington Chamber of Commerce in 1972 to study the country and attempt to get their Chamber of Commerce to arrange a "Sister City" connection with Wilmington. This assignment was completed on the positive side. A letter written to me and signed by R. Dexter, General Manager, dated Papeete, February 16, 1972, reads as follows:

"It is good of you to come to Tahiti. We appreciate your office as Chamber of Commerce official, and we are happy to make mutual membership connections with the Wilmington Chamber of Commerce. If your Honorable Board of Directors ratify the proposal for 'Sister City' connections, you will notify us for our official records with the Territorial Authorities. We are happy to extend you our friendship and courtesies on behalf of your President Bob Rocker and his Directors." Unfortunately, the Wilmington group had to table this because only the City of Los Angeles can officially make sister city connections.

In Papeete proper some restauranteurs and entrepreneurs bust their britches to please; others practice *laissez-faire* and care less.

In Papeete the main boulevard is "Rue Du General de Gaulle." Another impressive street is named "Rue Du Marechal Foch." They tell the story about the world's best-known Frenchman, supposed to be a roadbuilder and contractor, with the name of Detour, and they boast of their "Rue Du Detour" boulevard.

Tahiti is a French possession in the Society Islands, known as Polynesie Francaise. It is seven thousand miles from San Pedro, west of the Easters, and south of the Marquesas. Papeete is the main refueling station for most all trans-Pacific airliners and ships. They maintain a vital business relationship with the Los Angeles Harbor in tankers, and in South Sea commerce, and tourism. Tuna fishing in surrounding waters is particularly good, and trawlers from San Pedro and San Diego get full loads without strings attached.

It is said the South Seas are conducive to heavenly dreams. John Jacques Rousseau came and wrote *Children of Nature;* thus, the Romanticism cult was born anchored to an atoll. Louis Antoine de Bougainville came and had a flower named for him before he died in 1811. Paul Gauguin won fame painting native women, coral reefs, fertile gardens, and palm trees. Robert Louis Stevenson dreamed here and wrote *Treasure Island.*

Inventor Elias Howe came in 1845, after struggling in poverty for years on how to perfect a sewing machine. He dreamed some spear-waving savages captured him and threatened to cook him unless he perfected his sewing machine within 24 hours.

By the firelight Howe noticed their spears had eye-shaped holes in the tips, and Howe solved his bottleneck. He had been trying to make the machine sew threads running through the middle of the needle instead of the eye. He got his patent in 1846 and collected millions of dollars in royalties from all the sewing machine makers.

The cocoanut is the main export. In California we eat it, drink it, cook with it, wash with it, and from the husks we make fiber rope, carpets and mats, furniture, and baskets.

From the palm leaves, roofing is made for huts. The 60-to-80 foot tree trunks become lumber. As food and drink, cocoanut is served in more forms and is more widely accepted perhaps than any other product, save American corn.

Bananas were virtually unknown in the United States until the mid-nineteenth century, when sailing vessels began bringing a few bunches from the South Seas. By 1890, the import of bananas, now mostly from Central America, was big business. Today, Americans eat more bananas than any other fruit—30 pounds per capita per year. Tahiti produces a delicious red banana, dainty but small, which lends a gourmet touch to its cooking.

It was Bougainville who first claimed these islands for the French. And the French, bless them, fought for over 100 years every billowing wave fending off the pirates, buccaneers, marooners, cut-throats and fillibusters who dared to land. It has taken the French many generations to establish the colony and put it on a firm foundation. The natives hope it holds up, since the French government is now using some of the lesser atolls for their atom bomb experiments.

During the past few years there have been a few long-haired, moustacheod, deep-whiskered, guitar-playing Lochinvars strolling about the streets. Throughout the islands there are no locks or bars on the homes. This seems an obvious and an open invitation to the inevitable thief.

On the island of Bora Bora, Paradise of the Pacific, one is apt to succumb to the blandishments of the many titillating inducements where one may not resist the pulsating beating of bongo-bongo drums in the jungle, nor the poignant sound of an oboe in yonder hut, or the tuneful vibrations of a Hong Kong gong used for counting cocoanuts—the faster they drop from the trees, the faster the beat.

In the South Seas there is truly an aura of warmth and friendly camaraderie and hospitality where one feels a happy sense of well-being and an easy adjustment to environmental factors, where he can fully relax, meditate, fiddle, whittle or whistle.

In the distance one can almost hear the music of a calliope from a sheep ship, the bow waltzing the waters, heading for Fiji. Certainly, each wave carries a host of beautiful girls in phosphorescent, skin-toned bikinis, and a multitude of disappearing Aladdins.

On Bora Bora no one gets excitable, impulsive, or emotionally complex. And in the quiet sunset elegance of a thousand radiant hues one feels at peace with the world. Tonight it is exceptionally peaceful—a silent night quiet. No more bongo-bongo or oboe sounds, even the Hong Kong gong's gone.

It has been an overwhelming and wonderfully satisfying and self-fulfilling experience—a brief life cycle vacation interval to add to the sum total of an already exciting and intensely interesting senior-plus adulthood. Praise the Lord, and pass the cocoanuts!

104
Last Will and Testament of a Grateful Dog

Rosita was an unusual dog, and this is her unusual last will and testament.

THE LAST WILL and Testament of a Grateful Dog, with apologies to Eugene O'Neill.

I, Rosita, because of the burden of my 17 years and the infirmities that are heavy upon me, and realizing that the end of my life is near; Do, hereby bury my Last Will and Testament in the mind of my master, Oliver Vickery. He may forget until after I am dead, then remembering me in his loneliness, he will become conscious of this Testament and inscribe it as a testimonial to me.

When I came to live with Oliver and Grace, I was just a white-haired little pup, a half-breed Chihuahua, a nervous hybrid, alley bred and physically ugly. The genes of my forebears did not mutate properly, but I had eagerness, vigor, and personality, and they took me in.

I have little in the way of material things to leave. Dogs and cats and horses are wiser than men. We do not set great store upon things. We do not waste our days hoarding property, or ruin our sleep about how to keep the objects we have, and to obtain the objects we have not. The most for us dogs is a meaty bone, for the cats a saucerfull, for the horses some oats and a little hay. We do not talk back and we do not lie, but we all cherish attention and an occasional pat to assure our being wanted. This is all we ask.

There is little of value to bequeath except my love and my faith. These I leave to all who have loved me, to my Master and Mistress, Oliver and Grace, whom I know will mourn me most. But should I list all those who have petted me it would force my Master to write another book, if indeed he ever finishes the one he has been writing since the time I came to live with him, titled *Harbor Heritage.*

I hope my Master and Mistress will remember me always, but not grieve for me too long. Let them remember that while no dog has ever had a happier life, my pride has sunk to a feeble and bewildered humiliation with my being deaf and with arthritic pains. I feel life is taunting me with having overlingered my welcome. But I'm hanging on because I covet the kindness and the wonderful care my Master and Mistress have given me.

But I know it is time I said goodbye, before I become too sick and a burden on myself and on those who love me, including Dr. Denny Moore and Dr. David Huffman, the lovable veterinarians who have been most sympathetic and medically efficient in administering to my needs. I will be sorry to leave them, but not a sorrow to die. Dogs and cats do not fear death as men do. We accept it as part of life, not as something alien and terrible. What may come after death for us, who knows? But I like to think that anything so inevitable and necessary must be a glory. And I accept it as such.

I would like to believe with those of my fellow pets that there is a Paradise where one is always young and full-bladdered; where all the day one may smell, sniffle, diddle and daddle with an amorous multitude of our kin; where each blissful hour is mealtime, and during the long winter evenings there are a million fireplaces with scented logs forever burning, where one may curl oneself up and blink into the flames and nod and dream, remembering the old brave days on earth, and the love of one's Master and Mistress.

One last request I earnestly make. To you both I bequeath my collar and leash, and my overcoat, which I inherited from my predecessors Nan and Pancho, and ask you to hang them in the patio room as a reminder that I once lived in your home. I shall always remember how proud I was walking under the leash in our Vista del Oro neighborhood and romping around, smelling the pungent grass and exotic trees and flowers in Averill Park, when all eyes were fixed on me in admiration.

One last word of farewell, Dear Master and Mistress. Whenever you visit the parks in San Pedro with Sunny in tow, say to yourselves with regret but also with happiness in your heart at the remembrance of my long and happy life with you, "Here played Rosita." No matter how deep my sleep, I shall hear you, and not all the power of death can keep my spirit from wagging a grateful tail.

I am afraid this is too much for such a dog as I am to expect. But peace, at least, is certain. Peace and long rest for my weary old heart and head and limbs, and eternal sleep in the earth I have loved so well. Perhaps, after all, this is best.

105
A Bicentennial in 1776?

Our founding fathers would have been amazed if they had known the history of the world when they signed the Constitution.

IF THE FOUNDING FATHERS of our nation had a bicentennial celebration of their own in 1776, it would have revealed a golden age of art and literature, of explorations, discoveries and reformations that have affected every living person to this very day of 1976.

On our coast many major projects took place in the 1500s. Cabrillo came to our shore and discovered California in 1542. Sir Francis Drake hugged our coast in 1579 in his ship Golden Hind all the way to a bay just north of San Francisco, and overhauled his ship in a place now known as Drake's Bay. Most historians do not believe Drake saw the San Francisco Bay, and it is doubtful if he ever saw San Pedro Bay. If he had, history may have been different.

An active Indian Village known as Yang-na of some 1,000 population was established in the 1500s, and it was the center for the founding of the City of Los Angeles in 1781. The Indians had two paths to the ocean, one to San Pedro and one to a place now occupied by Santa Monica. These trails were used by later generations of explorers such as Portola and Fr. Junipero Serra.

In 1513 Vasco Balboa claimed for Spain all the lands bordering the Pacific Ocean. In 1534 Jacques Cartier discovered the Gulf of St. Lawrence, and in 1541 Hernando de Soto discovered the Mississippi River.

In 1500 the Portugal explorer Pedro Alverez Cabral landed in Brazil and claimed the country for Portugal. They still speak the Portuguese language.

In 1517 Martin Luther nailed his Ninety-Five Theses on the door of All Saints Church in Wittenberg and started the Reformation. It was extended in 1536 by John Calvin, who founded the Presbyterian Church. The Lutheran Church was founded a few years earlier.

King Henry VIII in 1529 demanded a divorce from his wife Catherine of Aragon, daughter of King Ferdinand and Queen Isabella of Spain. The Pope refused the request. Henry wanted to marry Anne Boleyn, Lady-in-waiting, which he did in 1533. Henry then declared the Pope had no authority in his kingdom and started the Church of England. In America it is known as the Episcopal Church. Henry's daughter by Anne Boleyn became Queen Elizabeth I and reigned from 1558 to 1603.

Elizabeth sent Sir Walter Raleigh to explore a large land mass in America, and Raleigh named it Virginia for Elizabeth, the Virgin Queen. The first white woman born in America August 18, 1587, was named Virginia Dare.

Queen Elizabeth granted Raleigh 12,000 acres in Ireland in 1596. He planted the potato on this land, which he found among the Virginia Indians. Thus, the Irish potato was born.

Drake and Raleigh were contemporaries. Both ranked high in historic annals as being foremost in crushing the Spanish Armada invasion of England in 1588. Drake was vice-admiral in charge. Both men eventually lost their heads in the Tower of London.

William Shakespeare lived during the Elizabethan period and produced 37 plays. Christopher Marlow, Francis Bacon, and Edmund Spenser all lived the same time as Shakespeare. It is said that in literature no other period has been so brilliant.

In the late 1500s London goldsmiths began to practice banking and furnished money for the first time for the expanding commerce and foreign trade. The Bank of England was thus started.

During the year 1500 many great artists lived and left their masterpieces created by Michelangelo and Leonardo Da Vinci. The Renaissance swept away many customs and attitudes that had dominated Europe for a thousand years. These new ideas and cultures still influence our lives. Pope Julius II rebuilt St. Peter's and Michelangelo painted the Sistine Chapel. Raphael, Titian, Bellini and Holbein all lived in this period. In 1534 St. Ignatius Loyola founded the Society of Jesuits.

Our dog lovers may be interested to know that the poodle, great Dane, Scottish deerhound, English setter and the Mexican Chihuahua were first bred in the 1500s.

The first hogs were introduced to America from Europe in 1595, and the first newspaper ad, no connection please, was published in Germany in 1525. It announced a medicine for sale.

106

Frank Alexander Is a Generous Host

This chapter goes back to the birth of the author in Bird Point, Missouri, with a tie-in with the Los Angeles Harbor Area and some details about the Delta Queen.

HANNIBAL, MO., June 1, 1978.—This is Tom Sawyer and Becky Thatcher country, made famous by the pen of Mark Twain. The mighty Mississippi River flows peacefully by, meandering 103 miles south to St. Louis and beyond.

The author is here on a research visit at the invitation of Frank Alexander of Wilmington, who owns 200 acres of prime farm land at nearby Saverton, a quiet village of barely 150 people, situated along the banks of the almost mile-wide Mississippi River. Here, Alexander is attempting to propagate a new breed of American beef cattle. Alexander told me that this is the first time any serious attempt has been made to breed a red Angus bull with polled (hornless) milking shorthorns, using only the bloodlines of cows originally brought from England to Missouri by early pioneers.

"You will note," Alexander said, "that they are all red cows, minus any Asiatic or Brahma blood, and unlike the Santa Gertrudis popular in Southern California, and other mixed Asiatic breeds being produced by other cattle breeders."

According to some local cattlemen and experts from the University of Missouri and Kansas, Alexander's system seems to be working. If he succeeds, his new breed will be officially registered under the name of "Vocas Coloradoes De

Los Americas." It would be a sensational breakthrough with the first authentic breed of American beef cattle that may one day roam the ranges of California, South America, and other parts of the world.

However, shortly after arriving from San Pedro, and before the author could closely observe these new breeds of calves, Alexander surprised him with a reservation he had previously made for him to be a passenger aboard the famous old stern-wheeler, Delta Queen, on its annual week-end cruise from St. Louis to Hannibal. The trip turned out to be two nights and almost three full days of leisurely, relaxing, and smooth sightseeing along the banks of the Mississippi. The Delta Queen was filled to capacity. It turned out that the author was the oldest person aboard, and during the voyage the captain managed to let him win the Missouri Waltz contest—not because of his age, he hoped—but because of his leg rhythm aided by his talented partner who happened to be the wife of a crew officer.

As the Delta Queen cruised along, the author could see the muddy waters and thought about its sources, from the canyons cutting into western prairies to the steep coal-bearing range of the Monongahela and the Cumberland valley of the Appalachian Mountains. Here, indeed, he thought, is the flowing summary of American geography and history. No river has played a greater role in the story of America.

Alexander gave the author a book about Mark Twain to read on the boat. It was interesting reading, but the author could not buy Twain's philosophy that living along the Mississippi River is the finest upon the globe. Personally, he'd rather live in San Pedro or the Palos Verdes. Yet millions of American boys have grown up enthralled by the stories and legends of the Mississippi River. It certainly is different. Someone on the boat remarked; "It is too thick to drink, and too thin to plow!"

The Delta Queen was not built for the Mississippi River, but for the Sacramento River. She is the only Mississipi River steamboat with a single smokestack—all the other steamers have two stacks. During World War II, the U.S. Navy used the Delta Queen, along with her sister ships, Delta King, to ferry troops and the wounded in San Francisco Bay. After the war, in 1946, the Delta Queen was purchased by Capt. Tom Greene, formerly of San Pedro, on a bid of $46,250. Green outfitted her for duty on the Mississippi River, where she has since been plying up and down the river from New Orleans to St. Paul, and up the Ohio River to Cincinnati.

From a bedroom window in the old mansion on Alexander's farm at Saverton, which was built in 1818 and resembles greatly the Phineas Banning Residence in Wilmington, the author observed miles of river barges loaded with grain and other important agricultural commodities being towed down the

Mississippi; coming all the way from St. Paul and other river ports in Minnesota, Wisconsin, Iowa, Illinois, and Missouri.

The author thus learned how New Orleans recently became the largest and busiest American port, with grain silos at Vicksburg, Natchez, Baton Rouge and New Orleans being kept filled for shipment of these grains to Russia, China, and other foreign countries.

Saverton, Missouri, is a one-street community, eight miles south of Hannibal. Every morning Alexander sent the author for the mail where Shirley Bomar, postmistress and storekeeper is in charge. One day Shirley sliced a few pieces of longhorn cheese, which he ate with crackers from what may be among the last of the old traditional country-store pickle and cracker barrels to be seen.

Shirley was quite knowledgeable about local memorabilia and offered more than a few historical gems. One of them was that Egbert Van Alstyne lived here in 1905 and composed his popular song, "Under the Shade of the Old Apple Tree," where Alexander's farm is now located. At that time, Shirley said, "the Saverton community was the center of the apple orchard country, and thousands of bushels were shipped annually by barge to St. Louis along with large quantities of hogs, sheep, and cattle."

Jim Thompson, reputed to be the best grain and hay farmer in these parts, stopped his mower long enough to tell about the large cement plant in the nearby village of Ilasco. "This factory shipped," he said, "almost 100 per cent of all the cement used in building the Panama Canal. About five million barrels of it was loaded on barges and floated down to New Orleans."

This bit of information prompted a visit to the factory. The plant manager was most courteous and related that most of the cement from his factory built most of the dams on the Colorado River, including the Hoover Dam near Las Vegas. He also offered a pamphlet that reads:

"When this factory was opened in 1900 the company brought in many families from Croatia, Dalmatia, and other Balkan countries. Their descendants are an asset to our country, and we are proud of them."

The author's being from the Los Angeles harbor area where there are so many Yugoslaves prompted ready concurrence about the good citizenship of the Balkan people, but it did sound like a San Pedro "connection."

After winning the Missouri Waltz contest aboard the Delta Queen, Captain Blum asked the author to try out on the steam calliope for a prize. His mind flashed back to the first music he ever heard, from a Mississippi River showboat calliope in 1901. The author was born in Missouri on December 30th, 1896, in a village called Bird Point, which since 1903 no longer exists because the mighty Mississippi River tore it asunder during one of its greatest onslaughts, washing away everything his parents owned.

He began to remember Bird Point well and to recall stories about Bird Point his parents used to tell. During their honeymoon in 1882, his parents drove a covered wagon from the hills of Kentucky to seek the western frontier. They stopped at Bird Point for a year, but remained for 21 years before the river ruined them financially. Bird Point was just across from Cairo, Illinois, where the Ohio River empties into the Mississippi.

At the Delta Queen calliope, the author's fingers became a little shaky. He hardly played a note, but the captain signed an impressive Vox Calliopus certificate that allows him to play any calliope on any river or swamp in America, including the waters of the San Francisco Bay and the Okefenokee Swamp. Thirty-four different waters were included but San Pedro Bay was missing. When Captain Blum was told of this ommission he whispered to the purser to hereafter type SAN PEDRO BAY in bold letters on all calliope certificates.

At the end of June the visit had come to an end. The author had been Alexander's guest for one full month, and it was urgent that he return to San Pedro. He had arrived by jet plane, and expected to return the same way. But his host insisted that they take the train instead, and he arranged that they return together to Los Angeles by Amtrak.

Only freight trains now come to Hannibal, so he had his nephew, James C. Vance, drive them to Fort Madison, Iowa—a 90-mile trip up the west and east bank of the Mississippi River. Vance is in charge of Alexander's farm at Saverton. It was a motor trip of many interesting sights and one that proved of unusual historical significance.

Along the way the two came to Nauvoo, Illinois, a Mormon community founded by Joseph Smith in 1839. Here an anti-Mormon mob killed Smith and his brother, Hyrum, in 1844. Their graves are in the local cemetery. After Joseph Smith's death, Brigham Young became the leader of the Mormons and led the faithful followers in 1847 to the Great Basin which became their headquarters, in what is now Salt Lake City, Utah. Every year, a huge caravan of up to 100 busloads of Mormons come to Nauvoo from Salt Lake to pay homage to the memory of their founder.

At Keokuk, Iowa, they saw the largest hydroelectric plant on the Mississippi River, with 15 generators each producing 9,000 kilowatts, enough energy to supply the City of St. Louis, 145 miles south. They were amazed at the smoothness of the operation. Many romantic songs have been written about the glories of "Old Man River."

When they arrived at Fort Madison to catch the old "Santa Fe Chief" for the trip, they observed three good-sized cemeteries almost in the center of town. There were many Indian battles here; some of them were massacres of non-Indian people. A chimney-like monument marks the site.

The author is not too sold on riding trains. Many think that because a train is on the ground it is safer than a plane; but newspapers are full of stories about frequent derailments and tank car explosions and other ghastly train mishaps.

However, the author was glad that he took train buff Alexander's advice to give Amtrak another chance. In Kansas, Colorado and New Mexico, one may observe evidence from the train window of some old markings and relics of the Santa Fe Trail.

From an historical point of view it was a rewarding experience.

107

Thomas Fitch—Silver-Tongued Orator of the West

Some anecdotes about the first Congressman from Nevada and his popular story-telling at the Banning Home in 1870.

THOMAS FITCH WAS KNOWN in his day as the silver-tongued orator of the Pacific, and as the foremost carpetbagger of the old West. He was a friend of many notables of his time, including Phineas Banning, Collis P. Huntington, Leland Stanford, Samuel Clemens, John Charles Fremont, Kit Carson, James G. Blaine, and others.

Fitch was born in New York City in 1838, a direct descendent of a colonial governor of Connecticut. He spent most of his life in California, Utah, Nevada, and Arizona, and at intervals lived in a dozen other states and territories. Finch tried his luck in law, politics, mining, journalism, land speculation, and even Shakespearian acting; like most of his contemporaries, he was constantly in pursuit of fame, power, and wealth.

Fitch became a well-known bon vivant and raconteur. He was a delegate at the 1860 convention in Chicago that nominated Abraham Lincoln for president.

When Phineas Banning ran for state Senator in 1865, he often invited Fitch to the Wilmington mansion to entertain his guests with some lively and colorful stories. Fitch enjoyed nothing better than telling about things he had done and seen, and about people he had known—tall stories and thrilling anecdotes.

Recently this writer came across a bundle of these stories. One of them had to do with the time shortly after Nevada became a state of the Union and Fitch was elected its first congressman. The Civil War was over, but reconstruction of the Southern states became a drain on the resources of the North, and carpetbaggers moved to the Southern states seeking plunder and political office. Here is the way Fitch tells the story:

"In 1868 I was elected representative in Congress from the state of Nevada, and in a quiet way felt my importance. Shortly after arriving in Washington and walking down Pennsylvania Avenue, I met an old friend, John S. Harris. We had been close friends in Milwaukee before the Civil War. John was head clerk in a clothing store and I was a bookkeeper in a grain commission house. We had lost sight of each other for many years. After a warm greeting, I asked Harris if he were in Washington looking for a government job, if so, I should like to help him.

"I said, now John, if there is anything you want, I'm sure I can help you get it." 'No,' John replied, 'but I thank you, Tom, for your generous offer of help. 'Now Tom, what if I may ask, is the object of your trip to Washington?' 'Oh,' I replied, swelling just a little with conscious pride, 'I am the new member of Congress from Nevada. 'And you, John, is your stay in Washington likely to be prolonged?' 'For some years it will be,' John said. 'I'll likely be here longer than you. I am the new United States Senator from Louisiana!'

Here is another Fitch anecdote:

"While a member of the 41st Congress I received a note from the postmaster general, requesting me to remove the postmaster at Dayton, Nevada, and appoint a successor. The postmaster at Dayton was a reputable citizen and I saw no cause of the complaint. The post office auditor, who made the complaint, came to see me with a portfolio under his arm. He was a dapper little fellow, with pink side whiskers and a hauty stride. 'This,' said he, pompously producing from his portfolio a letter which he read aloud from the corners of his twitching mouth:

"Dayton, Nevada, February 10, 1870–Postmaster General, Washington, D.C. Sir: I am in receipt of your critical communication directing me to change my method of returning accounts of box rents. Are you running this post office or am I? I have been postmaster here for six years, and until you got into office I never had any trouble about it. This is the third time you have written ordering me to change my method of keeping box office accounts.

"Where did you get the power to give me orders, anyhow? I will remark in closing, that before I will make the change you direct I will see you and the entire Post Office Department in hell beating tanbark.

"Yours, Albert Green, Postmaster of Dayton, Nevada."

"I requested time," Fitch said, "which was readily granted, to name a new man for the job. But somehow, I never could find time or the inclination to have him fired, and he may still be the postmaster there. I hope so."

108

Weymouth and Averill, Pioneers in Subdividing

Weymouth and Averill were from Maine. So were the Long Beach Bixby family. So were the clipper ships and whalers. So was Clarence Bailey.

THE VISTA DEL ORO section of San Pedro, approximately 1,000 acres, was purchased in 1919 from Rudecinda Sepulveda for prices ranging from $350 to $750 an acre by the Averill Weymouth Company, early land developers of San Pedro.

This area embraces all the land from Seventh Street to Sixteenth Street, and from Meyler Street west to near Western Avenue.

Rudecinda Sepulveda de Dodson was the daughter of José Diego Sepulveda. She and her brother Ramon Sepulveda at one time inherited most of the land in San Pedro. Louis Sepulveda, 85, still active, the son of Ramon, is the oldest living relative in the Sepulveda clan. He is the fiscal agent of the Sepulveda Land Co. and has offices at 821 S. Pacific Ave., in San Pedro.

According to a long-time San Pedro resident, Percy King, former superintendent of the Averill Weymouth Company, there were three Averills and one Weymouth connected with the Vista del Oro project. The financing came from the affluent Dr. George G. Averill, owner of the Keys Fiber Co. of Shawmut, Maine. He was the inventor and manufacturer of a prosperous paper pie plate business with a factory in both Shawmut and Waterville, Maine.

Dr. George Averill was the only one of the three Averills who never visited San Pedro until later in life, according to King, but he was content, after hearing glorious reports about San Pedro, to send his two brothers, Horace and Herbert, and his brother-in-law, Harry L. Weymouth, who married his sister, Effie, all the money they needed to promote the Vista del Oro project.

King also is quite knowledgeable about the early history of the 13-acre Averill Park, Thirteenth and Weymouth.

"There was a retired seaman," King said, "who became a director of the Los Angeles Department of Recreation and Parks and who was in charge of making this park an attractive center, complete with a stream flowing through the park. This former seaman frequented the foreign ships that came to this port, and persuaded the captains to bring back various exotic tree seedlings from all parts of the world."

The park was named for the Averill family. Harry Weymouth, along with the Averills, profited greatly from Dr. Averill's investments. They returned to Maine to help by extending the paper pie plate business and by inventing and adding paper drinking cups to the list of products.

Also in San Pedro both families left landmark street names, and a few years ago, *National Geographic* listed Averill Park as the 27th most beautiful in the United States.

The State of Maine has sent many of her citizens to California, some of whom have carved their names in harbor history.

For instance, the Rev. G.W. Hathaway of Maine gave four daughters who married four Bixby men, also from Maine. They were the developers of Long Beach. Jotham Bixby, one of the leaders, owned 15,000 acres in Palos Verdes, which he sold to the Vanderlips, who started the Palos Verdes mansion development of large estates in 1915.

Clarence M. Bailey, another long-time San Pedro resident, originally from Searsport, Maine, gave the author a book with the names of 100 sea captains who at one time or another sailed into the port of San Pedro. Some of these seamen retired to live in the Harbor Area. The book lists several old clipper and other wooden ships which were built in Searsport and Penobscot, Maine. Some of them developed considerable commerce in the hide and tallow business with San Pedro and Wilmington.

New Bedford, Maine, is recorded as the whaling center in the early days and some of its ships anchored in San Pedro Bay for provisions and supplies. Salem, Maine, was the center during the opening of the China trade, and San Pedro was one of the main ports where these ships obtained supplies, both going to and returning from the Orient.

Maine and shipbuilding went hand in hand for many generations. It is said that Maine built ships at Searsport and Penobscot Bay. They were some of the finest sailing vessels ever built. Some of these ships made voyages into distant lands, weathered many storms, outrode hurricanes, and brought fame and fortune to their owners and masters.

There is an impressive marine museum in Searsport, about as large as the San Pedro Ferry Building, which will become by 1979 a marine museum. Baily suggests that the museums could exchange certain artifacts of the sea that may help balance the marine knowledge and history of both museums.

109
THE MIRACLE OF OWENS VALLEY

This revealing story tells us that the Los Angeles Department of Water and Power owns more land in the Owens Valley than the corporate City of Los Angeles.

LANKY 22-YEAR-OLD William Mulholland jumped his ship, Wealthy Pendelton, in January, 1877, and hid for a week while Capt. William H. Blanchard went looking for him all over San Pedro. Young Mulholland could hardly have realized then that one day he would become the world's greatest water engineer and save the City of Los Angeles from thirst and starvation.

Nor could he realize that there would be a large and impressive Memorial Foundation, statues, and a long scenic Canyon Drive erected in his honor.

After Blanchard's ship left San Pedro, Mulholland, with his Irish brogue, asked directions on how to get to Wilmington and catch a train to Los Angeles. He had spent four years as a sailor after leaving Ireland at age 18. He had little or no education, but he could read and write.

Remi Nadeau's new book, *The Water Seekers,* says, "As young Mulholland rode the 23 miles from the harbor to Los Angeles he could see from the train window the cracked soil, the empty irrigation ditches, the withered crops, and the grass that should have been green in January but was brown and stunted. Within weeks cattle and sheep by the thousands would be dying of thirst and starvation."

This was the Great Drought of 1877 in which Edouard Amar lost most of his large sheep flock in the Palos Verdes Hills, where all water holes dried up, drifting sands and erosion followed when coyotes howled, mustangs neighed, and mules and burros let off brays of solemn distress. Not a blade of grass nor plant nor stubble was left.

After arriving in Los Angeles, Mulholland got a job as a ditch digger with the water department, lived in a one-room wooden shack, went to night school, studied geometry and engineering, and rose to head the Los Angeles Water Company in 1886.

He is quoted as saying; "Whoever brings water to Los Angeles will also bring the people." He brought the water alright, and people flocked to Los Angeles. When Mulholland arrived in 1877, the population was about 11,000; when he died in 1935 the population was over 1½ million people.

In 1900 Los Angeles was beginning to face a serious water shortage. The principal supply was the L.A. River, which was not polluted and provided large storage area. To halt water use by outside groups and to conserve the threatened supply, the City instituted a number of legal actions. But this was not enough, and Mulholland got busy with a bold plan.

By 1905 Mulholland, now regarded as the "Father of the Los Angeles Municipal Water System," guided an army of 5,000 men for six years in building the Los Angeles Owens River Aqueduct, which is the longest municipal aqueduct in the world. The Los Angeles Department of Water and Power, is, in fact, the nation's largest municipal utility operation. It owns, lock, stock, and barrel, as much land in the Owens Valley complex, as is occupied by the whole of Los Angeles City itself. Thanks to William Mulholland, it is the finest investment the City ever made. On the real estate market today, it would amount to several billion dollars.

Through the courtesy of DWP Commissioner Fred Heim, former president of the Los Angeles Harbor Commission, the author was recently invited to accompany a group of 24 Civil Engineers to personally view and inspect the whole Owens River Water and Power complex. It was a great revelation, and the trip added considerable knowledge from the historic point of view. Hosts Joe Hegenbart and J.M. Wool, DWP Engineers, were the most knowledgeable, cooperative and courteous field guides the author has ever met. Their commentary greatly increased the author's understanding and respect for DWP operations.

The party stayed two nights in Bishop. The author was assigned a likeable engineer, Dave Ellis, as his roommate. Dave told much about the many important items installed by the Aremco Steel Corp. which he and his partner, Engineer Harry Blaney, represented.

On the way up the party stopped at the Valley steam plant, Rinaldi Station, Sylmar DC-AC converter station, Castaic power project, and the Mojave yard. Then followed a pleasant drive to Lone Pine for a fine view of Mt. Whitney, but unfortunately the snow in the Sierras was about one-third of normal. Then to Independence Headquarters, Black Rock Rearing Ponds, and the Los Angeles Aqueduct intake. The next day the party saw Pleasant Valley Dam, the Gorge Hydroelectric Plant, Crowley, Convict, and Mammoth Lakes Ski area; an earthquake fault, June Lake Loop, Mono Lake, Buckley Ponds Wildlife Habitat, Mt. Whitney Fish Hatchery, Fossil Falls, Jawbone Canyon, and Alabama Hills Recreation Area.

It was a never-to-be-forgotten tour—one for which the author shall ever be grateful to Fred Heim, who fortunately is again a Los Angeles Harbor Commissioner.

110
Vincent Thomas Served Well at Sacramento

More about San Pedro High School and its proud graduates.

SAN PEDRO HIGH SCHOOL continues to rank high in the world of secondary education, not only for its scholarly attainments, but also for its many graduates who have attained prominence for themselves after graduation. Among them, are Maralin Niska, glamorous Metropolitan opera star, and Greg Bautzer, nationally known attorney, and former Governor Goodwin Knight.

But one of the most unusual success stories is that of Vincent Thomas, class of 1928, whose rise to political prominence is an example of early dedication and self-discipline. Thomas did it as an orphan from the streets and the wharves of San Pedro. His father died in 1918, his mother in 1925, leaving a family of six youngsters who moved into the home of their married sister, Mrs. Tom Nizetich.

In the early 1920s the Thomas family lived on Second and Beacon Streets, which was known as the Knob Hill area. To the west was an area known as Happy Valley. Thomas attended the Fifth Street Elementary School. The principal was a Miss Wickersham, sister of a prominent customs broker. One of his teachers was the mother of Greg Bautzer. His music teacher had Thomas form a glee club, which sang at several social gatherings throughout the harbor district. Another student at Fifth Street School was Goodwin Knight.

After graduation from the Fifth Street School, Thomas entered San Pedro High School in 1921, moved from Knob Hill to a house at 17th and Center Street, where they had a cow, chickens and goats, which was typical of many families living in San Pedro at the time, along with vegetable gardens in their backyard.

"I didn't particularly like to go to school because all of us had to work to make a living," Thomas said. From the streets, Thomas sold the *San Pedro News* and the *San Pedro Pilot* before they were merged in 1928. He also sold pies and bakery goods and other sundries. He had no assigned corner on which to sell his wares, which meant that he had to keep walking and roaming the streets to eke out his meager earnings. Thomas pays high tribute to B.B. Lippman, who had a store on Beacon Street. "On rainy days he would allow me to take a short-cut to Front Street. B.B., now 97, is a man of great compassion and understanding, and ever since that time he has remained one of my dearest friends," Thomas said.

While a student at SPHS, Thomas became active in student government, debating, oratory, drama, and sports, especially in football and baseball. In athletics Thomas was outstanding. The annual Black & Gold yearbooks carried several items complimenting Vincent Thomas on his high school activities, including his athletic prowess, his fisticuffs, his scholarship, his debating, and his school plays, especially when he acted as Mr. Winstead, in Booth Tarkington's "Station Y.Y.H.". It is still considered one of the most successful school plays ever put on in San Pedro. Thomas was nicknamed "Snakeoil" because of his "special" formula to cure all ills which he sold from door to door at 25 cents a bottle.

Coach Karl Haney, physical educational director at San Pedro High School, encouraged Thomas to stay in school and participate in sports, and at graduation in 1928 he obtained an athletic scholarship for Thomas at Santa Clara University, where Thomas also played varsity football and baseball. Thomas studied prelaw at Santa Clara, and in 1926 received the law degree from Loyola University.

After college Thomas went to work for Franco-American Packing Co., as private secretary to the company president, Joseph Mardesich. The following year he represented the Fishermen's Cooperative Association as a lobbyist at Sacramento.

Forest McDaniel, owner of a San Pedro men's store, urged Thomas to run for the State Assembly in 1940.

Thomas ran on the platform of "being against Los Angeles" and won. He almost succeeded in a bill that would have authorized San Pedro to secede from Los Angeles. Thomas now feels San Pedro fared better than it would have if the bill had passed. "The City began to wake up," Thomas said, "and for some years the stepchild, San Pedro, became the fair-haired offspring of Los Angeles. We acquired from them a new fish dock, and got most of our rutted streets paved. But they have no right to siphon money earned by the harbor department into the coffers of their general fund, and I'll fight to the last drop in the legislature to prevent it."

Thomas' political longevity is unprecedented. In 1978 he had served longer in Sacramento than any other elected official in California history. The Vincent Thomas Bridge was named in his honor, an unprecedented action for a living person. Since his school days, Thomas has possibly worked harder for the good of the harbor and is more closely tied to the community than any other graduate of the San Pedro High School. His beaming wife, Mary, daughter of the late Pietro Di Carlo, says," He has never turned anybody away from his office. He's the proverbial Good Samaritan."

111
PECK PICKS SAN PEDRO

When Peck came to the harbor in 1882 as a railroad conductor, he liked what he saw, remained and prospered.

AS A LONG-TIME STUDENT and researcher of the old adobe days in California, and of the early development of the Harbor Area, the author finds it easy to romanticize, dramatize, and humanize those dedicated pioneers who built homes and lived in our community.

One of the greatest of these was George H. Peck, San Pedro's leading philanthropist and benefactor. Before coming to San Pedro, Peck had an unusual career that spanned from hardship to riches. He was born in San Francisco in 1856. When 18, he worked in a fish factory in Astoria, Oregon. He moved to California and became a rancher, "punching cows" in El Monte.

For eight years, he was employed by the Southern Pacific Railroad in Los Angeles. He gradually worked up to baggagemaster; when he arrived in San Pedro in 1882 as a conductor, he liked what he saw. He quit his job and entered the real estate business, became a subdivider, home builder, lumberman, and contractor and started the Bank of San Pedro in 1888.

Within a short time, Peck had enormous land holdings. Among tracts he laid out were Harbor View, Grandview, Barton Hill, West Basin, East View, and Rudecinda–South Shores. He also owned a large tract on Terminal Island, where he started his profitable building and construction industry.

In San Pedro, he erected several hundred homes, a number of business blocks, including the Post Office block, the Peck block and the Ferl blocks. Moreover, Peck owned three miles of oceanfront property in Manhattan Beach and plotted the town after building a suitable wharf facility to permit some of his fleet of lumber barges plying between Eureka and San Pedro to unload lumber there. Most of the old homes now standing in the Harbor Area were built by Peck and his associates.

In addition to his local land holdings, Peck controlled large parcels of Los Angeles proper, and 1,200 acres of prime Palos Verdes land bought from the Sepulvedas from which he laid out 50-acre ranches selling them on easy terms to home seekers.

Most of the financing was handled through his Bank of San Pedro. This bank and its assets later became a part of the United California Bank of San Pedro. Its original site was at Sixth and Beacon and for years was known as the "Bank Cafe." Recently, it was bulldozed into rubbish and the site now is in the hands of the San Pedro Redevelopment Agency.

The old Peck home, built in 1887 on a bluff about where Fourteenth and Beacon Streets meet now, was in the vicinity of Timms' Landing activity. The home was moved many years ago to 380 W. Fifteenth Street and rebuilt on a concrete foundation. It is a landmark that should be preserved.

Peck had three children, Alma, Rena, and Leland. All of them became well-known landmark names of streets and parks—all built on land donated by their father. The largest and most valuable park in San Pedro is, of course, Peck Park. In his will, Peck left a special trust fund of almost $2 million to the City Department of Recreation and Parks. Peck died in 1940.

Ten years ago, this writer was a member of the San Pedro Chamber of Commerce Peck Park Committee trying to decide on a suitable memorial honoring George H. Peck. The Peck Auditorium Building in Peck Park was the final result, as recommended by Chairman Ed Patterson.

On August 16, 1909, George Peck and Elks Club Exalted Ruled Edward Bautzer, were hosts to President William Howard Taft when he came to San Pedro for dedication ceremonies as the Harbor Area became part of the City of Los Angeles. Peck drove Taft and his entourage around the harbor in his Locomobile. It was a gala affair amid flag-draped streets and cheering crowds. That evening, the festive group was entertained by a lavish grand regale at the Masonic Auditorium on Beacon Street, after which they went to Barton Hill with Los Angeles Mayor George Alexander to view the awesome sight of the first legal fireworks display in the Harbor Area. This event announced that San Pedro and Wilmington belonged to the City of Los Angeles by right of peaceful conquest, due albeit to the joker trump card—a strip of land that still connects the harbor with the City of Los Angeles.

George H. Peck's proud grandson, Herbert Peck Culler, lives in San Pedro and is an active member of the new San Pedro Bay Historical Society, which is currently trying to catalogue old landmark homes and places that should be preserved. Ed Hauck, Dick Wolfe, Bill Olesen and this writer have catalogued a few old buildings in the Harbor Area for future reference and study. Here is a partial list:

The half-way house at 1060 Paseo del Mar, between Point Fermin and White Point; the Grace McDonald home, 4074 Bluff Place; the Butterfield House, Thirty-sixth Street and Pacific Avenue; the Jesse Bourgeois home, 511 Shephard Street, the Charles Perham house, 3541 Kerckhoff Avenue; the church at Tenth and Mesa Streets; the old brick house at Seventh Street and Grand Avenue; the residences at Sixth and Meyler Streets, at 325 W. Tenth Street, at 728 W. Fifth Street, and at the corner of Third Street and Cabrillo Avenue; the building on the northeast corner of Second and Gaffey Streets. The Dodson home, Drum Barracks, and the 115-year-old Banning Mansion are referred to elsewhere in this book.

Jim Renzona wrote calling our attention to the old Bank of Italy building at Sixth and Center Streets. "It is an architectural and aesthetic curiosity," he said. "The doorway portal is one of the best examples of iron casting I have seen."

Anyone with ideas on preserving San Pedro's local heritage is invited to drop a line to the author in care of the *San Pedro News-Pilot.*

112
The DiRocco Family Have Deep Roots

It can be truly said that the pioneer DiRocco family helped greatly in making San Pedro a great port. It is a highly respected and leading family.

WHEN TWO BROTHERS, Anthony and Frank DiRocco, from the quaint fishing port of Gaeta, Italy, sailed their small fishing boat into San Pedro harbor from San Francisco in 1883, it presaged the start of five generations of the DiRocco clan, all born and reared in San Pedro.

At an early age, these brothers left their home in Italy and became sailors on foreign ships, Anthony on a British vessel and Frank on a French ship. Fortunately, both ships plied the waters of the Atlantic and Pacific Oceans in foreign trade pursuits, but the brothers had lost all contact with each other for many years, until, quite by accident, both of their ships happened to tie up in San Francisco at the same time in early 1883. Even then, they met by the merest of chances, when both were in Sanguinetti's cafe on the embarcadero.

They left their ships, pooled their finances, bought a fishing boat, named it Two Brothers, and headed for the fishing shoals off San Pedro. By coincidence, both of them had seen the San Pedro bay when their ships, at different times, anchored in the harbor and both were delighted with what they saw—the inlet and the contour of the bay reminded them of their old home port of Gaeta, including the geographic similarity to the adjacent Palos Verdes Hill and shoreline. Besides, there were plenty of fish to be caught and harvested in these waters.

The DiRoccos were from a prominent family of experienced fishermen who had taught the boys valuable techniques in catching and curing salt water fish long before they left home to become sailors. These brothers were the first to establish a wholesale and retail fish market in Los Angeles in 1885. No doubt, this business venture went a long way to popularize San Pedro as an important fishing center. Later, the DiRocco markets were extended to other communities.

At Harbor View Cemetery, 24th and Grand Avenue, is a five-acre plot of ground, donated to San Pedro by Augustus Timms in 1883. Within these confines are the graves of six DiRoccos, among them Anthony, who died in 1896 and his brother, Frank, who died in 1934.

Frank's son, Vincent DiRocco, made history as a San Pedro tugboat captain and Port Pilot for over 40 years, retiring in 1962. He skippered at one time or another all of the Wilmington Transportation tugs and served as First Officer on their passenger ship which sailed to Catalina Island, and towed three popular glass-bottom boats. The glass-bottom craft had to be brought back to Mormon Island during the winter months to protect them from stormy seas and billowing waves.

Since that time, however, a protective cove has been created near Avalon to harbor these boats. Vincent was the skipper aboard Wrigley's tug, Captain William, which was used for towing barges loaded with rock quarried on Catalina Island and used to build Los Angeles harbor, and made many offshore and salvage trips as far as San Francisco. "These were long and exciting tows, and I wouldn't mind doing it again," Vincent muses.

During the widening and deepening of the harbor in 1916, government engineers had Vincent row a skiff over all the mud flats to keep a chain taut so they could determine where the dangerous submerged rocks, shoals, reefs, and sandbars were located.

During his early sea-faring experience, Vincent was the Captain of the towboat responsible for maneuvering several ships used for filming such thrillers as "Mutiny on the Bounty," featuring Clark Gable, "Corsair," with Chester Morris, "I'm in the Navy Now," with Lillian Gish, "Treasure Island," featuring Wallace Beery and Jackie Cooper, and "Tugboat Annie," with Marie Dressler. When the author read this list back to him, Vincent smiled and said, "These were all happy assignments in my career, and I'd like to relive those days over again."

Vincent's reputation as a careful pilot was also well-known to the U.S. Navy. He was assigned to pilot the most famous ship ever to enter the San Pedro harbor, the U.S.S. Constitution ("Old Ironsides" from the War of 1812) on her memorable voyage from Boston to San Pedro and way-ports, in February 1933.

Frank's brother, Antonio, had four sons, Salvatore, Sylvestre, Joseph, and Frank. They all became identified in some capacity with the harbor and the sea. Salvatore and Sylvestre were the first ferry boatmen, rowing passengers across the channel at five cents a head, until a gasoline ferry was available; and Sylvestre was the Captain of the Islander, the last ferry which was decommissioned when the Vincent Thomas bridge was completed and opened for traffic to Terminal Island in 1961, at which time Sylvestre retired.

Frank became a tugboat captain after his return from WWI, in which he had served on the SS Great Northern—later the H.F. Alexander, a troop carrier which plied the Atlantic without destroyer escort. Joseph allied himself with the harbor pilots and was the first to run a gasoline pilot boat, the Hester. Before the breakwater was completed in 1915, each night he placed a flickering red light on the breakwater trestle to warn ships away from danger. His brother, Sylvestre, had done the same thing, on makeshift beacons and buoys off Deadman's Island, when ships were due to arrive at night.

In the Bynner Martin column in the *News Pilot* in 1948, he wrote: "Capt. Joseph A. DiRocco will retire as one of San Pedro's best-known port pilots, after 36 years as pilot boatman on ships in and out of the Harbor."

Joseph's son, Anthony DiRocco, is Councilman Gibson's Field Deputy for the Harbor area in the San Pedro office. This year, out of curiosity and filial desire, Tony and his wife, Lucy, took their first trip to Italy to meet their Italian relatives and inspect the port from which the DiRoccos came to America.

"You can mention," he said, "that the physical outlines of Gaeta, Italy, are indeed like a picture postcard of San Pedro."

113
WALLS HAVE DEEP ROOTS

Captain Reynold Wall from Denmark arrived in San Pedro in 1894. He was skipper of several Banning ships, and the father of two sons: Dr. George Wall and Andrew Wall, both leaders in the development of San Pedro.

WHEN DANISH CAPTAIN Reynold Anderson Wall, father of San Pedran George Wall, M.D., and Andrew Wall, president of Al Larson Boat Shop, arrived in San Pedro in 1894, to look for his brother Andrew, he made maritime history in the harbor.

In 1890 Captain Wall sailed to Rosalea, Mexico, on the British bark Dynsyre. There he jumped ship and boarded the American bark Yosemite, which took him to San Francisco, where he heard through the seamen's union that his brother was in San Pedro. He came to San Pedro and rejoined his brother. The two of them sailed for several years in the Alaska Packer ships, one of them being the Star of India, which is now on display in San Diego.

These Star ships would sail from San Francisco in the spring, and when they arrived in Alaska the crew became fishermen for the summer. This became a profitable undertaking, because the crew worked on a percentage basis.

Andy Wall told the author about an interesting part of the trip when the ship and its crew returned to San Francisco loaded with canned salmon.

"The ship carried a large group of Chinese who did most of the packing and canning of the catch. Some of them were addicted to opium, and during the return voyage some would die," he said.

"My dad's job in addition to his sailor duties was to go down through the hold and see if any had passed away. If they had, my dad would tie a Holy Stone to the dead man's feet and sew the body up with canvas and throw it overboard. For each funeral, he got an extra five dollars."

Captain Reynold Wall graduated from navigation school in 1910 and received his unlimited master's license. In 1913 he married Louise Petersen in San Pedro. She was a sister of the late Ottina Soderman, a history buff, who recently died at 92 years.

Captain Wall was skipper of Phineas Banning's S.S. Crickett. Later he became master of three other Banning ships, the Compañero, the Hermosa and the Cabrillo, all of them carrying passengers to Catalina Island.

When the Bannings sold Catalina to the Wrigleys in 1919, Capt. Wall started sailing in steam schooners again. In 1924 he became Port Pilot for the Harbor Department. In 1925 he brought the ferry boat Islander to San Pedro from Santa Monica and was its skipper for several years. The Islander ran between San Pedro and Terminal Island until the Vincent Thomas Bridge was completed.

Captain Wall retired in 1946. During his retirement, however, he often sailed as chief mate in the last wooden steam schooner on the coast, the Daisy Grey, hauling lumber from Eureka to San Pedro. He died in 1960.

His son, George, was born in 1914 in San Pedro, and his other son, Andy, was born in 1917 on First Street in the area known as "Happy Valley." Both sold magazines, the *Los Angeles Times* and the *San Pedro News-Pilot,* and both were caddies at the Royal Palms Golf course on weekends. They are graduates of San Pedro High School. George also worked for a time as a longshoreman to help pay his way through UCLA Medical School in 1939.

George has practiced medicine in San Pedro since that time. He was one of the founders of the Bay Harbor Hospital and presently is its board chairman. In 1964 under Mayor Yorty, George was president of the Los Angeles Harbor Commission.

In 1938, Andy became a cadet aboard the Panama Pacific ship Virginia, later transferring to the Dollar Line ship President Hayes. In 1942, during the Second World War, Andy became an Ensign in the Coast Guard reserve. In 1943 he was graduated from Pensacola as a Coast Guard aviator and flew various planes until the end of the war in 1945. He is now retired from the U.S. Coast Guard Reserve with the rank of Captain.

In 1946 Andy went to work for his father-in-law, John Rados, who owned the Harbor Boat Building Company. During the Korean War, Andy served in the Coast Guard at San Diego, Guam, and Honolulu. After the Korean conflict, Andy went back to the Rados boat building business and entered law school at night.

In 1959 Andy was graduated from Southwestern Law School and bought the Al Larson Boat Shop, which he still owns. The roots and the spirit of the Wall family of San Pedro run deep in harbor heritage.

114
Roy D. Smith, Pioneer

Dr. Smith is a vibrant and knowledgeable San Pedran who has seen the community grow and prosper as few living men have seen it.

ROY D. SMITH, M.D., is one of San Pedro's most lovable pioneers. He came to San Pedro with his parents and older brother, Harry, in 1903 when they moved from Baker, Oregon. Roy is adept in remembering names, places, and events of the community.

He is the oldest living past president of the San Pedro Chamber of Community Development and Commerce. Since 1906 there have been 59 different presidents of the chamber, three of them Smiths: Fred W. served two terms, 1932 and 1936, T.G. Smith, one term, 1965, and Roy D., 1939. Roy also remembers the formation of the San Pedro Chamber in 1906, and the building boom which the chamber aided during the harbor breakwater construction, when San Pedro was a mere 5,000 population.

Soon after arriving in San Pedro, Roy's father opened the Smith Shoe Store at 435 S. Beacon Street. It prospered and for several years was the only store in the harbor district devoted exclusively to shoes. It can be said that Roy's father fitted more shoes on more feet than anyone else in a radius of 25 miles.

As always, some feet are hard to fit. But when a new customer, Clyde H. Foote, found that Smith's shoes gave him more foot comfort than he ever had, he told everybody in town how lucky he was. After that, people began to call him "Lucky" Foote. In 1937 Foote founded the popular 30-Year Club, which has grown to over 1,000 members.

When the first street paving started on Beacon Street, "It attracted a large crowd of grateful citizens. Before that, depending on the season, it was a dusty or muddy San Pedro," Roy said. Roy remembers the old nickelodeon movie houses that charged a nickel admittance, and the jitney craze when one could hail and board a taxi and ride all over town for five cents.

Smith was present during the ground breaking for the new San Pedro Peninsula Hospital in 1925, and expresses his warm gratitude to the doctors: Archibald Warnock, Jess L. Block, Vernon Dunbar, Leonard Thompson, and William Guidinger, and others, for being the main forces in getting a modern hospital built with fine beds, efficient nurses, a courteous staff, and specialized operating room equipment.

Dr. Smith is still practicing medicine and has a large following in the community. He administers principally to old timers, ranging in age from 60 to 100 and still makes house calls when necessary. He is the proud father of two sons, both doctors practicing in San Pedro specializing in orthopedic surgery.

Richard designed and patented an intricate device for ankle and knee operations, equipment that has been accepted and nationally recognized by the medical profession. Richard is married to the former Belia Olguin, head of the Cabrillo Museum. Robert is a board director of the San Pedro Peninsula Hospital.

Both sons and their father are graduates of San Pedro High School. Even more impressive, both sons and their father are all honored graduates of the University of Louisville School of Medicine, Louisville, Kentucky, founded in 1832.

Roy is a linguist, speaking French, Spanish, Italian, Greek, Chinese, and the patois of the South Seas. He is often sought by the hospital as an interpreter for foreign patients.

Moreover, Roy has been an important factor in many worthy projects, including the establishment of the San Pedro Peninsula Hospital.

Smith is also an inveterate reader of books and magazines on many and varied subjects, including philosophy, psychology, economics, international relations, and government policies, besides keeping abreast of modern medical techniques. During World War II, Roy saw duty with the U.S. Navy, reaching the rank of commander.

He lives in one of the most attractive and beautifully decorated homes in the San Pedro Hills, with two loyal watch dogs, four grateful black cats. The residence occupies an acre and has an exquisite ocean view. The yard is generously sprinkled with fruit trees, berry bushes, vegetables, and other yielding plants, plus a hoard of honey bees that show up in search of flowers and nectar.

An aura of cultured elegance surrounding is sensed upon entering his home. His voice is younger than his years, and his thoughts seem to express simple truths rooted in deep humility. Roy is a widower. His wife died in 1974.

One thing is certain: Roy loves San Pedro. He has seen it grow and prosper for three-quarters of a century. In the sunset years of his active and productive life, he can now savor the rich cornucopia of the San Pedro he helped create. Certainly, the history of San Pedro cannot be written without the name of Roy D. Smith looming large on its heritage horizon.

115
The Amar Family

Amar was the first sheep owner in the San Pedro district. His large flocks roamed all over the Palos Verdes Hills and beyond. His son, Eloi, was superintendent for many years of Banning's Catalina Island property.

NO HARBOR HERITAGE would be complete without recording something about the life of Edouard Amar and his son, Eloi. They both made history. Edouard was born near Grenoble, France, March 6, 1852. When he arrived in San Pedro in 1875, Los Angeles was a village of about 15,000 population. Before he died in 1929, Edouard was honored with the coveted French Legion of Honor with Ribbons.

In 1873, Amar got a job from M. Vilet on a farm near Wilmington, worked for two years, and took his pay in sheep. His success as a sheepman was phenomenal. He went into sheep raising in San Pedro in 1875, starting about where Gaffey Street is now located. Within four years, he had a flock of some 50,000 sheep grazing on many hills stretching to Miraleste, Rolling Hills, Palos Verdes, and beyond.

In 1884, he had a sheep camp where Ft. MacArthur is now located, and the hill where the Masonic Temple stands at 1640 W. 9th Street, was known as Chuck Wagon Knob, from where Amar's grazing sheep could be counted in the thousands.

Amar's objectives were based on increased efficiency and performance in sheep and wool culture. Sheep and lambing required special care and attention. His Basque herders made a daily count of the flocks and losses due to coyotes or other depredations.

Amar provided for all foreseeable contingencies—shearing, spraying, dipping, accidents, and sickness. His sheep came first. His wool was prime at the auction block.

But, alas, Monsieur Edouard faced many vicissitudes. Lethal shadows hovered in the terrible drought year of 1877. For three days and nights, the worst windstorm ever recorded in Southern California hit his unprotected flocks. All water holes dried up in the hills and on the plains. Herders' tents fluttered and flapped, and general gloom pervaded the camps.

Drifting sands and erosion followed. Throughout the hills, coyotes howled, mustangs neighed, mules and burros brayed in dire distress. The effect on the land was devastating. Not a blade of grass or plant nor stubble was left. Even the Sepulveda honey bees left their hives never to return. Edouard drove what was left of his flock to the Owens Valley.

It was the constant tramping and impact of sheep that destroyed the Palos Verdes serenity and the solitude usually enjoyed by cattle grazing. These fragile Palos Verdes soils were rejuvenated by the Vanderlip subdividing in 1915 for home construction and gardening as now can be observed.

There is an anecdote attached to Amar's sheep. On July 4, 1876, San Pedro gave a centennial celebration of American independence and invited Phineas Banning to deliver the oration on the "Glorious Fourth." Banning began with a prayer asking heads be bowed giving grace to God and thanking Him for the Union Victory in the Civil War.

Banning's clear, persuasive eloquence aroused the audience to a high pitch of patriotic feeling. Just as he was reminding his audience to remember Paul Revere's ride down the New England Pike to arouse the populace that the "British are coming," a dozen recalcitrant burros driven through town by Edouard Amar passed close to the speakers platform. All of them, almost in unison, let out a braying chorus loud enough to be heard all the way to Rattlesnake Island.

Banning thought this was a good omen that should echo approval of his patriotic oration. He would put this episode to good use. He ended his speech by telling his audience that there was nothing lower than jackasses and that was exactly what the rebel soldiers had been in trying to divide our National Heritage "conceived and consecrated in the American Declaration of Independence on July 4, 1776."

Edouard's son, Eloi, was born in 1891 in the showplace home his father built in 1887 at Twelfth and Mesa. This landmark home was bulldozed two years ago; it had character, sentiment, and history. To his family, Edouard was a sincere amorist, and there was no question about Eloi's filial devotion.

The father was one of the founders of the Elks Club of San Pedro, along with his friend George Peck, who incidentally persuaded Edouard to buy 30 acres, which he laid out as Vista Del Mar.

Son Eloi became a contractor and real estate broker with his father. He built the Elks Club building that still stands at Seventh and Palos Verdes. Eloi became Exalted Ruler of the Elks in 1925. He was highly educated and fluent in English, French Basque, and Spanish. In 1922, he built three blocks of bungalow courts which can be seen now, all rented and in good repair, on West Twelfth Street between Pacific and Mesa.

For many years, Eloi was general manager of Catalina Island, before and after the Banning heirs sold it to William Wrigley in 1919. Eloi died in 1963 and is buried in Avalon.

In 1912, he went to Banning, California, to marry Bessie May Booher. His son, Edouard, is married to Helen Becker, sister of Wilmot Bird.

His daughter, Rose, is married to Duane Walsworth. Eloi's wife, Bess Booher Amar, divides her time between Avalon and Twenty-nine Palms.

During his lifetime, Eloi was president of the Los Angeles Harbor Commission, and also general manager of the Long Beach Harbor Department.

The Amars, father and son, are a pioneer family whose roots are deeply embedded throughout the harbor area.

116
THE RADOS FAMILY— PIONEERS IN SHIPBUILDING

One of the great families in the harbor area. For 55 years their faith and investment in the community gave jobs and economic stability to thousands of local people.

MEMBERS OF THE LOCAL Rados family have been pioneers and have played an important part in the overall progress of the Harbor Area. John Rados (1896-1968) and his father, Romolo Rados, founded the Harbor Boat Building Company 60 years ago on Terminal Island. John had three brothers, Myles, James and Al.

In 1914, before World War I started, they migrated to Canada from Losinj, Austria, Hungary, now Yugoslavia. In Canada the Rados built stern-wheelers for the Yukon. While in Canada, John enlisted in the Canadian Army in World War I. In 1917 he married Etta Romy, whom he met in Canada. Their daughter, Gloria, was born on Terminal Island in 1920. Their twin boys, Bob and Jack, were born in San Pedro in 1922.

There were few whites living on Terminal Island at the time, and when Gloria was in grade school, she was the only non-Japanese in the school. A few years later, however, Art Almeida, prominent labor leader, and his brother attended this school. Gloria is married to Andy Wall, owner of the Al Larson Boat Building Shop on Terminal Island. They live in San Pedro, where both Andy and Gloria are active in community activities and welfare projects.

Andy recently became chairman of the 16-member board of directors of the Los Angeles Bay Maritime Museum headquartered in the old Ferry Building, at the foot of Sixth Street in San Pedro, for which an appropriation of a million dollars was set aside by the federal government for all necessary repairs, painting, and room additions. According to Councilman John S. Gibson's office, the museum should be open to the public in 1979.

John's brother, Myles, became a prominent naval architect; the other brothers, James and Al, became part of the management of the shipyard. "In the beginning," Andy said, "there were just a handful of employees. They increased to over 500 workers during World War II."

During their 50 years of experience in building ships and serving the maritime industry, the Rados family developed many improvements in design, construction, test, overhaul, and repair techniques. Other boat builders copied them through the courtesy of Vice Admiral Howard Vickery and Admiral Land of the U.S. Navy, who were in charge of all shipbuilding during World War II.

The Rados Company was honored with many contracts for the U.S. Navy, the U.S. Coast Guard, and other branches of the armed forces, and in the commercial field for various kinds of ocean-going yachts.

Prior to World War II, Harbor Boat Building Company designed and built 17 yachts, 32 fishing vessels, and 20 military vessels, including 80-foot patrol ships, and 64-foot mine layers for the U.S. Navy, plus many other strategic craft.

During this period the company was instrumental in design changes and improvements that led to the wholesale conversion of the California fisheries to build the purse seiner and the tuna clipper style of boats. A large prototype tuna clipper was first built in the Rados yards on Terminal Island; it was the nucleus around which large fishing companies placed their orders for whole fleets of fishing vessels, most of them plying South Pacific waters off Peru, Ecuador, and Chile.

The Harbor Boat Building Company was operated by John Rados and his family from 1920 until 1960, when they sold their interest to Ling-Tempo-Vought, Inc. In 1963 LTV sold it to John Weinstock, who operated the Company until end of 1965. Then, in 1966 the firm became a wholly owned subsidiary of the Tyler Corporation, who in 1971 sold it to Omega-Alpha, Inc.

It is significant to know that during this period of several different owners, from 1960 until 1975, the Harbor Boat Building Company maintained a blood link with its beginning in that its president, Ronald J. Rados, was the son of the late Myles Rados.

In 1975 bad times hit the boat building business, and in December of that year the company closed its doors for the last time. But throughout the 55 years of existence, Harbor Boat contributed greatly to the economic and social development of the San Pedro and Wilmington community and to national defense. The Rados' won many awards for excellence by both the Army and the Navy.

John's son, Jack, was killed in the line of duty at Okinawa during World War II. John's son, Bob, is the president and owner of Rados International, a marine engineering company in San Pedro. John's daughter, Gloria, is secretary-treasurer of the Larson Boat Shop, helping her husband, Andy, along with their four sons who also work there, all helping out in a family tradition of local boat builders.

Keeping alive the close blood relationship of a noble industry of ship building that started in San Pedro is a fitting tribute to the founders, John Rados, and his father, Romolo.

117
Judge Joe Raycraft, Pioneer

Raycraft recalls early days in San Pedro, and his long friendship with Ramon Sepulveda.

WHEN JUDGE JOE RAYCRAFT became president of the San Pedro Chamber of Commerce in 1940, he was just 33 years old—two years younger than Sandy Neill, president of the San Pedro Junior Chamber of Commerce.

Raycraft continued to create precedents and break records as being among the youngest, if not the youngest, in his many endeavors in his busy professional career. When the late Governor Earl Warren appointed Raycraft in 1947 to the judicial bench, he became the third youngest in Los Angeles County, and the first San Pedro lawyer to become a judge.

In 1937 Raycraft became the youngest president of the San Pedro Optimist Club. He served on the bench for more than 20 years, the last five years as presiding judge of the Long Beach Superior Court. Raycraft never lost an election. In fact, no one wanted to run against him.

In 1960 Warren, Chief Justice of the United States, left a busy desk in Washington, D.C., to aid Raycraft in dedicating the new Long Beach Courthouse. Raycraft retired from the bench in 1967, at which time his colleagues gave him a deserved party attended by over 100 prominent professional persons.

When Little Joe, as he was affectionally called by his parents, first arrived in San Pedro in 1913, he was an observant 6-year-old lad. They came on the ship Nellie, a popular vessel that ran regularly for a few years with passengers between Long Beach and San Pedro.

The breakwater had been completed three years before. Raycraft said he saw everything and liked what he saw, and determined then and there that one day he would like to live here.

"The Nellie tied up at the foot of Fifth Street, I remembered it well," Raycraft said. "Front Street, which is now Harbor Boulevard, and Beacon Street marked the center of town. There was no Gaffey Street, and Pacific Avenue had only an occasional house or two; west of there one saw only grazing sheep and a few braying donkeys."

"The Southern Pacific Railroad had an imposing depot at Fifth and Front. They also had a large freight pier protruding out from the old Timms Landing. I also remember seeing several sailing vessels and schooners loaded with lumber."

Records of 1913 show Long Beach with a population of 17,000 people. San

Pedro had 3,300 inhabitants. This was a period when San Pedro began its steady climb to become the most active lumber port in the United States. It also was a year of floods in Wilmington, when high tides in the estuary washed upon the land.

The Southwest Instrument Company, a long-time institution in San Pedro, has rare photographs showing all the stores and houses along what is now Avalon Boulevard, with a plank boardwalk 10 feet above street level. This situation prevailed until the water was pumped back into the channel after the installation of cement bulkheads along the Wilmington wharf. Anaheim was the only through street to Long Beach and often was impassable due to water and mud hazards. Also in 1913 there was an old dirt wagon pass known as the old Salt Road from Wilmington to Redondo Beach.

Raycraft's father was an architect and contractor and built the roller coaster and Silver Spray Pier in Long Beach. Young Joe practically cut his teeth on the doings of the Pike. When he was 16 his parents had died, but Raycraft was determined to get an education. He worked his way through high school, and USC, four years in undergraduate studies, three years in law school. He created another first by passing the bar examination before graduating from law school.

In 1932 Raycraft opened his law office in the Sepulveda Building at Sixth and Palos Verdes Streets, San Pedro. He specialized in waterfront cases to start with, and became the attorney for the Sepulveda and Dodson families. He also did legal work for B.B. Lippman and for the Di Rocco family, and many other prominent firms and individuals.

Raycraft numbered among his close friends most all the old community leaders, including George Peck, Joseph Atchison, A.P. Ferl, John T. Gaffey, Ray Mitchell, C.W. Cleveland, Frank A. Vanderlip, Roy J. Becker, Cecil Thomas, Dr. George Wall, Dr. E.C. Spires, and Dr. Roy D. Smith.

Raycraft delights in telling how Ramon Sepulveda would visit him almost daily. After hitching his horse, he would come in for a chat and discuss how the harbor has progressed since his father, Jose Diego Sepulveda, laid it out in varas.

"I love San Pedro and the Harbor Area," Raycraft concluded. "It is still an attractive and intriguing district that has always been alive and alert and on the move and has never existed in a definitive form. The air is always invigorating and sweet with the exhilarating smell of land and sea."

Judge Raycraft is still active in San Pedro with his law business specializing now in probates.

118
The Irvine Ranch Story

This is possibly the richest ranch per acre in the world. Drought conditions enabled James Irvine to get control in 1868 from the Sepulvedas.

IN RECENT MONTHS the 100,000 acre Irvine Ranch has had prominent news coverage because of its sale to a combine of investors who paid around $300 million for the property. But little was written about the original ownership and how the Irvine family came into possession of this strategic landfall.

"Lucky" Baldwin, in his land speculation in Artesia and Santa Anita, was a piker compared with James Irvine (1827-1886), who left Ireland at the age of 19 years in 1846, landed in New York where he did odd jobs for two years. After reading about the gold strike in California, he boarded a sailing ship in steerage and landed in Panama. Irvine then walked across the Panama Peninsula to the Pacific side, boarded the bark Alexander Von Humboldt which took him on a three-month, storm-swept voyage to San Francisco. The ship anchored briefly in San Pedro Bay for urgent supplies.

From San Francisco Irvine became a passenger on the sidewheel steamer Senator for Sacramento. He panned for gold up the American River, saved enough nuggets and gold dust to buy into a wholesale grocery business, and became rich not only in grocery items, but in selling miners a "simple-to-calculate" gold weighing scales.

Irvine left the gold diggings and went to San Francisco, where he successfully speculated in real estate and home construction. At one time he owned 25 rentals housed there. In 1866 Irvine married Nettie Rice of Cleveland, Ohio. In 1867 their son, James Irvine II, was born in San Francisco.

During Irvine's mining camp experience he met Llewellyn Bixby, and Bixby's cousins, Dr. Thomas Flint and his brother, Benjamin Flint. They entered into a partnership known as Flint, Bixby, and Irvine, and became sheep growers on a big scale in Northern California. Sheep require less pasturage than cattle, and the firm was eager to expand into Southern California and would take their chance on periodic cattle-killing droughts. During the Civil War and for several years afterward, wool brought high prices because cotton crops were neglected or destroyed in the southern states, and wool became an excellent substitute.

By 1868 Irvine and his partners bought 108,000 acres of rancho land, including Newport holdings from Jose Sepulveda and a portion of the bay shoreland owned by Bernardo and Jose Antonio Yorba, and their cousin, Juan Pablo Peralta. Originally, this land belonged to the San Juan Capistrano Mission and extended from the Santa Ana Mountains to the sea at Newport. Irvine and his partners, Flint and Bixby, wanted to obtain this land cheaply, possibly by a bankrupt sale, and stock it with sheep. They did both. How?

Louis Sepulveda gave the author the answer by letting him read J.M. Guinn's book, *Historical and Biographical Record of Southern California.* It reads: "Herds of gaunt, skeleton-like forms moved slowly over the plains in search of food and water. Here and there, singly or in groups, poor brutes, too weak to move on, stood motionless with drooping heads, dying. It was a pitiful sight. The loss of cattle during the famine years of 1864-1865 was fearful. The plains were strewn with their carcasses."

"In marshy places and around the cienegas where there was a vestige of green the ground was covered with their skeletons; and the traveler for years afterwards was often startled by coming suddenly upon a veritable Golgotha, a place of skulls, the long horns standing out in a defiant attitude, as if defending the fleshless bones."

This ended the prosperous and free-living days of the Dons. Colorful Jose Sepulveda, owner of 47,000 acres, after selling his land and paying his debts ended up with $18,000. At one time he owned over 20,000 head of cattle and over 3,000 horses.

In 1876 James Irvine bought out his partners, Flint and Bixby, for $150,000. The Bixby family was already interested in the Ranchos Los Cerritos, and Los Alamitos, as grazing grounds for their sheep, horses and cattle.

The land Irvine controlled became known as the Irvine Ranch. The property was converted during the century from sheep grazing to one of California's prime agricultural centers through the introduction of irrigation, citrus orchards, residential, and industrial locations.

The land now includes parts of the cities of Newport Beach, Tustin, all of Irvine, and contains about one fifth of the whole of Orange County. During their last fiscal year ended April, 1977, the Irvine Ranch Corporation earned a gross profit of $103.8 million.

James Irvine II (1867-1947) once rode a volocipede from his ranch to San Francisco, just to prove it could be done. Unlike his father, young James devoted his life in developing the agricultural potential of the ranch. Large cargoes of their produce in grain and fruit are shipped every year through the Ports of Wilmington and San Pedro.

119
Nikola Tesla, Yugoslav Genius

Finally, Nikola Tesla, the Yugoslav, has been recognized as one of the greatest electrical genuises of all time.

THE SCIENTIFIC GENIUS OF Nikola Tesla (1856-1943), a Yugoslav, whose inventions amazed the scientific world in the 1880s, when he invented the magnetic fields of electric induction on motor coils, came to international attention recently when the Pentagon and NASA announced that Tesla's principles are being used in laser beam techniques.

According to Pentagon officials, Tesla's formula creates a sharp magnetic field that rotates at a predetermined speed, capable of producing high-voltage laser beams calculated to be sufficient to protect our missiles and astronauts against any known enemy assaults or aggression from outer space. A NASA spokesman believes this factor may prove, possibly, one of the greatest scientific breakthroughs for the overall maintenance of world peace in modern times.

Tesla came to the United States in 1884 and engaged in independent research in his New York laboratory, where he made rapid advances in the fields of high-voltage and high-frequency apparatus. He patented the Tesla coil and a system of arc lighting, still used on our streets, and a generator for high-frequency currents. Also, according to the American Encyclopedia. Tesla invented an improved system, over Marconi's method, of wireless transmission, plus a high-potential magnifying transmitter.

Tesla's most famous and profitable invention, however, was the electric alternating-current induction motor, introduced at a time when advocates were seeking such a motor. Tesla, pressed for finances, sold the invention to George Westinghouse in 1888. Westinghouse invented the air brake in 1868 for railroad trains. Westinghouse also invented the gas meter, which is attached to almost every home in the nation.

Research indicates, however, that it was Tesla's motor invention that was the basis for the success and establishment of the Westinghouse Electric Corporation. Westinghouse also invented the rotary engine and other items, but even so, the electric motor proved to be the most popular product in the Westinghouse conglomerate. It is the most useful and provides the greatest utility; in fact, all business utilities are based on its power; it changes electric energy into mechanical power to perform work and is used for almost every purpose that requires electric power to run machinery.

The size of the electric motor ranges from the tiny devices that operate watches, sewing machines, and household appliances, to powerful locomotives. In all modern factories each machine is run by its motor. Even a machine that generates its own electricity, such as at power dams, is driven by a motor. It takes electric motors to keep the *San Pedro News-Pilot* presses going. Newspaper presses actually have several electric motors, each performing a definite task. Motors feed the rolls of paper to the presses, turning out the printed pages, folding the papers together and binding them in small packages for distribution.

On the local waterfront, electric motors power many kinds of machinery including fork lift trucks, winches, air conditioners and fans. Commercial fishing boats need motor propulsion. In the home electric-motor-driven refrigerators and freezers preserve food. Housewives use dishwashers, washing machines, mixers, and driers powered by electric motors.

Even a wrist watch can receive its power from a tiny motor instead of a mainspring, thanks to the inventive genius of Nikola Tesla.

These thoughts inspire grateful thanks to Realtor Marty Medak and to Restaurateur Ante Perkov for their suggestions for researching the life of Tesla—a kindred spirit to approximately 50,000 people of Yugoslav blood living in San Pedro and in the South Bay area of Los Angeles.

120
Famous Cult of Helena Modjeska

The Helen Modjeska commune was one of the most interesting communes ever established in America. It failed as a cooperative farm effort, but produced the man who wrote Quo Vadis? *and who went on to win the Nobel Prize for literature in 1905. The Cult was in Anaheim.*

COOPERATIVE CULTS AND COMMUNES are not new in California. From 1850 to 1950 there were several kinds of Utopian colonies established in California by zealous, charismatic leaders and reformers, seeking the ideal society and the perfect state. They all failed.

During these 100 years, at least 17 Utopias embarked on an idealistic experiment. Of these 17, six were religious and 11 were secular. Some of them started in Southern California. One of the most interesting started in our own backyard in Anaheim in 1876. It was under the direction of Helena Modjeska (1840-1909), who enlisted several intellectual Poles in Krakow, Poland. They pooled their resources and started a cooperative in California, modeled after the earlier Brook Farm Utopia in Massachusetts, where Nathaniel Hawthorne, and other intellectuals lived.

The group from Poland consisted of Count Chiapowski; his wife, Madame Modjeska; Rudolphe Modjeska, son of their first marriage; Julian Sypniewski, his wife and children; Stanislaw Paprocki, classical painter; a few poets, authors and writers. Helena Modjeska was already a famous Shakespearian actress. One of the group, Henryk Sienkiewicz, wrote the immortal *Quo Vadis?* after his sojourn in California, which won the Nobel Prize in literature in 1905.

This was not a phony group; they were all intellectual radicals bitter over Russian domination of their homeland who were looking for freedom of expression. They were Polish patriots to the end.

In the spring of 1876, Modjeska sent Sypniewski and Sienkiewicz to explore the farmland possibilities in Southern California. After investigation they chose the area of Anaheim, "because most of the people of this area speak German." This was a familiar language for the Polish clan.

Sypniewski returned to Poland with glowing accounts. Sienkiewicz waited at Anaheim Landing, also at Wilmington and San Pedro, writing enticing letters for Modjeska and her group to come on to San Pedro and Anaheim.

In July 1876, the intellectuals sailed aboard the Donau from Bremen on the first leg of their voyage to their Utopian home in California. After landing in New York, they took an excursion to Washington, where they obtained boxes of pamphlets on farming. The group then proceeded to the Isthmus of Panama on a steamer and braved the 50-mile stretch through the murky jungles to the Pacific, where they boarded an old side-wheeler ticketed straight through to San Francisco. The ship's captain refused to stop at San Pedro or Wilmington.

From San Francisco the Utopians boarded a steamer for Wilmington, where Sienkiewicz was waiting for them with horses and wagons obtained from Phineas Banning for the last lap to their farm near Anaheim. There they found a wooden house with two bedrooms, a dining room, a kitchen, and a parlor with an upright piano and a sofa. There also was a large barn with hay.

By lottery they negotiated for their respective room assignments. Sypniewski and his family were assigned the large bedroom, while Count Chiapowski and Helena took the small bedroom. Ralph slept on the sofa and Anusia, a teen-age Pole who joined the group in Poland to look after the children, made her quarters in a nook of the kitchen. Sienkiewicz and Poprocki took the barn.

Modjeska became the cook. She was soon disillusioned; even preparing breakfast for this group of intellectuals was no easy task. Each one wanted something different: tea, coffee, milk, chocolate or wine-soup.

According to Modjeska's *Memories and Impressions,* the first few days of work in the fields were glorious, but complaints about sore arms and lame backs soon kept the geniuses confined to the house and barn. Sienkiewicz gradually divorced himself from farm labor, setting up a table under the trees in a far corner of the farm where he read, smoked his pipe, and wrote most of the day.

It is possible that in Sienkiewicz's reflective moods the genesis of his masterpiece, *Quo Vadis?*, took root. The story is patterned on an episode in the life of Jesus Christ. Here at the farm near Anaheim Sienkiewicz lived where he was exposed to an environment in a barn closely akin to the birth of Christ in a manger.

Modjeska recorded that their spirits began to lag from boresome toil and homesickness. To compensate, the whole colony often took to its buggies and horses for a picnic or a drive to Anaheim Landing and along the shore. Modjeska wrote that it required the combined efforts of three intellectuals to kill a turkey.

"After six months we all came to the conclusion," Modjeska wrote, "that our farming was not a success. We had several cows, but no one would milk them. We had to buy milk, butter, and cream from our neighbors. We had chickens, but our dogs made meals of the eggs. We had a vineyard which yielded beautiful muscat grapes, but nobody bought them, and often people would come and fill their wagons with grapes without more ado; they said such was the custom of the country, and our winter crop of barley disappeared in the mouths of the cattle."

Money from the sale of the farm provided return passage for those colonists who wished to return to Poland. Modjeska, however, remained. In 1878 she returned to the stage she loved. Edwin Booth and Otis Skinner helped to raise Modjeska to a prominent place in the history of the American theater.

Modjeska's Forest of Arden in Santiago Canyon is now a state preserve. It is open to the public. Anyone in Anaheim can direct you to it.

121
No Secrets in Masonic Brotherhoods

The Wilmington Masonic Lodge, established in 1869, was the first in the harbor. The membership in turn founded first lodges in San Pedro and in Long Beach.

THERE ARE THREE Masonic Lodges in San Pedro and one in Wilmington. People often wonder about their secrets, their functions, and what they stand for.

As a long-time Mason, the author can say there are no secrets inconsistent with belief in God, a belief in high moral standards, fidelity, and brotherly love.

The Masonic rituals are inspiringly beautiful, teaching the richness of life and how to live by the square, acting on the level, and within the points of the extended compass, so that when away from the lodge we might redeem ourselves to the principles of brotherly love, truth, charity, and compassion. These are the essence of so-called Masonic secrecy.

Being a Mason, denied to some, beyond the reach of many, is a high privilege. There is no religious discrimination. Catholics as well as any other denomination may apply for membership. No Mason will ask anyone to join, the decision being left solely with the individual. Masons everywhere glory in the high quality of membership and they look with pride on past achievements of the Masonic order.

The history of Masonry in the Harbor Area dates back to May 25, 1869, when Wilmington Lodge No. 198 was installed. This lodge has created many unusual precedents in creating and installing many other lodges, including the first San Pedro Lodge No. 332, June 17, 1897.

Lodge No. 332 in San Pedro enjoys its own temple building at 1640 W. Ninth Street and is the largest of the three. Wilmington Lodge also installed one in Anaheim in 1870 and in later years, in Long Beach, Compton, Redondo Beach, Lomita, and the A.F.E. Irwin Lodge No. 645 in San Pedro, plus many more lodges in Los Angeles County.

The Wilmington Lodge is known throughout Masonry for its former worshipful master, George Hinds, who served longer in this office than anybody in Masonic history.

He is the same George Hinds who adopted James H. Dodson, Sr., and enlisted him as a junior partner in the firm of Vickery and Hines, meat packers of Wilmington in the 1880s. Dodson later married Rudecinda Sepulveda.

Hinds was worshipful master of the Wilmington Lodge 15 years, starting in 1871. In 1887 Dodson was worshipful master. At the time, Rudecinda ranked high in the Catholic hierarchy, but perfect harmony reigned throughout their marriage. Dodson and Rudecinda are buried together in the Rudecinda Chapel at the Harbor View Cemetery in San Pedro.

In the early 1920s Grand Lodge officials thought San Pedro Lodge No. 332, founded in 1897, was becoming too large to service the steadily growing San Pedro community and recommended the creation of a new lodge. They founded Pt. Firmin Lodge No. 332 on May 2, 1923. Hubert Kaltenbach, former publisher of the *San Pedro News-Pilot* is a former worshipful master of this lodge.

The lodge minutes show that the 24 charter members of Pt. Firmin Lodge were of exceptional merit. Many of them later served as worshipful master. Most of them have left an inspiring heritage in the community.

For instance, Gilbert Bell who served in 1923 and 1924 as worshipful master of Pt. Firmin Lodge was the founder of the San Pedro Hospital, the San Pedro DeMolay and the Alpha Pi Beta Fraternity. Moreover, Bell was active in sponsoring degree teams in the U.S. Naval Fleet, at the time stationed in San

Pedro. In addition he conferred degree work among the U.S. Army at Ft. MacArthur. During this time, Bell was president of the First National Bank of San Pedro, which later merged with the Bank of America.

Point Firmin Lodge is unique in acquiring an old landmark name, and spelling it with two "i's" instead of one.

The lodge gets its name from Fr. Fermin Lasuen who, after setting up a small building in San Pedro, left to establish the San Fernando Mission. The area retained his name, however, and the lodge decided to adopt it when it was established in San Pedro.

But a secretary, in making the documents of the lodge misspelled the name. By the time it was discovered it was too late to change before the lodge was established. And now, after so many years, the lodge says it will stick with the Firmin rather than Fermin.

The degree work in Masonry is important, but when one reaches the third degree it is the peak degree in this particular lodge, known as his Blue Lodge.

After he reaches the third degree, he is eligible to join the Scottish Rite or the Arch Bodies; then through ritual he can become a 32nd degree Mason. The only degree higher is the 33rd, rarely bestowed. In the Harbor Area, there are only four 33rd degree Masons: William Wood of Wilmington, and Reuben Kove, William Marron, and Walter Kemmerer of San Pedro.

One of the outstanding annual activities of San Pedro Lodge No. 332 is Mariner's Night dinner, an evening of fellowship and refreshment to honor all Masons of the sea. It is under the guidance of Walter Kemmerer. In 1978 over 1800 attended.

122
Judge W.H. Savage and Drum Barracks Anecdotes

Armed bartenders served spirited drinks at Banning's Exchange Hotel in Wilmington. An exciting time at Drum Barracks.

IN STUDYING LOCAL HISTORY of the pioneers, the name of W.H. Savage pops up from time to time. Records show he was a real character of the old school—ambitious, determined, imaginative, and courageous—a self-made man who became important in the early progress of Wilmington and Drum Barracks. He became a judge, and his talents as story teller are legend.

Savage arrived at Drum Barracks in Wilmington in 1864 from New York as quartermaster of a regiment of toughs of the East Side and from Brooklyn, many of them ex-pugilists with battle-scarred faces and cauliflower ears.

Most of them already had experience fighting in the Civil War, but their officers could not control them on the battlefield of the South. They were transferred to Savage to go west and fight the Apache Indians, yet unconquered after three centuries of Spanish and Mexican rule, and terrorizing the Southwest along the Colorado River settlements.

Apparently the reputation of their regiment traveled ahead of them. When they arrived at Drum Barracks, Col. George P. Curtis, Jr., a son of George Patrick Curtis, a stepson of George Washington, was in command. Curtis assigned the regiment to quarters outside the barracks in tents and kept them separate from the other soldiers.

The first night the regiment arrived, the men couldn't wait to paint the town red—drinking, singing, carousing, and fighting. Some of them were locked up in the guard house. But let Savage tell the story:

"There were 22 stores in Wilmington, 20 of them saloons. The most famous was Phineas Banning's Exchange on Canal Boulevard. Banning was proud of his facility and advertised it in the newspapers and on ships as the finest hostelry south of San Francisco, with spring beds and spring water."

Savage described the hotel and bar with its outbuildings and corrals in the rear, carriage houses, and barns, totaling several blocks. The hotel building was two stories. A large balcony was usually lined with guests in tilted-back chairs, their feet dangling over the balcony rail, enjoying the view of marsh flats, ocean, valley, and mountains. Downstairs was the restaurant, bowling alley, pool room, and bar.

"There were two bartenders," Savage wrote, "busy mixing drinks. One of them, a grim, desperado-looking man by no means smiled at us. He looked as if he had not smiled since his father was hung. Mind you, I don't say that his father was hung, but if he was not he should have been, becoming the father of such an ill-looking fellow. His linen was badly soiled. Beneath his flowing army coat could be seen a pair of ugly Colt pistols while with the red fringe of his Mexican sash could be seen a chain of golden nuggets connected to his watch fob. The other bartender was more amiable, although strapped to his belt was a heavy Colt and a Bowie knife. On the back bar rested the wooden mallet known as the bum-starter, used in maintaining order when customers become too noisy or boisterous. In the corner stood a double-barrelled shotgun and an old musket, also two more large Colts of the Drum Barracks pattern called batteries. Banning's bar was not to be taken by surprise."

Obviously Banning planned that his Wilmington Exchange should be the main meeting place for soldiers, sailors, longshoremen, miners, cattle and sheep people, ranchers, stage drivers, gamblers, and prairie schooner emigrants. No doubt, Wilmington was a busy and profitable place for him. Here the pioneers of the surrounding settlements came to buy their goods, get money orders, and post mail. Banning owned the only wharf; ships were ever alongside. He also controlled blacksmith shops and a wagon-manufacturing company.

Streets seethed with the ebb and flow of commerce; wagons, ox-carts, canopied schooners with high tired wheels, and camel caravans driven by turbaned Egyptians and Arabians, Indians, soldiers, sailors, loafers, and bums, made up the cast for this remarkable scene.

One of Savage's tall tales is woven around a popular ex-scout and Indian fighter who went on periodic drunks. One day the scout brought in a bottle, sold to him by mistake since it was full of muriatic acid used in polishing brass.

When the mistake was discovered, an alarm was sent out and a search began for the scout. Wilmington was in an uproar. Banning gave orders to find the scout before he could drink the stuff. Every place was searched, but he was not found. Everyone thought he was dead.

About 10 days later the victim tottered to the bar and shouted, "Say, son, have you any more of that whiskey left? It's great stuff, it took me over a week to sober up!"

After the Civil War, Savage worked for Banning as a freight driver while studying law. He became a member of the State Legislature and the author of several laws. He died about 1931. His son, Municipal Judge William M. Savage, relieved Judge Walter Binns at San Pedro Municipal Court recently during the vacation period.

123
Juana Maria

Abandoned for 18 years on lonely San Nicolas Island, the last of the Channel Island Indians, when Juana Maria died their history and culture died with her.

RECENTLY, WHILE RUMMAGING THROUGH some old books, reports, and leaflets at the Santa Barbara Mission, the author found a sad but heroic story about an Indian woman who fought desperately for survival after being abandoned for 18 years on the inhospitable, cold, barren and windswept Island of San Nicolas.

In 1835, Capt. Charles Hubbard, master of the small schooner Peores Nada, sailed to San Nicolas, the outermost of the Channel Islands. He was to evacuate the remaining Indians to the mainland at San Pedro, where they would be met by the Franciscan Fathers and transported to the San Gabriel Mission for safety and recuperation.

Just as the loaded boat was about to leave the island, there was a scream, an Indian woman leaped overboard and swam to shore. She had forgotten her baby.

Meanwhile, a sudden squall forced the schooner to leave without her. Hubbard, however, vowed to return and pick up this Indian woman and her child. Unfortunately, a few months later, on a sea otter trip to San Francisco, his ship was lost with all aboard.

Years passed. Every so often seal and otter hunters asserted they saw some kind of a figure run away at their approach every time they made camp on San Nicolas. Searches were made, but without success.

Although both San Gabriel and Santa Barbara Missions had records that an Indian woman and her child were on San Nicolas Island, few people believed the woman or her child had survived for long.

The island was overrun with packs of vicious wild dogs. The rescued Indians told how difficult it was even when they were all together to fend off the snarling and yapping wild dogs. In 1850, George Nidiver and Thomas Jeffries, with a crew of Santa Catalina Indians, went to San Nicolas in a small sailboat to hunt sea otter and to find, if possible, the remains of the Indian woman and her child. They were there for six weeks. Then, just before they were ready to leave with a boatload of furs, one of the Indian crew, who was hiking all over the island, returned to the camp flushed with excitement.

He told of seeing a figure running in the distance. He tried to catch up with the island phantom, but failed. They sailed back to San Pedro without the Indian woman or her child. Three years later on another otter trip, Nidiver and his companion, Carl Ditman, spotted a basket containing a robe sewn with birds' plummage.

Incredible as it seemed, they knew the Indian woman who swam back to the island 18 years earlier to find her misplaced baby was still there and very much alive. Nidiver ordered his men to join him in searching the island, canyon by canyon, cave by cave, knoll by knoll, until the mysterious woman was found.

It was Ditman who finally discovered a lean-to atop a knoll, and a figure inside it. It was the Indian woman. As their report later revealed, she was dressed in a cloak of cormorant feathers. She was friendly, and talked in sign language. She was willing to go to the mainland with her discoverers. She explained how she had lived off abalone, fish, bird eggs, and seal. Fresh water came from several springs found on the island.

She also explained that her baby died the day she came back for it, and that she buried her child deep in the ground with some beads, the body dressed in bird feathers. The woman had trained a pack of wild dogs to answer her command. The dogs lived with her and protected her. Two pet ravens also nestled on her shoulder.

The report further noted, "Despite the fact that Ditman was the first person she faced in 18 long years, she did not become alarmed. She seemed to be in excellent physical health, and there was a large supply of food in her grass hut, which she shared daily with the beasts and the birds."

"She knew every inch of the island, had walked its breadth through the years with her loyal dogs at her side. Her life was lonely, but in time she came to accept it and for years fled in fear from every visitor. She was a quiet, shy person, amazingly attractive despite her unique ordeal."

At night, as she lay in her hammock, she could see castles in the sky. She related that the shining stars appeared as bountiful gods guiding her destiny. As Nidiver's frail craft left San Nicolas Island, the Indian woman waved a last farewell from the bow of the tiny boat to the group of bewildered, but loving wild dogs, howling their heart out from the makeshift wharf as their beloved mistress disappeared over the water.

Civilization proved to be a greater challenge than living alone on San Nicolas. In spite of her new diet of proper food, or perhaps because of it, she failed rapidly. On the island she was fully attuned to the environment of nature in the raw. The animals and the birds understood her; they were part of her life. She could talk to them, and they with her. She was nature's child. It was her world.

Within three months of her discovery she died at the Santa Barbara Mission. She was the last of the Channel Island Indians. Their history and their culture died with her. On her death bed, a priest baptized her, giving her the name of Juana Maria.

Her robe of cormorant feathers was sent to the Pope of Rome, where it now rests in the Vatican Museum. She is buried in the mission graveyard. A plaque erected to her memory reads:

Juana Maria
Indian Woman Abandoned on
San Nicolas Island Eighteen years
Found and brought to
Santa Barbara
By
Captain George Nidiver
In 1853
Daughters of the
American Revolution
1928.

Bibliography

Adobe Days, Sara Bixby Smith, Jake Zeitlin, 1931, Los Angeles
Six Horses, George Hugh and William Banning, 1930, Century Company
Port Admiral, Mayme Krythe, California Historical Society, 1957
Two Years Before the Mast, Richard Henry Dana, Boston, 1840
Reminiscences of a Ranger, Horace Bell, 1927, Wallace Hubbard, Santa Barbara
California Mission Days, Helen Bauer, 1957, Sacramento
From Wilderness to Empire, Robert Glass Cleland, Alfred A. Knopf, 1944
Men to Match My Mountains, Irving Stone, Consolidated Book Publishers
Wesward to Promontory, Harry B. Combs
Harbor District of Los Angeles, Ella Ludwig, History Record Company, 1972
Sixty Years in Southern California, Harris Newmark, Houghton, Mifflin.
Pathmaker of the West, Allan Nevins, 1939
History of Los Angeles City, Charles Dwight Willard, 1901
Crusader in Corduroy: Dudley Gordon, Historical Society of Southern California, 1972
Official Correspondence, Thomas S. Larkin, Bancroft Library
Personal Reminiscences, John A. Sutter, Bancroft Library
City-Makers, Remi Nadeau, Trans-Anglo Books
Personal Memoirs, U.S. Grant, 2 Volumes, Webster & Company, 1885
Harpers Monthly, Volume 50 to 65—1850 to 1882
California's Story, Herbert E. Bolton, Allyn and Bacon, 1922
Various Booklets, Published by Los Angeles Title and Trust Company, 1937

GRAVEYARDS VISITED

Banning Plot (Now Wilmington Cemetery) Rebecca Banning grave
Calvary Cemetery
Compton Cemetery (15 soldiers from Drum Barracks)
Evergreen Cemetery (Bixby's grave)
Forest Lawn Cemetery
Green Hills Cemetery
Harbor View Cemetery
Inglewood Cemetery (Phineas Banning's Three Sons)
Rosedale Cemetery (Phineas Banning grave)
Santa Barbara Mission Cemetery
San Fernando Mission Cemetery
San Gabriel Mission Cemetery
San Juan Capistrano Cemetery

Index

Italic numerals indicate plate numbers.

C

D

M

N

O

P

R

S

T

U

V

W

Y

Z

NOTES

NOTES

NOTES